WITNESSES
TO THE
HOLOCAUST

An Oral History

TWAYNE'S
ORAL HISTORY SERIES

Donald A. Ritchie, Series Editor

EDITED BY RHODA G. LEWIN

WITNESSES
TO THE
HOLOCAUST

An Oral History

TWAYNE PUBLISHERS · BOSTON
A Division of G. K. Hall & Co.

Witnesses to the Holocaust: An Oral History
Edited by Rhoda G. Lewin

Twayne's Oral History Series No. 2

Copyright 1990 by Jewish Community Relations Council/
Anti-Defamation League of Minnesota and the Dakotas.
All rights reserved.

Published by Twayne Publishers
A division of G. K. Hall & Co.
70 Lincoln Street, Boston, Massachusetts 02111

Copyediting supervised by Barbara Sutton
Book design and production by Janet Z. Reynolds
Typeset by Huron Valley Graphics, Ann Arbor, Michigan

Printed on permanent/durable acid-free paper
and bound in the United States of America

Library of Congress Cataloging-in-Publication Data

Witnesses to the Holocaust : an oral history / edited by Rhoda G.
  Lewin.
    p.   cm.—(Twayne's oral history series ; no. 2)
  ISBN 0-8057-9100-0 (alk. paper);
  1. Holocaust, Jewish (1939–1945)—Personal narratives. 2. Oral
history. I. Lewin, Rhoda G. II. Series.
D804.3.W47   1990
940.53′18—dc20

89-15642
CIP

10 9 8 7 6 5 4 3 (hc)

IN MEMORIAM

*Recha Lewin of Berlin, Germany. Her son, Fritz, volunteered
to fight for his country in World War I and was killed in battle
in 1917. Recha cherished the Iron Cross her son received
posthumously; it was inscribed, in German, "The eternal gratitude
of the Fatherland is yours." In 1943 Recha Lewin also died for
Germany, her Fatherland. She traveled to Auschwitz locked in a
cattle car and on her arrival was sent immediately to the gas chamber.*

SERIES EDITOR'S NOTE

Historians since Herodotus have interviewed eyewitnesses to great events, but twentieth-century technology provides the opportunity for more widespread and systematic collection of oral history. First on wax cylinders, then with wire-recorders, reel-to-reel and cassette tape recorders, and video cameras, modern interviewers have captured an enormous quantity of reminiscences, from presidents to pioneers, literati to laborers.

Oral history may well be the twentieth century's substitute for the written memoir. In exchange for the immediacy of diaries or correspondence, the retrospective interview offers a dialogue between the participant and the informed interviewer. Having prepared sufficient preliminary research, interviewers can direct the discussion into areas long since "forgotten," or no longer considered of consequence. "I haven't thought about that in years," is a common response, uttered just before an interviewee commences with a surprisingly detailed description of some past incident. The quality of the interview, its candidness and depth, generally will depend as much upon the interviewer as the interviewee, and the confidence and rapport between the two adds a special dimension to the spoken memoir.

Interviewers represent a variety of disciplines, and work either as part of a collective effort or an individual enterprise. Regardless of their different interests or the variety of their subjects, all interviewers share a common imperative: to collect memories while they are still available. Most oral historians feel an additional responsibility to make their interviews accessible for use beyond their own research needs. Still, important collections of vital, vibrant interviews lie scattered in archives throughout every state, undiscovered or underutilized.

Twayne's Oral History Series seeks to identify those resources and to publish selections of the best materials. The series lets people speak for themselves, from their own unique perspectives on people, places, and events. But to be more than a babble of voices, each volume will organize its interviews around particular situations and events and tie them together with interpretive essays that place individuals into the larger historical context. The styles and format of individual volumes will vary with the material from which they are drawn, demonstrating again the diversity of oral history and its methodology.

Whenever oral historians gather in conference they enjoy retelling experiences about inspiring individuals they met, unexpected information they elicited, and unforgetable reminiscences that would otherwise have never been recorded. The result invariably reminds listeners of others who deserve to be interviewed, provides them with models of interviewing techniques, and inspires them to make their own contribution to the field. I trust that the oral historians in this series, as interviewers, editors, and interpreters, will have a similar effect upon their readers.

Donald A. Ritchie, Series Editor
Senate Historical Office

CONTENTS

FOREWORD

The Quality of Memory

David Cooperman

The work of memory in our lives is so much a part of human existence that we easily take it for granted. We rely on it for the most simple of everyday matters—remembering a birthday, a telephone number—and we draw on our remembrances to bind our present acts with past experience. We also share the memories of loved ones, of kin, of close friends. Without such sharing our lives would be impoverished. Without such sharing a people loses its way. This book is, then, a very special act of sharing—a recapturing and a sharing of sharp memories by people who lost their own loved ones, their kin, or their close friends in the Holocaust.

This book is meant to enrich our lives. It is not intended to be simply a story about the past. There are many remarkable histories of the Holocaust in which the serious reader can study every aspect of that overwhelming event. In this book the voices of people who felt the full force of the Holocaust speak out as if their memory were able to give birth to the events themselves. It is common to speak of "the dead past" as a way of saying that things that happened then are merely stories told and retold, stories that have no real effect on our lives today. This cannot be the case, however, with the people who speak in the pages that follow. Whether they were victims or liberators who helped to snatch the victims from death, they breathe into life the events they experienced.

The people who speak so eloquently in this book have two things in common. They were part of the Holocaust, and they happened, in one way or other, to be living near one another in Minnesota and Wisconsin years afterward. The liberators came home; the survivors reshaped broken lives and became involved in a settled pattern of everyday life and memory. Now, years afterward, we understand that what they experienced earlier in this violent century can so easily be lost unless their remembrances are recorded. These eyewitness accounts permit us to imagine how it must have felt in human terms and allow us to share such remembrance.

There have been many genocides in human history but only one Holocaust. Between 1939 and 1945 about six million Jews and five million non-Jews were forcibly removed from their homes, humiliated, and murdered in cold blood. How could this conceivably have been accomplished? At first, with conventional means—mainly rifles and machine guns in the hands of special army units or other armed representatives of the Nazi regime. From 1942 to 1945 it was done with the aid of a vast Nazi bureaucracy and carried out by a combination of forced starvation and assembly-line gassing in the notorious death camps. Never before had such a gigantic, complex social organization been invented, and science and technology utilized, for the sole purpose of completely murdering a people. When it was over, a formerly thriving, richly developed culture—Jewish life in Europe—was essentially destroyed.

Jews and Christians alike suffered and were murdered. But Jews were murdered only because they were Jews. Why this obsession with killing Jews?

Expulsions and pogroms, most of them sparked by false beliefs about Jews and Jewish worship, had occurred regularly in many European countries since the Middle Ages. But by the late nineteenth century new patterns of anti-Semitism had developed. In France, Germany, Austria, and Russia there were political parties and social movements based on anti-Jewish racial myths. Then, in the aftermath of World War I, severe social and economic problems arose in the defeated nations, particularly Germany and Austria, and in the new states reinstated or established by the Versailles Treaty, such as Poland. Extremist nationalistic parties and movements attracted followers who found the new parties' simple-minded programs satisfying—programs that blamed the Jews for losing the war and for the severe economic depression that followed. As these groups grew in membership, their political power increased, and more and more citizens found them "respectable." Meanwhile, there was little friendly, sympathetic contact between Christian and Jew because of the religious organization of the larger society and because in many central European countries the Jewish communities were by tradition isolated both geographically and socially.

When the Nazis under Hitler gained power in Germany early in 1933, they initiated legalistic attacks against Jews, which included firing Jews from civil service jobs and restricting their access to public clubs, sports facilities, and other places. On May 10, 1933, Jewish books and books by non-Jewish opponents of Nazism were destroyed in huge public bonfires. The Nuremberg Laws of 1935 provided the racist standards for defining Jewishness; all people with any Jewish ancestry within at least three generations became outcasts. By 1938 most Jews had been deprived of economic means of existing, having been expelled from the professions, arts, schools, and unions. Business, marriage, real estate, and other legal obligations between Jew and non-Jew could be legally broken whenever the non-Jewish partner wished to do so.

November 9 and 10, 1938, signaled the beginning of the Holocaust. In what has come to be known as *Kristallnacht,* the "night of the broken glass," the Nazis encouraged rioters in Germany and Austria to destroy synagogues and Jewish shops and businesses. More than 100 synagogues were destroyed and hundreds more damaged, 20,000 Jews were arrested and taken to concentration camps, and hundreds more were killed, and 7,500 shops and businesses were smashed and looted.

On September 1, 1939, Hitler took the first steps toward his dream of building a "master race." The German attack on Poland was the first step in the official slaughter of Jews outside Germany, while at home, in Germany itself, the authorized "mercy killing" of deformed and mentally ill persons began. Almost 80,000 were murdered, until protests from Protestant and Catholic leaders stopped the killing. But when detailed plans were drafted on January 20, 1942, for the so-called Final Solution, there were no official protests. The Jews were to be exterminated.

This was no simple job. It required systematic planning, coordination of many organizations, among them the Gestapo, S.S., police, army, government agencies, and Nazi party leadership groups. As country after country fell to the Germans, Jews all over Europe were concentrated in ghettoes and systematically starved. Those who survived were sent to slave labor camps or to gas chambers at mass killing centers whose names have come to stand for the most hellish constructions of mankind: Chelmno, Treblinka, Sobibor, Majdanek, Belzec, Auschwitz. More than two-thirds of Europe's Jews were murdered in this way. Toward the end, when Germany was losing the war, railroad cars, manpower, and materials desperately needed in combat continued to be focused instead on the killing of Jews.

In Poland 90 percent of the Jews were murdered. In Denmark non-Jews in the Danish underground evacuated 7,000 Jews to Sweden, and only 475 were captured by the Germans. Where there was comparatively little anti-Semitism, where Jewish and Christian communities had wide contacts, the Nazis were less effective.

In every country in Europe, some Jews survived. Germany surrendered, ending the war in Europe, on May 8, 1945. Slowly the survivors began to piece together what remained of their lives and families. Yet few of those who survived understood the astonishing intent or extent of the Holocaust. But when they speak of their own lives, before, during, and after these events, their stories can be pieced together and related to the larger forces that swept them up. And there are lessons to be learned, among them the efficacy of the big lie, the use of scapegoats, the inability of many victims-to-be to believe what could happen, and the failure of many good people, and most of the governments of the free world, to see what was happening, to care, and to act.

The comparatively small proportion of survivors made their way, for the most part, to Israel or to the United States. Whether their new lives in any way are a commentary on their past experiences is a Job-like question, not addressed here. The task for the reader is to take what follows, know that these are live sparks, and not ghosts of the past, and to remember. In remembering, perhaps one's own life and community can be deepened and enriched.

David Cooperman is professor of sociology at the University of Minnesota.

PREFACE

There were no guarantees for survival in Hitler's Europe, especially for Jews. A carpenter or a mechanic had a better chance than a shopkeeper. It helped to be young and physically fit, and sometimes to have blond hair and blue eyes, or to have money or jewelry with which to buy forged papers, black market food, or the route to freedom.

Luck was often the most important factor, and the luckiest ones left Europe before or during the war. Almost 240,000 of them came to the United States in the 1930s and early 1940s. Another 50,000 survivors came later, after the war was over.

Many of the new Americans, especially the postwar survivors who had suffered in camps or in hiding, did not even tell their own children what had happened to them, why there was a number tattooed on Mother's arm, or why the children had no grandparents, no aunts and uncles, no cousins. Some could not, or did not want to, tell their children what cruelties human beings could commit, what they had suffered, or what they had to do in order to survive. Others remained silent because they could not answer their own questions: How could human beings treat their fellow human beings with such cruelty? Why was I chosen to survive? Moreover, they were silenced by well-meaning people who did not want to listen, who said, "It's over, and we must put the past behind. Forget those terrible things, begin a new life."

Then, in the mid-1970s, historians and survivors began to realize that the Holocaust story had not been told and that the survivors, an aging generation, would not be here to bear witness for future generations. Some, most notably Elie Wiesel and Primo Levi, had begun to write about their experiences. But tens of thousands who could give eyewitness testimony had not done so.

In New York, Los Angeles, Dallas, Washington, Milwaukee, Kansas City, Oklahoma City, and other communities, survivors and children of survivors began to interview each other, and oral historians began to interview them. In Minneapolis we, too, began to collect testimony from survivors and from those who had liberated the camps. Our goal was to create teaching materials for high schools and colleges, churches, interfaith groups, and other organizations, in part to discredit the so-called scholars who were saying that the Holocaust was wholly imaginary, that there were no gas chambers or no crematoria, that the Jews who died had been killed by Russians, except for the subversives, partisans, spies, and criminals (1.5 million murdered children among them) that the Germans, unfortunately, had had to kill themselves.

Staff at the Minnesota–Dakotas Jewish Community Relations Council/ Anti-Defamation League recruited interviewers, constructed an interview questionnaire, located funding, then turned to the most important aspect of the project: finding the interviewees.

There were no records showing how many survivors or liberators lived in Minnesota. Social service agencies that had assisted survivors when they arrived in the United States had not kept records of their whereabouts, and survivor organizations like the New World Club and the New Americans had long since disbanded.

However, the Minneapolis Public Library had recently prepared an exhibit for school children based on the nationally televised miniseries, "The Holocaust." Twenty local survivors had answered a communitywide call for tour guides. Relying on the "snowball" sampling technique, a questionnaire was sent to the volunteers and to a few other survivors who were lecturing or had written on the Holocaust. The questionnaire was a simple one: Where were you born? Did you spend the war years in a ghetto / camp / in hiding / as a partisan, where, and for how long? Would you be willing to be interviewed? Do you know anyone else who should receive notice of this project?

Interviewing began in April 1982. By February 1985 thirty-nine interviews had been completed, three of them with American liberators of the camps. One of the first lessons had been learned: volunteer interviewers were so traumatized by their listening experience that few were willing to do more than one interview. Twenty of the interviews had been done by a paid journalist.

In February 1986 I was asked to edit the transcribed interviews, which ranged in length from 43 to 185 pages, into three- or four-page "Survivor Packets" that could be used as teaching materials. Each brief summary had to preserve the speaker's language, personality, and viewpoint, and present the speaker's most important experiences.

I began by listening to the tapes, transcript in hand, to make sure that the transcripts were accurate. Some interviewees spoke with foreign accents, and many had used foreign words and phrases and references to events that were misunderstood by the transcribers.

I soon realized that several countries were not represented at all, among them France, Hungary, and Greece. In addition, more survivors and liberators were coming forward, and each had a new story to tell. Some identified themselves at Holocaust commemoration programs. Some heard about the project and wanted to be included. Children of survivors began to sign up for Holocaust history courses at University of Minnesota and metro area colleges. When I spoke on the Holocaust, people would tell me, "You must interview so-and-so . . ." A friend surprised me by saying, "You know, I was born in Cracow . . ." A hotel porter said, "I go fishing with this guy who talks about this German camp he saw, and he starts to cry."

We now have the stories of forty-four survivors, two Polish Catholic women, who were interviewed with the two Jewish friends whose lives they saved, and fourteen American liberators, men and women who were among the first to enter the camps.

Holocaust oral history can be used in many ways. One is to investigate how social behavior reflects violence in popular culture and governmental policy. Another is to explore the implications of German-born social psychologist Kurt Lewin's theories and research on authoritarian practices in child rearing.* A third is to study validity and the "practiced" response, noting that where several family members or close friends survived together, each tells the same stories, in the same words, even when they are interviewed at separate times or repeatedly by different interviewers.

Still another research question worth exploring is why male survivors who agreed to be interviewed outnumber women, more than two to one. Educational psychologist Carol Wirtschafter, who has developed classroom exercises using these interviews, has noted that many high school students seem to find nudity more difficult to deal with than death, which they see so often on television or in movies. Perhaps, then, most women do not want to remember, much less describe, being forced to strip naked in the presence of hundreds of men, women, and children, family and friends and neighbors, while being observed by male and female guards, showering en masse, then waiting together for hours, still naked and shivering, until they were permitted to put on their prison uniforms, and having to live for years with never a moment's privacy or safety from harassment.

We also learned, or relearned, some facts about oral history practice that could be of help to people planning similar projects.

We learned how difficult and emotionally draining it is to interview

---

*See Kurt Lewin, *Resolving Social Conflicts*, ed. Gertrud Weiss Lewin (New York: Harper & Row, 1948), esp. Part I: "Problems of Changing Culture."

survivors of tragedies about events that are as real and as painful to them today as they were more than forty years ago. We learned how important training is for interviewers. The "intuitive" and "empathic" approach may sound good, but when an interviewer stops a survivor in mid-thought to ask, "Where is Kiev?," serious damage is done to the rapport necessary for a good interview. We also learned that, technique and training notwithstanding, an interviewer must adapt to each interview situation, sometimes setting aside the questionnaire when the floodgates of memory open and a survivor talks nonstop for hours.

In editing the transcripts, I sought at all times to keep what was unique about each person and each person's experience and to let that person tell the story in his or her own words, with the following exceptions. I usually made no attempt to imitate foreign accents or to replicate common usage, as in 'em instead of *them* or the repetitious use of phrases like *you know.* I translated most foreign words and phrases into English. I sometimes replaced an *and* or other connecting word with a period or changed the order of speaking in order to draw together comments relating to a specific topic or event. I corrected inadvertent errors in geography, names, and dates. I tried to omit hearsay and to focus instead on eyewitness testimony.

Complete transcripts and the taped interviews are archived at the JCRC/ADL, 15 South Ninth Street, Suite 450, Minneapolis, MN 55402. The interviewees have given permission to use their interviews for scholarly and educational purposes, and I hope they will be pleased to see themselves in print and to know that they have made this substantive contribution to Holocaust education and to their collective history.

Certainly I am pleased. This book, to me, is what oral history is meant to be—"history as if people mattered." Because the Germans were methodical keepers of records, historians have access to a great deal of quantitative information about the Holocaust. However, oral testimony tells us what actually happened to those who died and those who survived. By doing so, it gives us the human dimension of an event unparalleled in human history.

Rhoda G. Lewin

ACKNOWLEDGMENTS

We are deeply grateful to those who shared their lives with us in the taped interviews for this book—the survivors, who somehow learned to live with their memories, and who built new lives and new families for themselves in the United States, and the liberators, who struggled not to weep, and sometimes the tears did come, as they remembered those few hours more than forty years ago when they were the first Americans to see what so many Germans had done to human beings like themselves, in concentration camps and labor camps.

Many people worked on this project. Overall direction was provided by Morton W. Ryweck, executive director of the Jewish Community Relations Council/Anti-Defamation League of Minnesota and the Dakotas (JCRC/ADL), and by Professor David Cooperman of the University of Minnesota. JCRC/ADL staff assigned to the project included assistant director Carol Wirtschafter and her predecessors, Samuel I. Horowitz and Michael Greenberg. Initial funding was provided by the Fingerhut Family Foundation, the St. Paul Foundation, General Mills Foundation, and private donors. Interviewers included Don Bernstein, Maddy Braufman, Bonnie Dickel, Steven Foldes, Michael Garelick, Michael Greenberg, Harlan Jacobs, Jane Katz, Sandy Kibort, Rhoda Lewin, Stuart Markoff, Riv-Ellen Prell, Lynn Rosen, Nina Samuels, Gary N. Shapiro, Rosalyn Smith, Gary Stern, Joni Sussman, and David Zarkin. Secretaries Barbara Schneider and Mary Sue Miller tended to myriad details, and Carla Cruzan and Ellen Lewin performed the tedious and often difficult task of transcribing the interviews. The map of Europe is the work of Professor Cooperman and cartographer Gregory Chu, funded by the Edelstein Family Foundation, University of Minnesota. Also generous with their assistance and encouragement were Professor Stephen Feinstein of the University of Wisconsin at River Falls and Professor Robert Ross of the University of Minnesota.

Special mention, too, should be made of William Borth, a high school history teacher in Willmar, Minnesota, who began in 1980 to teach a separate and self-contained thirteen-week course on the Holocaust. Borth received anonymous hate mail and threatening telephone calls, but he continued his class, and the harassment eventually stopped. When his students sponsored a Night of Remembrance in October 1986 to introduce the community at large to the events of the Holocaust, more than 1,000 people crowded into the local auditorium, and several hundred more had to be turned away. Our children need more teachers like Bill Borth.

My personal thanks go also to Professor Cooperman, who encouraged my early research in oral history and the lives of Jewish immigrants to the United States; to my Berlin-born husband, Tom Lewin; and to my late father, Louis Greene, who was also an editor, a writer, and a historian.

Rhoda G. Lewin

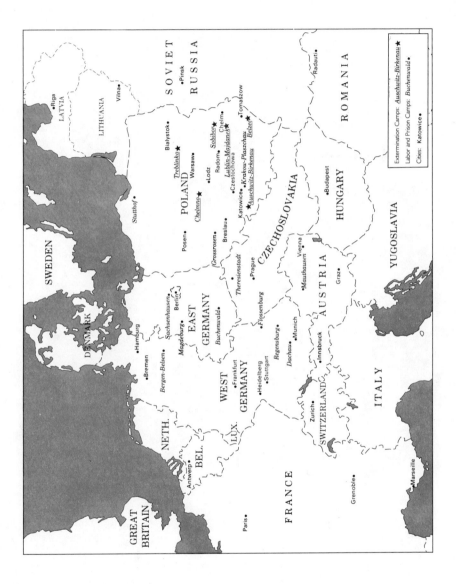

PART I

*Survivors of
Concentration Camps*

Many people have come to use *concentration camp* as a generic term to describe the places where the Germans imprisoned or exterminated Jews before and during World War II.

Actually, there were many kinds of camps, and many kinds of prisoners. There were slave labor camps in ghettoes and other locations, where Jews and non-Jews from countries occupied by the Germans worked in factories, quarried stone, built roads and tank traps, and performed other work for their German captors. There were prison camps intended at first for the Nazis' political opponents and, later, for prisoners of war. And there were the extermination camps, where millions, almost all of them Jews, were systematically put to death. Death came in many forms. Men, women, and children of all ages were gassed, burned alive, starved to death. They died of typhus, tuberculosis, or other diseases. Or they were killed in other ways by sadistic guards or by doctors performing medical experiments.

Here are the stories of twenty-one camp survivors.

SAM BANKHALTER
Lodz, Poland

> In Auschwitz I had to pick up people with ty-
> phus, still living, take them to the gas chambers,
> then to the crematorium. You don't think, you
> just try to survive. I was fourteen years old.

Sam Bankhalter's father was a manufacturer of prefabricated wooden houses, a Hebrew scholar, and an ardent Zionist who helped young Poles who wanted to go to Palestine. Sam was running an errand for his father when the Nazis caught him and sent him to Auschwitz.

There was always anti-Semitism in Poland. The slogan even before Hitler was "Jew, get out of here and go to Palestine." As Hitler came to power, there was not a day at school I was not spit on or beaten up.

I was at camp when the Germans invaded Poland. The camp directors told us to find our own way home. We walked many miles with airplanes over our heads, dead people on the streets. At home there were blackouts. I was just a kid, tickled to death when I was issued a flashlight and gas mask. The Polish army was equipped with buggies and horses, the Germans were all on trucks and tanks. The war was over in ten days.

THE GHETTO   The German occupation was humiliation from day 1. If Jewish people were wearing the beard and sidecurls, the Germans were cutting the beard, cutting the sidecurls, laughing at you, beating you up a little bit. Then the Germans took part of Lodz and put on barbed wire, and all the Jews had to assemble in this ghetto area. You had to leave in five or ten minutes or half an hour, so you couldn't take much stuff with you.

The Jewish community chose my father to run the cemetery, to organize burials and clean up the streets, because dead people started smelling on the streets. They brought in frozen Jewish soldiers, hundreds and hundreds. I helped bury them.

AUSCHWITZ   We were the first ones in Auschwitz. We built it. What you got for clothing was striped pants and the striped jacket, no underwear, no socks. In wintertime you put paper in your shoes, and we used to take empty cement sacks and put a string in the top, put two together, one in back and one in front, to keep warm.

If they told you to do something, you went to do it. There was no yes or no, no choices. I worked in the crematorium for about eleven months. I saw Dr. Mengele's experiments on children, I knew the kids that became vegetables. Later in Buchenwald I saw Ilse Koch with a hose and regulator, trying to get pressure to make a hole in a woman's stomach. I saw them cutting Greek people in pieces. I was in Flossenburg for two weeks, and they shot 25,000 Russian soldiers, and we put them down on wooden logs and burned them. Every day the killing, the hanging, the shooting, the crematorium smell, the ovens, and the smoke going out.

I knew everybody, knew every trick to survive. I was one of the youngest in Auschwitz, and I was like "adopted" by a lot of the older people, especially the fathers. Whole families came into Auschwitz together, and you got to Dr. Mengele, who was saying "right, left, left, right," and you knew, right there, who is going to the gas chamber and who is not. Most of the men broke down when they knew their wives and their kids— three-, five-, nine-year-olds—went into the gas chambers. In fact, one of my brothers committed suicide in Auschwitz because he couldn't live with knowing his wife and children are dead.

I was able to see my family when they came into Auschwitz in 1944. I had a sister, she had a little boy a year old. Everybody that carried a child went automatically to the gas chamber, so my mother took the child. My sister survived, but she still suffers, feels she was a part of killing my mother.

I waved to my mother and I went over to my father and said, "Dad, where's God? They kill rabbis, priests, ministers, the more religious, the faster they go! What has happened?" His only answer to me was, "This is the way God wants it." This was the last time I spoke to my father.

THE TRANSPORT   The Germans liquidated Auschwitz a few months before liberation. They put us in railroad boxes, 125 guys in there, hundreds of cars. You cannot sit, you cannot stand, you cannot lie down. You're sealed in, going in one direction one day, back the same direction the next day. No food, nothing. This was January, and I was so thirsty I licked the frost off the metal, even when my tongue got stuck and pieces ripped off.

We wound up in Buchenwald. But when they tried to clean out Buchenwald, I wouldn't go. I could barely walk, and I knew I wouldn't make it. There's another fellow alive today in Germany, and one in Israel, because the three of us crawled into a septic hole under the barracks and hid.

LIBERATION   For three days I was in that hole, listening to the guns, closer and closer. Then I passed out. I guess it was the American military that dragged me out of the hole and flew me to Marseille, to a hospital.

After I recuperated I went all over, looking for people. I was nineteen years old, and I had nobody. I couldn't even remember my grandparents' names, so I could look for them. Then one night in a dream the name came to me. This is the way I found my aunt, who lives now in Paris.

You start to put your life together. I was living in a D.P. camp, then I went out on my own in Frankfurt. I worked for the American military as an interpreter. I picked people up in Poland, smuggling them to Palestine, smuggled food, clothing. I sent people from Hamburg to Haifa, but the British sent them back. I got married, and my wife was working with me.

In '49 we settled down in Israel. I worked smuggling ammunition, got into buying mechanical equipment for *kibbutzim*, built one of the biggest irrigation plants in the world. I had a job that took me all over the world—Burma, Africa.

As a Jew, I don't think you can feel as good anywhere as you can feel in Israel. But there are terrorists all the time. We were coming home from a birthday party and had an ambush with machine guns shooting at us, killing three people. My daughter, ten years old, was scared to death, couldn't sleep at night, couldn't concentrate in school. The doctor said, "You have to get away from this atmosphere." I wanted to stay in Israel, but we came to the United States in 1956 and I'm still here.

LOOKING BACK   Once you start fighting for your life, all the ethics are gone. You live by circumstances. There is no pity. You physically draw down to the point where you cannot think any more, where the only thing is survival, and maybe a little hope that if I survive, I'm gonna be with my grandchildren and tell them the story.

In the camps, death actually became a luxury. We used to say, "Look at how lucky he is. He doesn't have to suffer any more."

I was a lucky guy. I survived, and I felt pretty good about it. But then you feel guilty living! My children—our friends are their "aunts" and "uncles." They don't know what is a grandfather, a grandmother, a cousin, a holiday sitting as a family.

As you grow older, you think about it, certain faces come back to you. You remember your home, your brothers, children that went to the crematorium. You wonder, how did your mother and father feel when they were in the gas chamber? Many nights I hear voices screaming in those first few minutes in the gas chamber, and I don't sleep.

I talk to a lot of people, born Americans, and they don't relate. They can't understand, and I don't blame them. Sometimes it's hard even for me to understand the truth of this whole thing. Did it really happen? But I saw it.

The majority of the people here live fairly good. I don't think there's a country in the world that can offer as much freedom as this country can offer. But the Nazi party exists here, now. This country is supplying anti-Semitic material to the whole world, printing it here and shipping it all over, and our leaders are silent, just as the world was silent when the Jews were being taken to the camps. How quick we forget.

When I sit in a plane, I see 65 percent of the people will pick up the sports page of the newspaper. They don't care what is on the front page! And this is where the danger lies. All you need is the economy to turn a little sour and have one person give out the propaganda. With 65 percent of the population the propaganda works, and then the other 35 percent is powerless to do anything about it.

FRED BARON
Vienna, Austria

I was liberated in Belsen. I remember clutching
a can of condensed milk in my hand. I sat in the
mud and slime among the dead, and I found a
rusty nail and tried to punch a hole in the can.
Then I took a pebble, but the pebble was to me
like a rock. I didn't even have the strength to
open a can of milk.

Fred Baron was fifteen when the Germans marched into Vienna in 1938. His parents were well-to-do, assimilated Jews; both died in the Holocaust.

I had a wonderful youth. I went to concerts, to the opera, my parents sent us to camp in the summertime. But in Europe even small children were aware that life is not always peaceful. The first thing we learned in school was military history—the wars and rebellions and constant occupations.

My father was really an agnostic and my mother was not observant any more, and my Jewish education came once a week in the public schools, the same as Catholics and Protestants had. We were born in Austria and spoke German and felt and looked just like anybody else.

In March 1938 the Germans marched into Austria. What had evolved in Germany over five years happened in Austria within a matter of weeks.

THE OCCUPATION   One of my best friends became overnight an outspoken Austrian Nationalist and an anti-Semite. I was kicked out of high school. My father's store was closed down. Bank accounts were closed, people lost their jobs, Jews were not allowed to practice as professionals. We were penniless, forced to share our apartment with other Jews.

Jews could not go to any public building or any parks. We could not go to a library or movie. We were not allowed to ride on public transportation except under certain conditions, and then only on the rear platform. We could not go into a store, except one hour a day. Even if we had money we were not allowed to buy many things, including some foods, because they were just not sold to Jews. I went to a soup kitchen every day to bring home our only meal.

On *Kristallnacht* I went downstairs to see whether it was safe to go out, and a lieutenant spotted my yellow badge and took me to a makeshift jail. My mother found me after a few hours. She had relatives in Hungary, and she managed to free me by waving some kind of Hungarian document in the Nazis' faces.

My father had friends in England, and they were all trying to help us get out, but like America or any other country, England made tremendous difficulties for Jews to immigrate. The only exception was for a few Jewish children. These friends made it possible for my sister to join one of the children's transports early in 1939. My parents felt very sad about sending their twelve-year-old daughter away to a strange country, to live with a strange family in a small town.

September 1, 1939, war broke out with Poland, and after a few weeks they took Jewish people on trains and dumped them in ghettoes in Polish cities. Many of our friends were taken this way. My father saw his family, everything, going down the drain. He became very sick, and there was no medical treatment for Jews, so he didn't get any treatment and soon died.

My mother and I were hiding one night here and one night there, with non-Jewish friends. Anybody hiding a Jew was subject to terrible penalties, so to ask even a close friend to hide you was not an easy thing to do. We also tried to hide in Jewish apartments where the people were already deported.

Then I found work at the railroad station and was given security for myself and my mother. I worked carrying pig-iron on my shoulders.

In fall of 1941 the German extermination policy really got running. Transports to the east were increasing, so my mother and I went over the border at night to Hungary.

In Hungary I was trying to get legal documentation so we could get food stamps. I traveled to a little town where somebody with connections was supposedly able to give us the necessary papers. But a crime was committed in the town, and as soon as they saw me, a stranger, they put me in jail. The judge said I was innocent but wanted to send me back to Austria! I tried to explain that being sent back there was like a death sentence, and finally the judge dismissed me because I had some papers from my father, who was a volunteer and an officer in the Austro-Hungarian army in the first World War. I was given papers that I was a legal resident of Hungary and could get food tickets.

Then the Hungarian authorities got hold of my mother and put her in jail in Budapest. Because we entered the country without papers, they told her they would deport her unless I would join her.

This was December 1941. We were sent to an internment camp in northeastern Hungary. There were separate buildings for men and women, but I saw my mother from time to time. Later all the male Jews were sent to a prison camp near the Slovakian border, and my mother was freed to live with relatives in Hungary. She sent me letters, a package containing some clothing, even a cake. Then the German S.S. completed the occupation of Hungary in the spring of 1944, my mother again was put into a camp, and that was the last I heard from her.

DEPORTATION   I was marched with the local Jewish population—men, women, and children—eight or ten hours, to a small railroad station. Nobody told us where we were going. We were forced into railroad cars, 100 to 120 in one car, like sardines, without food, without water, without any sanitary facility. The cars were sealed and we stood there for maybe half a day before even moving. Finally, began the slow trip to nowhere.

There were children in our car, and old people. People got sick, died, and some went insane. It was an absolute, indescribable hell. I really don't know how many days and nights we were in that living hell on wheels.

When we finally stopped, they tore open the railroad cars and we were blinded by light, because our eyes were just not used to light any more. We saw funny-looking characters wearing striped pajama-like uniforms with matching caps, with great big sticks in their hands. They were screaming and yelling in all languages to jump out of the cars.

I didn't know where I was. All around us were barracks and barbed wire and machine gun towers, and in the distance I saw what looked like a huge factory with black smoke coming out of chimneys. I noticed a peculiar smell in the air and also a fine dust, subduing the light. The sunshine was not bright but there were birds singing. It was a beautiful day.

We were marched through a meadow filled with yellow flowers and one of the fellows next to me just turned and walked straight into the meadow. The guards cried out to him to stop, but he didn't hear or he didn't want to. He just kept slowly marching into the meadow, and then they opened up with machine guns and the man fell down dead. And that was my reception to Auschwitz.

AUSCHWITZ   We were separated, men and women, and formed rows of fives. I found myself in front of a very elegantly dressed German officer. He was wearing boots and white gloves and he carried a riding whip, and with the whip he was pointing left or right, left or right. Whichever direction he pointed, guards pushed the person in front of him either left or right. I was twenty-one years old and in pretty good shape, but older people were sent to the other side and marched away.

We had to undress and throw away all belongings except our shoes. We were chased through a cold shower, and we stood shivering in the night air until we were told to march to a barracks. We were handed prisoner uniforms—a jacket, pants, and a sort of beanie—and a metal dish. We didn't really know what happened yet. We were absolutely numb.

A non-Jewish kapo, an Austrian with a hard, weather-beaten face, told us, "You have arrived at hell on earth." He had been in prison since 1938, and he gave us basic concepts on how to stay alive.

"Don't trust anybody," he said, "don't trust your best friend. Look out for yourself. Be selfish to the point of obscenity. Try and stay alive from one minute to the other one. Don't let down for one second. Always try and find out where the nearest guards are and what they are doing. Don't volunteer for anything. And don't get sick, or you will be a goner in no time."

Auschwitz was gigantic—rows and rows of barracks as far as the eye could see, subdivided by double strings of electric barbed wire. There were Hungarians and Polish Jews and a great number of Greeks, many Dutch Jews, some French, Germans.

Food was our main interest in life. In the morning we received what they called coffee—black water. We worked until noon, then we got a bowl of soup. In the evening we received another bowl of either vegetable or soup, a little piece of bread, and sometimes a tiny little piece of margarine or sugar or some kind of sausage. And that was the food for the day.

Suicides happened all the time, usually by hanging, at night. One fellow threw himself in front of a truck. It just broke his arm, but the S.S. guards beat him to a pulp, and in the morning he was dead.

A tremendous number of transports were coming in. The gas chambers could not keep up, so they were burning people in huge pits. Some of the smaller children were thrown in alive. We could hear the screams day and night, but sometimes the human mind can take just so much and then it just closes up and refuses to accept what is happening just 100, 200 feet away.

LABOR CAMP   I was sent to Silesia, to a small town belonging to the Grossrosen administrative area. The Germans built bunks in an empty factory, encircled the area with barbed wire, built machine gun towers, and presto!—one slave labor camp for a thousand people.

We were working right in small German towns, widening the roads and making them stronger so the Germans could bring in heavy equipment against the Russians. I don't like to have anybody tell me the German people did not know what was going on because I could see hundreds of them every day and they could see us. We couldn't be mistaken for anything but prisoners! We were walking skeletons, we had our hair shorn, we had these blue and white striped uniforms. And we were guarded by heavily armed S.S. as if we would be the most precious possession the world would have to offer.

When their wives and families came to see them, our guards were concerned husbands, normal human beings. But when it came to the prisoners, they were absolute animals, and they became more and more vicious as they saw their own end nearing. Toward the very end, when these dregs of humanity were sent to war, the Germans brought in old people or severely wounded soldiers as guards, and these showed us much more humanity.

In December 1944 we could hear the rumbling of the approaching Russian armies and guns firing. We saw German refugees, civilians, coming from the east and going west. And pretty soon we saw them going east from the west. Germany was being compressed, and they were running from the Russian and American armies.

THE TRANSPORT   In February we were marched on foot to Czechoslovakia, over the mountains. It was cold, snowing. Everybody that lagged behind was shot, so we learned to sleep while walking, to urinate while walking. Then we were put in open railroad cars, without provisions, freezing. A sympathetic German in charge of this train kept us alive by giving us hot water from the engine.

BERGEN-BELSEN   They took us to Bergen-Belsen, a nightmare of a different sort. It was crowded, there was hardly any food, water was nonexistent. But we were not hounded by guards or worked to death. We starved to death.

At first people who died were put in mass graves. It took four of us to drag one body to the graves, four dying people dragging one dead one. Then there were so many, they were put like cordwood at every corner of the barracks. Mountains appeared, mountains of bodies.

They sent me to Stettin to build fortifications against the Russians. But the military commander took one look at us and told the S.S. to take us back because we were more dead than alive.

LIBERATION   I was liberated in Belsen. I was in very bad shape, no longer able to walk. We received a package from the Red Cross, some hardtack and a can of condensed milk. I was liberated, the Germans were defeated, but all around me people were still dying, and I didn't have the strength even to open a can of milk. That was the first time in my life that I started to cry.

A British soldier asked what am I doing. I was showing him that I was trying to punch a hole, and then I remembered my sister who went to England, and I asked whether he knew anybody in his outfit from that area. A few minutes later he came back with a nurse and an officer.

The nurse was from Bedford where my sister was, and she was writing down my sister's name and the people she stayed with. The officer was a physician, and he took away that can of milk, and picked me up and carried me to the nearest barracks, and made a clear space in one of those filthy bunk beds.

He brought me a huge can of zweiback toast and a five-gallon can of English tea and he says, "That's all you're gonna drink or eat if you want to stay alive. Don't move, and I'll come see you every day." And he did. He saved my life.

The British brought in German prisoners to carry the bodies and dump them into mass graves. Then they brought in the bulldozers and set the camp on fire.

A Swedish Red Cross official came to take down names of former inmates who were in bad shape, to be taken to Sweden. He asked each one their nationality, and when I said "Austrian" he said he can't take Germans or Austrians. I said, "I was put into this mess because I am Jewish, not Austrian!" A day later I was on the ambulance train to Bremen and then went by ambulance boat to Sweden.

I wanted to leave Europe behind me. In 1947 some friends helped me come to the United States. I stayed on the East Coast for about half a year and was on the verge of going back to Sweden when somebody told me, "What you see here is not really the United States." I found out there are Scandinavians in Minnesota, and I figured if they could stand the cold, maybe I could too!

LOOKING BACK   Until three or four years ago I even avoided talking to my own children about the Holocaust. But lately I have felt an
absolute need to pass the experiences I had on to the next generation.
We must learn from mistakes that were made, must be aware of how low
a people can sink. Germany was not a backward country; it had given us
many great minds and outstanding people. And in Austria, particularly
Vienna, with its long history of anti-Semitism, it didn't take much for
German propaganda to take effect.

Fred Baron (*left, front*) recuperated in a Swedish hospital after liberation from Bergen-Belsen, 1945.

Fred and Judy Baron with their children, Gary and Susan, 1988. Judy Baron is also a survivor.

REIDAR DITTMANN
Tonsberg, Norway

I must have been there in summer, fall, winter, and spring. But looking back at Buchenwald, I feel as though the month of November existed always. There's nothing grayer and more miserable than November.

Reidar Dittmann is a Lutheran. He was only eighteen, a music student studying choral conducting, when the Germans occupied his country in April 1940.

I was the first political prisoner in the history of my home town, and my home town is 1,100 years old! In October of 1940 I demonstrated against the Germans by leading 4,000 young people singing anti-German songs, and I was arrested and given a six-week jail term. But my father came, and the judge let him take me home.

When the underground was organized that same fall, it became reasonable for the organizers to use someone who had already showed his loyalty. As a clerk in a shipyard building ships for the Germans, my task as a member of the resistance was to see to it that work would go very slowly. One day a major merchant vessel was being officially baptized by the admiral of the German fleet in Norway. His wife cracked the champagne bottle on the prow, the ship sailed down the bedding—and then it sank! We had removed the plates the night before. I was sentenced to life imprisonment for that and sent to build coastal fortifications.

Then the puppet premier of Norway, Vidkun Quisling, pardoned 1,000 political prisoners according to age, and since I was only nineteen, I was sent home. I immediately got back into the underground, and I was apprehended again. This time I was sent to Germany, to Buchenwald.

BUCHENWALD   The first concentration camps in Germany were built to get members of the political opposition out of the way. The senior inmate in my barracks was a German Social Democrat, a member of the city council in Kassel. He was imprisoned on April 15, 1933, six weeks after the Nazi takeover! He was a professional survivor, number 431. I had number 32,232.

The corpse carriers were one of the more active working teams in Buchenwald. From 800 to 2,000 people died every day. We estimated that if you were Norwegian, Dutch, Danish, you might survive. If you were Belgian or French, your chances were slightly poorer. If you were

Czechoslovakian or Hungarian, they were even poorer. As a Polish prisoner, you had a life expectancy of three weeks. The Jews, of course, were a totally separate category, brought into Buchenwald for the express purpose of being exterminated.

We wore our numbers in a triangle on our left breast pocket. A red triangle meant political prisoner, and we had *NO,* which meant *Norwegian.* Criminals were wearing green triangles. Jewish prisoners had a purple triangle. The tattooing of numbers was reserved for Jewish prisoners.

On my card was written "Germanic intellectual material." I was Lutheran, Protestant, I was a university student, I was "Germanic"—blue eyes, blond hair. I was like an S.S. recruitment poster! So in a sense, that card said I was destined to survive.

I can close my eyes and know every little corner of this camp. In the center was a beautiful oak tree, and on the tree was a brass plate. It said, "Under this tree, Goethe sat and wrote some of his most beautiful poetry." And above the wrought iron gates when we marched through as prisoners was the motto of the camp in brass lettering, "Right or wrong, my country." I didn't know that was an American phrase, a statement made by Stephen Decatur during your war of liberation. And across the gate was another statement—the Nazis were grand about statements and mottos—which came, I think, from Ovid: "To each his own."

As you entered you came to the roll-call area. The gallows were the geographical center of the roll-call area. They were not used a great deal because hanging was impractical and slow, too inefficient for the Germans.

One of the most prominent features in the camp was the smoke stack from the crematory. There was never a time when it wasn't belching black smoke, and never a time when there wasn't an odor in the camp easily identified with the crematory.

We had roll call twice a day, at five in the morning and at six at night. The numbers had to agree, and we were kept on roll call until they did. Sometimes this could take six hours, during which there was no food, no comfort. The weather didn't matter. The guards wore furs and heavy boots, but we had only our very poor striped outfits on. People died at roll call every day.

Everything you did in camp, you did through responding to the public address system. One morning we were informed that roll call was delayed. We could hear the grinding of trucks, the mobile gas chambers that were waiting. And we knew that the night before some 10,000 Jews had arrived from Hungary.

We were hovering out in front of our barracks, and we heard this shuffling of wooden shoes against the gravel, from the lower part of the camp. The sound came closer and closer, and in the grayness of this November morning we saw masses of people shuffling toward the roll-call area.

They were all males. There were some so old they couldn't walk by themselves but had to be supported by younger individuals. And there were some so young they hadn't yet learned to walk, and they were carried in the arms of their fathers, their uncles, their grandfathers. They were all walking toward annihilation.

And on this particular day, the smoke poured forth so voluminously from the crematory chimney that daylight didn't break through.

As the war approached its end in the spring of 1945, we hardly got any food at all. I was convinced I wouldn't survive, because we were all thinking, "The Germans are not going to let us get out and tell about it."

LIBERATION   To be called to the gate meant to be exterminated. On March 18, 1945, the announcement came over the public address system, "All Norwegians to the gate." We were 349 Norwegians. We shuffled up the walk to the roll-call area, and the commander-in-chief—he was hanged in Nuremberg—came in with two people in dusty uniforms. He was smiling. To see him frown was horrible. To see him smile was even worse.

One of the two young men in the dusty uniforms said to us in Swedish, "I have come to take you to neutral Sweden." We didn't believe it. We thought that this is a trick. And then he said, "Go back to your barracks and pick up your belongings."

If he had been part of the system, he would certainly have known that we had nothing but our striped suits, and a triangle with a number, and our wooden shoes! So we shuffled back to the barracks, and into the barracks, and out again, and back to the roll-call area. And there they were, the two in the dusty uniforms, and the commander was gone. And the same young man said, "All right, boys. Let's go."

That's when it dawned on us that this was really true, because there wasn't a German in all of Europe who would simply say, "Let's go." Even if it were a German who liberated us, he's say, *"Achtung! Achtung! Macht schnell! Sofort!"*—"Attention! Attention! Step on it! Immediately!" So we walked under the gate, looking back at "To each his own" and "My country, right or wrong," and there were seventeen white buses with the Red Cross and Swedish flags on them and a little banner on each bus, "Welcome to neutral Sweden."

I weighed ninety-two pounds. May 8 was V-E day. If my stay in Buchenwald had lasted for another two months, I wouldn't have.

LOOKING BACK   When I first came to the United States on a scholarship to study at St. Olaf college and then came back to teach, I did find a tendency among certain people to disbelieve what had happened in Europe.

Norwegian Americans were very conscious of the extermination of the small Norwegian Jewish population, of which twelve people survived out of 2,000. But I had people say, "You experienced these things. How much of it is not true?" And I had to disappoint these people and say, "Whatever you have heard is true, and a great deal more." I had colleagues of German background expecting me to say, "Oh, the Germans were nice to me." Of course I couldn't do it, and some of them never spoke to me again.

After my liberation, I became a member of the Norwegian Army Intelligence Corps, preparing documents for the Nuremberg trials, with a nice little apartment in a military camp where we had 15,000 German prisoners. I had a German colonel who was my "boy" and was very happy to do it.

One of the weaknesses of American society in its relationship to Nazi Germany is that the Americans met the Germans when the Germans had been defeated. Americans have not experienced the Germans as their rulers!

DAVID EIGER
Radom, Poland

A cousin, maybe seventeen, decided he has to have
freedom. He dressed like a Polish peasant and
smuggled himself out of the ghetto. A day later his
body was brought back, with a bullet between his eyes.

David Eiger studied business management at a Catholic high school, graduated at sixteen, and was on his way to college when Germany occupied Poland in September 1939. In 1949 he came to the United States, learned English at the movies, and married an American girl he met on a blind date.

My father was president in Radom of the Jewish National Fund and was very friendly with men who formed the first government in Israel. I always belonged to a Zionist organization, and my plan was to wind up in Palestine.

In high school we had military training two or three hours every week. We wore blue slacks and a khaki blouse with a wide belt. One day I took off my belt and found written in ink, by my classmate who sat behind me, "You dirty Jew." I did not let that go by without a fight!

At graduation you were entitled to be admitted to an officers' school, but Jews usually received "deferments." When the war started, I asked to be mobilized. I was refused.

The Germans came to Radom on September 7, 1939. All radios had to be turned in. We could not walk on the sidewalk. We could not walk by a German with our hat on; we had to take off the hat and greet the German. We had to wear armbands with a blue star on the right arm. You could not be found outside after curfew without a permit. And all this was under penalty of death. The Germans would just shoot, no questions asked, and send the body back to the ghetto.

FORCED LABOR   In the Radom forced labor camp six of us lived in one room—my mother and sister and I, an uncle, and our friends Jules and his mother, in a room probably ten by fifteen feet. We had to stay in line all night to get bread, and we would maybe wind up with no bread but caught by the Germans to go to work.

In April 1942 there was a knock on our door at three in the morning, and my father was arrested by the Gestapo. I went to the Jewish Council to find out what happened with my father, but some Gestapo saw me and started to shoot. I hid and finally got to police headquarters after 6 A.M., when curfew was over. About 200 people had been taken, and more than half were executed on the spot. The bodies were at the Jewish hospital, so I went to look at all those lined-up bodies. My father's body was not there.

Within a day or two we were advised that people who were not shot were sent to Auschwitz. About a month later a packet came to my aunt from Auschwitz of her husband's clothing, followed by a telegram that he had died.

In the fall a German in the tanning factory where my father and I used to work came one day to tell me there's a letter in that factory, addressed to a worker who used to work there, but it was my father's handwriting and style of writing. That letter was for me, from my father in Auschwitz, to tell us he's alive!

Meanwhile, in July of 1942 the sending of people to Treblinka started, the first liquidation. Almost everybody in my family was shipped out that night to the gas chambers, and about 1,000 people were shot. A friend of mine was picked for a work crew to bury the bodies.

About ten days later the Germans installed big floodlights around the ghetto. Gestapo men were checking work passes—a card that one is working, what place, and in what industry. Then they made the decision whether that person would go or stay.

My sister Dora was out with a work crew and I had a work pass, but mother didn't. But I saw one Gestapo man who had been in our apartment to visit a relative of my mother's. I pushed my mother forward to that Gestapo man and he let her stay.

The following night they came again. I gave this German my gold watch, and again he put us with the group who stayed. Later I heard he was lenient with other Jews, too, and the Gestapo sent him to the Russian front.

In January of 1943 I was sent with two others to Gestapo headquarters to count the German loot—money and gold from people who had been deported. We overheard a lieutenant saying the ghetto should register all the Jews who had relatives in Palestine or who had been to Palestine. We did not know whether that list was good or bad, but we took a chance. My father had once visited Palestine, so all three of us asked the lieutenant to put us on the list. He did, and we were left behind when the others were sent to Treblinka.

One day in spring 1943, all the doctors and lawyers and leaders of the forced labor camp had to report to the gate. The Germans put them on trucks, and in a forest about fifteen miles from Radom, they shot them with machine guns. One survivor came back to tell us.

That fall the Germans transferred us to barracks at the munitions factory. This was a division of Majdanek, with barbed wire, watch towers, and armed S.S. guards watching us all the time. But we were basically not treated much different than before, except that women and men were separated, and we were counted twice a day.

THE TRANSPORT   We stayed there until the Russians got close to the Vistula river. It was July of 1944 and hotter than hell, but we walked, 3,000 of us, from Radom to Tomaszow, three days. Then we were put in cattle cars and sent to Auschwitz.

I saw somebody from my home town and I called to him, does he know whether my father is around, and he brought my father to the barbed wire! I told the S.S. guard that's my father, and I haven't seen him in three years. He says, "Go on the other side of the train and let your pants down so people think you go to the bathroom, and you can talk to him." We visited that way for fifteen minutes!

My mother and sister were kept in Auschwitz, but the men were put on trains to Vaihingen, a labor camp. In Vaihingen there were no gas chambers or crematoria, but we were hit with a typhus epidemic. People who died were buried 100 to 200 in a grave, with lime in between.

DACHAU   In April 1945, as the French came close, we were shipped to Dachau, probably 250 miles. In Dachau it was not a matter of "Am I going to die?" but "When am I going to die?" The biggest optimist was thinking, "I would like to survive Hitler by one hour."

Dachau was a mixture of everything—criminals, political prisoners, homosexuals, Jehovah's Witnesses, Germans, Poles, Russian soldiers. In the month we spent in Dachau, though, we were mostly isolated, and when we were evacuated from Dachau they evacuated the Jews only, to completely eliminate us.

They put us on a passenger train to Innsbruck, but at the Austrian border they refused to let us in. The radio was blaring that the freedom-fighting people had taken Munich. It was cold, deep snow, and they herded us into barns for the night. In the morning we were put back on the train.

This time we crossed the border in the afternoon and were unloaded in the middle of nowhere, somewhere between Mittenwald and Scharnitz. That night our guards disappeared.

LIBERATION   We hid in the mountains without any food for two days and two nights. The artillery bombardment was right over our heads. Then we saw soldiers in different uniforms speaking a language I did not understand, English. It was May 1, 1945, our liberation.

My friend Jules and I stayed in Garmisch, working in an American mess hall. Meanwhile, a Jewish chaplain from the American army realized the need to accumulate information about the survivors, so about the middle of June we get information from a friend that he saw a list from Bergen-Belsen, that my mother and sister survived.

Jules went on the train to fetch them. Then, about six weeks later, there was a knock on the door and there was my father! He was liberated by the Russians in Theresienstadt and went to work for the Red Cross. He met a fellow I was liberated with, and the fellow gave him my address in Garmisch! So now we were all together.

If you live in a country where you were born, you know the streets and the houses. You know what you have to cope with, the anti-Semitism and the possibilities. It's comfortable. It's very difficult to come to a strange place. But in Auschwitz we had agreed that we will never go back to Poland.

There was nothing for us to go back to, in Poland. I know people who went back, stayed maybe six months, then got out. I always cut the past and look to the future.

I lived in Germany four years, went to school, worked, taught accounting. In 1949 my father and I decided to come to the United States and HIAS assigned us to Minneapolis. I'd never heard of Minneapolis before. Jewish Family and Children's Service met us at the train depot, gave us a check, and put us up in a hotel. My only thought was to learn how to speak English and to get a job, so I would not need charity.

I was an accountant and a teacher, but I got a job pressing pants. It was a hot summer, and with that big pressing machine it was maybe 160 degrees! There was a cheap movie theater downtown, and I would go to that movie and see every feature twice, once for the action and once to learn English.

LOOKING BACK   If I came out with anything from the Holocaust, I came out with the thought that you cannot hate a group as a group because hate breeds hate. When there were two Germans together, they were bad, but there were incidents of Germans, as individuals, who were pretty good.

I remember a professor in Poland who said there would be no anti-Semitism if the number of Jews would decrease. He was wrong, because there is still anti-Semitism.

ROBERT O. FISCH
Budapest, Hungary

We had to walk from Graz to Mauthausen.
Sometimes we didn't get anything to eat or
drink. An Austrian peasant threw us apples and
a German guard shot the peasant. One day we
saw a lot more bodies than usual. One S.S. sergeant just decided he is going to shoot every
fifth person in line!

*Robert Fisch wanted to be an artist or an architect when he grew up, but when he
was released from Mauthausen at age twenty he went home and enrolled in
medical school. During the Hungarian revolution in 1957 he treated both
wounded Russian soldiers and the Hungarian schoolboys who were fighting
against them.*

My grandfather came to Hungary from Poland when he was six years
old. He was very poor, but he went to the amusement park and got a
bucket and started to sell water. Later he and my father got geese,
chickens, ducks and sold them to market, and became very wealthy in the
poultry business.

We lived among Catholics, and I had Jewish and non-Jewish friends.
The most dear person to me as I grew up was a Catholic woman who had
been with us since I was eight months of age. She eventually had a great
role in our lives because her parents were hiding my mother during the
German occupation, although to help Jewish people was risking their
own lives.

History, unfortunately, never avoided Hungary. It's very difficult for
a small country where Hungary is to be independent. Through the
centuries the Turks came through Hungary, the Tartars, the Russians,
the Crusaders. When Germany invaded Russia, the Hungarians were on
the side of the Germans, but by 1944 the Germans had lost their winning
start and the Russians were coming. So on March 19 the Germans officially occupied Hungary, even though the Hungarians were supposed to
be their allies!

THE OCCUPATION   The Germans established a Jewish advisors
group for communication with the Jewish community. We had to wear a
yellow star on our coats, ten centimeters in diameter. University student
demonstrators were openly anti-Jewish. About ten days after the Germans occupied Hungary, I was in the building that was the center of the

Jewish religious community, and a very upset person arrived. I sneaked into the room and was listening.

He described deportations taking place in the villages, how they go to the outside of the village, every Jewish person, with a little bag of clothes and food. In freight cars with room for twenty people they put 100 people, without any water, locked them in, and the train eventually went somewhere. From then on, I had no expectations from the Germans, except to be killed.

LABOR CAMP   June 5, 1944, I was sent to a work camp to build bridges. We were some 240 men in that camp. They were taking away our photographs, and they tore the pictures and said, "You're never going to see your family."

We had to work very hard, but we were reasonably well fed. My parents brought a radio to me, so we were able to listen to the BBC, and with maps we followed very precisely what was taking place. We knew the war is going to be ending, and the Germans have no way to win. We were called to dig out unexploded bombs, but when we saw the American air force flying, we knew that every bomb they drop is actually our freedom.

Then in January 1945 we were moved out. We came to this brick burner, and suddenly a smell hit me. Inside were hundreds of dead and dying people, bone and skin, defecating, full of lice, unable even to sit up. We were forced to sleep three nights among these people, and we were invaded by thousands of lice.

Then they took us by train to the Austrian border, and we stayed in a little village, digging ditches to defend Austria against the Russians. When we arrived, they gave for every five of us a bread. A German military man actually tried to help, and gave us one bread for every three men. Some S.S. also hid food behind their coats and gave it to us. One guy was hitting and kicking people, even women and children, and one day I was assigned to him, and I was so scared, but when we get out in the forest he said, "Relax, sit down," and gave us food. Then when we went back he started to scream and hit people again.

Then one day a person just collapsed. They started to kick him on, and then they recognized that something's wrong. From the lice in the brick burner we got typhoid, a typhoid epidemic. From the end of January until May, more than half the men were dead.

I was very young and I was in extremely good physical shape, but I was running a high temperature. The Germans established a room for sick people and one day an S.S. truck came, and they said the twenty sickest individuals could go to the hospital, that the food was wonderful. I was not trusting the Germans, but one of my friends went. They were shot at the edge of the village, in an hour of when they left that room.

We walked from there to Graz, an industrial area. If someone was not able to walk, they shot him right there. In the morning some of us threw our blankets away, and in the afternoon picked things up from the dead people, so we would not have to carry the blankets all day.

MAUTHAUSEN   Mauthausen was a political camp and also a military prison camp, and there were still some American prisoners there. Ten decagrams of bread—about one-fourth of a pound—with fungus on it, and one cup of coffee, that was our food for the whole day. Next day we were taken to Gunskirchen, a subcamp. They put us in a long wooden building. We had to sit on the ground, with people leaning on our knees, and somebody was sitting next to us and behind us. When people started to sleep or tried to lie down, they lay on other people. Many people died, just suffocated.

We had to be in line every morning, noon, and evening to be counted. For six hours we were in line, twelve hours we were in the barracks, and the rest we could go to the bathroom. For 30,000 prisoners they had two bathrooms. One day I could not wait for my turn, so I just urinated in the field. A German guard saw me and beat me with his rifle.

Our food was usually bitter coffee, a little bread, a little soup. The Jewish kapos were very cruel with us, and they had food, and we hated them so. One day we received something extraordinary, an International Red Cross gift, little food packages, and these kapos were eating a whole bar of chocolate while fifty people had to divide a can of sardines and six lumps of sugar. If I had the opportunity, I would have killed them to get that chocolate away from them.

LIBERATION   The American army came May 4, in the evening. I was so weak I had to crawl up the stairway.

Liberation was incredible, chaotic. The Americans threw food, candies, everything they had. American medical people tried to help us, but we were dehydrated, starving. I'm a doctor, and I don't know what I could do with this kind of situation. It was absolutely unreal. The American army knew the Germans very well, and yet they asked us what happened to us, why are we here? They could not believe the Germans were doing this only because someone has a different religion.

The Americans took us to the Russian zone. It was still about thirty miles to the next railroad, so I stayed overnight in a little ruined home. I had some liquor to take to my father, and a Russian soldier said he would like to buy it. I said, "Fine, give me some money or take me to the railroad." An hour later he came with a machine gun!

I also had some cigarettes and was able to buy a ride to the next railroad station with them. So that's how I got home.

With the help of Wallenberg and some Russians, 50,000 of the 100,000 Jews in the ghetto were saved, but my father and all my relatives in small towns had been killed. My brother left before the occupation to study engineering in Switzerland, and my mother was hidden by our Catholic friend, so they were saved. They emigrated to Israel, but I stayed in Budapest in medical school.

When the Communists took over, it was as bad as under the Nazis. Then in 1956 we had the revolution. I was seeing the Russian tank division coming into Budapest, and Hungarian students, twelve years old some of them, holding hands and marching against the tanks. We organized to provide medical assistance for the revolutionaries.

I heard they had medical supplies at the Austrian border. We stole four trucks from a government garage, put red crosses on, and started west to the border. We see a caravan coming, French, American, English relatives of embassy people fleeing into Austria. So we broke into the caravan, and with these foreign diplomats we went to the border.

The Austrian border guards were very friendly and we went on to Vienna. Outside Vienna the Austrian police waited for us, and the chief said, "You cannot go any further. Ask for political asylum, or go back to Hungary."

I knew it was the craziest thing to go back to Hungary, but we packed the trucks with medical supplies and food and went back to the hospital, which was now the communication center for the revolution. Then the revolution was over, and I was completely out of my mind, how stupid I was when I went back. Many people were being executed.

I lost weight, I looked not too good, and a doctor friend recommended I should go to a sanitarium near the Austrian border. I said to the doctors there, "I want to get out," and they brought someone who led me to the border. In Austria HIAS was waiting for us, and in 1958 I came to New York.

LOOKING BACK   When the war ended, I had a lot of hatred in me, and I thought I would be able to be cruel with the Germans. But when I met Germans who were hungry, I had two choices. I do either the same things they did to me, or I will be different. And I didn't feel that to let them suffer would be the answer.

Responsibility is a very complicated issue. Eichmann was originally assigned to make emigration possible for the Hungarian Jews, for $400 each in trucks or other merchandise, but no country would "buy" the Jews. You cannot blame a Hitler when millions of people were taken by trains, "assisted" by local guards and train engineers. Roosevelt knew exactly what was happening, so why were the trains not bombed, to stop the concentration camp activities?

When things become critical, then you are for yourself. You are on your own. But we should raise our voices when a mass extermination is taking place—Cambodia, Afghanistan, regardless of where it is—because they are human beings, and we are.

HENRY FREIER
Lodz, Poland

In the ghetto, when one father's son died, he
kept him in the cellar for weeks, to collect the
kid's rations. I was there. I saw it, I smelled it.
How can you forget something like this?

Taunted from childhood by Polish boys saying "your houses, our streets," eighteen-year-old Henry Freier, whose father was an ardent Zionist, set out for Palestine in 1932. He and four teenage friends hitchhiked to the Italian coast but were turned back by the British authorities.

We were eight children at home, and I was the oldest boy. I was eleven when I quit school and started working where my father worked as manager for an office supplies company. Every penny I made was to help feed the children.

In 1939 Polish radio said, "We won't give the Germans even buttons from our coats." The newspaper in Lodz said, "Our Polish heroes are forty kilometers from Berlin." But in ten days the war was over.

In our building there were seventeen Polish families and seven Jewish families. I was born and raised with this guy, a Catholic. I used to go with him to church. I was a boxer, and we belonged to the same sport club. But when the German army walked into Lodz, two days later this man was wearing a swastika. He said, "Don't talk to me. I found out my Grandmother was German."

THE GHETTO   To get 300,000 people into the ghetto, every *Volksdeutscher* and German in uniform was chasing and killing and beating us.

I was twenty-five and married. I got a horse and buggy to move my furniture, and they took the furniture, the horse, the buggy, and the guy

I hired, too. Our apartment was one room. In one bed was my wife and me, and the other bed was my wife's sisters. Bathrooms were outside.

In the beginning in the ghetto, we had concerts. We had very good musicians. We had intellectuals, a lot of them, and there were schools, but not for long.

I opened a little store selling cheese, butter, smuggled food. One morning the police came and took everything out from the store. They gave me a good "lesson"—ten on one side, ten on the other side. I could hardly move. My wife ran to a very prominent man in the ghetto, officially a Gestapo agent but I knew him from before the war, and he saved my life.

Then I was a watchman. My job was to watch the potatoes. We had people digging out the potatoes and covering them with straw and putting sand on it, that the rations should last through the winter. One October day hundreds of tons of potatoes came in and at night came a frost. The potatoes froze and got rotten. We put lime on them, but people were starving and they were digging out those rotten potatoes and eating them. You could see people in the ghetto crawling on all fours, swollen from hunger.

Then came the first evacuation. They started with the children and the hospitals. Next, 66,000 Jews were evacuated. They took them on trucks to Chelmno. They told us they are going to work, but I saw my Catholic friend in the ghetto, and he said to me, "Henry, they are killing your brothers and sisters in Chelmno." Then their belongings came back, so we knew they didn't go to work.

I witnessed one episode, a beautiful blond Jewish woman with a daughter eleven years old. They took the daughter because she didn't have a certificate that she was working. The girl was screaming, "Mama, help me!" and the mother ran to this Nazi and started kissing his dirty boots. He kneeled down and raised her beautiful blond hair, and he put a bullet in her brain.

AUSCHWITZ   When we were taken in 1944 to Birkenau, Auschwitz, men who knew me were unloading the trains. Old people would go one way with the children, the men one way, the women one way. My friends saw my wife carrying the baby, and they said to me, "Henry, take away the baby, give it to an old lady because your kid is going right into the fire with the person carrying him." We did, and they threw my son in the fire.

I was digging, pushing wagons with sand, building highways. In the ghetto I had connections, I had given this man an apartment with furniture, and in Auschwitz this same man was our kapo, our man for death or life. So he brought me bread, and he said, "You're not going out to

WITNESSES TO THE HOLOCAUST

work." So I was watching in front of the barracks, and if an S.S. guard walks by, I let the kapos know. Then I was in back to watch that nobody runs to the electric wires to commit suicide.

From Auschwitz, we were sent to Grossrosen, about 2,000 people. We were passing the women's camp, and I saw my sister and my wife. It was the last time.

GROSSROSEN   Coming to Grossrosen by train, we didn't have food for three days. When we got there we got a little bit soup and maybe three slices bread, and they said this is for twenty-four hours. I finished it almost with one bite. We went to sleep on bare boards.

In the morning a kapo, a Jew, was selecting men to work in the kitchen. I said I was a butcher because next to me was standing a real butcher I knew from Lodz. The meat was horsemeat, hanging quarters. A butcher knows how to unhook and take it on his shoulder, and I didn't, but the kapo let the real butcher show me how to do it and how to take the meat from the bone. The meat was for the S.S., the bones went into soup for us. I was the cook for the S.S. guard, potatoes and thick soup, and I ground the meat. I ate the meat, too, and I would steal the thick soup and bring it to the sickroom.

This kapo, I was "his Jew." I was beaten up by this man every day. First he beat me up, then he fed me. That's the way it was.

I was healthy, very healthy, and stronger than most of them. Of six men who were never ill, I was one. The whole bunch from Lodz was still there, and a doctor from Lodz died in my hands. Before he died, he took out his upper plate of false teeth, platinum, and said, "Henry, take this, and maybe this platinum will save your life." And it did.

THE TRANSPORT   I was in Grossrosen until 1945. The Soviet armies were five kilometers away, and we heard shooting day and night. Only 600 of our 2,000 men from Lodz were left alive. They took everybody from all the camps around, and we went first one place, then another. We were walking through a town, and I heard a German woman ask an S.S. guard, "Who are those people in the stripes?" The guard said, "Jews." She said, "Why don't you kill them?"

FLOSSENBURG   We were on trains for nine days, sitting on bodies. Finally we wind up in Flossenburg. Of 8,000 people in the train, we have 3,000 bodies. It was warm. The bodies were green, falling apart. The smell was indescribable. The crematorium could take only so many, so we had to dig ditches and put in wood and tar and people, wood and tar and people.

It was cold, drizzling, mud up to our knees. People were dying like flies. I had these platinum teeth, and I said to the guard in charge of the barracks, "This is worth a lot of money. Take it." He asked me what I wanted, so I said that you don't chase me out to work at three in the morning, and my good friend, I want him to work with me. So we got to work where transports come in and they take away all their clothes, to look through the clothes for money and valuables. The guards, kapos, everybody, they were dancing around you, this one needs socks, another needs a pair of pants, they give you orders. You bring these things to them and they feed you.

From Flossenburg we went to Regensburg. We were cleaning up, picking up the bodies where the Americans were bombing, and every day we lost fifty or sixty men, hungry, sick, shot by the guards.

One day the chef picked me up to go to the butcher shop. I had in my striped prisoner uniform a pocket I had sewn inside, and I put a piece of sausage in my pocket. A German guard, the biggest killer, found out and took me down to the end of the line. If they take you to the end of the line, it's to death, but my brother-in-law ran to the cook, who ran to one of the officers, who came running and pushed the rifle, and the bullet went into the ground instead of into me. That was April 28, 1945.

LIBERATION   We were 150 guys from Lodz, still together, sick with typhus, but we knew Hitler is dead and the Americans are coming. The S.S. guard ran away, and we hid for two days. Then I saw American tanks, and I jumped on the first tank, and there were tears, and singing, and hugging.

We took some revenge. One of the biggest killers from the S.S. guard, we were tearing pieces from him and buried him right there in Regensburg. Later, in Laufen, I was president of the Jewish committee, taking food from the Germans and giving to the Jews. It made me feel good. I was also working for the military government in apprehension of S.S. and war criminals and Austrian border smugglers.

My dead wife's niece found out where I was, found my brother in the Polish army, and found her sister, my present wife, in Mauthausen. One of my brothers was a very devoted Zionist. When the Germans came in, he and his best friend pulled straws, who's supposed to go to Warsaw and fight, who goes to Palestine. His friend "won" that one, to go to Warsaw. My brother married his friend's fiancée, and today he is an agronomist in Israel.

I didn't go to Palestine, because I didn't want any wars any more. In 1949 I came to the United States.

LOOKING BACK   I am very hard, I can take any punishment. But what it was is coming back all the time. My parents, five of my brothers and sisters, their families, all died in Majdanek. The reunion of survivors in Israel in 1985, it wasn't for us, it was for you, for Americans, for the youth.

PETER GERSH
Miechow, Poland

Many times in the middle of the night, I scream.
I lived through the Holocaust and I can't believe it yet. You have to try and live a normal
life, but you can't forget.

Peter Gersh was eighteen when the Germans occupied Poland. He and his family were Orthodox Jews, and he belonged to the Zionist youth movement. He was a skilled mechanic who could repair cars and trucks, and he learned how to shoe horses. These were survival skills during the Nazi occupation.

My parents, grandparents, great-grandparents were all born in Wlod-zislaw, where nine out of ten were Jews. In our town, one out of four were Jews. Tailors, shoemakers, capmakers, all Jews, and Jewish doctors, dentists, lawyers. My father was the town's machinist and locksmith, and we employed at times up to ten gentile people.

News from Germany about the treatment of the Jews grew bleaker from day to day. Skirmishes between German and Polish border guards got to be more frequent. We were expecting war, and on August 31, 1939, our world stopped completely and everybody tuned in to radios, waiting. September 1, early in the morning, the Polish president read a proclamation: "Last night our mortal enemy, the Germans, crossed our borders. We are determined to repulse the attack." That was wishful thinking. September 7 the Germans marched into Miechow. September 10 the Polish armed forces collapsed. Poland was now under German occupation.

My older brother and I and a few friends set out on foot to escape to Russia. But we were overtaken by a German motorized division about 150 miles east of Miechow, and there was nothing to do but return.

For the first two or three months, it wasn't too bad because the *Wehrmacht* was in control. Then they handed their power over to the Gestapo, the local Polish police, and the *Volksdeutsch*.

THE GHETTO   A few streets around the synagogue were set aside for a ghetto. They put walls up and barbed wire. There would not have been even enough standing room for all of us, but elders and small children were disposed of. The Germans promised the Poles free sugar for exposing Jews in hiding—sugar was in short supply—and every day Jews were killed. Lack of food and medicine also took their toll.

I had a dozen helpers, all Jews, and we worked fifteen to eighteen hours every day to take care of German cars and trucks. It gave us food to survive, and I could keep my family together.

Then, in July of 1942 they marched all the remaining Jews to the train station and loaded them into boxcars. The young and strong were sent to labor camps. The rest went to Belzec to be exterminated. My father was a professional, so he was spared. My brother was a tailor, which they needed also, and my younger brother, he helped me.

Now we had no doubt about what was awaiting the Jews in Poland. It was time to try to save whoever we could. For men that was almost impossible. They could recognize us as Jews because of circumcision. But with a little help and luck, women could save themselves.

We met a man from Germany who was a construction engineer in Cracow, forty kilometers away. He found a place with a family for my mother and the older of my two sisters. I got false papers for my mother and sister, that they weren't Jewish, but the Gestapo caught me with the papers. I was interrogated and beaten so badly that when I went to the toilet, only blood came out. I was lucky a major stopped the beating, because how could I tell them the papers were for my mother and sister?

LABOR CAMP   They transported me to the jail of the Plaschau labor camp on Jerusalemskaya street, in a suburb of Cracow. In jail they came in every few days and took out thirty or forty to be shot, but I was lucky. I got out of jail because a friend of my father was in charge of the horses and wagons at the labor camp, and he told me to say I knew how to shoe horses.

There had been a Jewish cemetery on Jerusalemskaya, hundreds of years old, but the Germans took away the tombstones. Now it was just barracks, about 800 Jews in a camp where everybody worked. Most worked in agriculture, went to factories in the city. A small group were mechanics, machinists, welders.

Then the Germans liquidated the ghettoes in southern Poland, and in three months we were about 35,000. They brought in Dutch, Germans, Belgians, and the camp population swelled to about 70,000.

At 5 A.M. they made Jewish musicians play reveille on the trumpet to wake us up. Then we had some bread or a little soup. A person was hungry all the time, and always the fear. The guards were *Volksdeutch* from Poland, Romania, Hungary, Yugoslavia, the Ukraine. They lived outside the camp, unscrupulous beasts in black uniforms. The camp commander, Amnon Goeth, was born in Vienna, appreciated art and music, had a Jewish orchestra, but if he saw a man hitting an unruly horse, he would shoot the man on the spot or tell his two Dalmatian dogs, "Get him," and they would tear the man apart.

Every day you saw people shot, torn by dogs. Nobody knew if their last minute was approaching. It was hell there.

In January 1945 the Russians were near, so we were put in buggies and went west about thirty miles to Auschwitz. In two weeks the Russians were approaching there, so we were transported to Buchenwald. From Buchenwald we marched to Flossenburg. Hundreds died on those marches.

LIBERATION   The Americans were approaching Flossenburg, so we were marching to Dachau. It was dark, raining. I saw my chance and ran into the woods. I came to a farm and climbed on top of the wooden silo, very high. I hid there four days, eating corn and grain. Then American tanks were rolling by! There were Jewish soldiers, American Jews, and I could talk to them in Yiddish. They took me to Floss, a little village nearby, where there were maybe a thousand Jews who had been marching to Dachau. They put us with German families and told them to give us food.

This was April 1945. The war ended May 8. In June I found my younger brother in Waldenburg, Germany. I got news that my sister survived Bergen-Belsen, and we went there and picked her up. My father had been sent to Grossrosen, so we went there but couldn't find any sign of him. Liquidated. My older brother, too. None of my other relatives survived, nobody. Then I heard my mother and my other sister were in Cracow.

To go to Cracow was 700 miles. I took a motorcycle. Just after Prague, I saw a Russian soldier and asked him if there's a place I could stay overnight. He and his friends took away my motorcycle and threw me in a cellar where they keep potatoes, a hole in the ground with a door on top, and locked me in there for two days. Then they took me to head-quarters, guns cocked. Luckily there was a Jewish officer there, a Russian Jew, who let me free, but he didn't want to give the motorcycle up, so I walked and went by train to Cracow.

I decided to take my family to Bavaria, in the American zone. I knew it would be a lot better than Poland under the Russians. We traveled by train, in open boxcars. You didn't even buy tickets, you just got on, and nobody checked. The bridges were destroyed, so a trip that would nor-mally take one day took ten days.

In Feldafing, Germany, a D.P. camp, UNRRA gave us food and clothing. The beginning of 1946 I moved to Munzberg, near Bayreuth, where I had some friends. I didn't want to live any more in camps, didn't want anybody giving me welfare. A friend and I established a company, buying steel from the mills, selling to hardware stores and builders. I married off my two sisters, made nice weddings. My mother and I had a nice apartment, bought nice things, clothes. In 1948 I registered to go to the U.S. They "processed" us with pictures, X-rays, hundreds of questions. Some seemed infested with anti-Jewish feeling, especially people from the state department. They didn't hide it. Finally, we sailed for America on an old military ship.

LOOKING BACK   It's unbelievable to be a survivor of the Holocaust. Films, books, nothing can describe it. There were a lot of people more capable, more deserving, but I had the right profession, so I survived and they did not. It was just by chance.

I hate no one. But if I hated anyone, I would hate the Polish people. The priests and the Catholic Church, they instilled hate in the Polish people, every Sunday and every day. Poles beat up Jews before the war, and in the war they had a field day. They were guarding the Jewish work force, and some were just brutal, filled with hatred. The Germans didn't give them weapons, so they killed Jews with shovels.

When I heard that the Russians occupied Poland, I thought, God should see to it that they're there for a thousand years!

EDWARD GROSMANN
Medzilaborce, Czechoslovakia

The kapo said, "Listen, I'm a brother of yours, a
Czech. I'm here because I was a Communist. In
the presence of the S.S. I'll yell, I'll kick, I'll beat
the living hell out of you. Otherwise I'll leave
you in peace." I survived because of him.

Edward Grosmann began Hebrew school at age three, finished his secular educa-
tion at fourteen, but continued his Jewish studies until the Nazis took over Czecho-
slovakia. He was seventeen years old when the war began.

My ancestors were farmers even before the Jews were allowed to hold
land. Legend goes that they had settled in Medzilaborce many centuries
before, that they may have been refugees from the Inquisition.

My father was already in the United States, came back to Czechoslovakia in 1919, left again in 1925. My mother stayed and carried on in a very
small general store.

In Medzilaborce 70 percent of the townspeople were Jews. I had non-
Jewish friends and I never felt any anti-Semitism, but we realized, for
example, most of us would not have a chance to go to the university
because there was a secret quota system and only so many Jews were able
to attend. I was very active in this small business we had, and most of our
customers were non-Jews from outlying areas. Later some of them even
tried to hide my sister during the deportations.

We had a very small group of Zionists, continuously fighting with the
elders of our community, who could not see the need for a political state
in Palestine for the Jewish people. Their very traditional approach was
that when God will decide that the Messiah should come and redeem His
people, the people of Israel, at that time we will be ready to go. Then,
when we saw the fall of Austria in 1938, I tried to escape to Palestine. But
Slovakia declared itself independent from Czechoslovakia and became
an ally of Nazi Germany, Hitler marched into Prague, and it was too late.

THE OCCUPATION   There was no Nazi occupation. Our neighbors
became the Nazis. They started immediately to force us to wear the
yellow stars. I was kicked out of school, and our non-Jewish friends
stayed away from us because associating with Jews was punishable by
penalties and imprisonment. The regime Aryanized our little business,
kicked us out, and gave the licenses to the non-Jew who took over our
store.

All the young Jews were taken away from their homes and families and had to do public labor—cleaning streets, helping build roads. You were not paid and had to provide your own food.

There was a great celebration in Slovakia when Hitler marched into Poland. We Jews, meanwhile, could not believe the things we had been hearing on BBC about Germany and Austria taking Jews to prison and torturing them, but we were afraid and very worried. Then some relatives came from Poland and were telling us about the Nazis taking people out in the street and murdering them in cold blood, and about the ghettoes.

We heard a big ghetto was being created near Prague, called Terezin, and that many Jews were taken away to the east for labor. We went to the synagogue, praying and entreating the Almighty to save us.

LABOR CAMP   In 1941 I was drafted into the Slovak army, just like the non-Jews. I went through basic training like all the other soldiers, except we used a shovel instead of a gun. Then we were sent into labor battalions in uniform, to build roads, railroads, other war-important projects.

There were over 2,500 of us in Jewish battalions. There was absolutely no persecution, other than we were wearing a blue uniform instead of a green uniform, and gypsies wore a brown uniform. Our living conditions were as good as any other soldier. We were allowed to worship in our barracks any way we chose, and on Jewish holidays we could arrange with the supervisors to make up our quota of time during the evening or on Sunday. We got the same pay, the same food, and it was agreed that we would not have to accept non-kosher food. There was no kosher meat available, but we were able to get beans and peas and bread, which made up in dollars and cents the money allocated to feed us.

By now, our families were already gone, and we were the only Jews left in Czechoslovakia, 2,500 out of maybe 100,000.

After the war we learned the Slovak minister of defense knew what was going on in Poland and he felt at least he can save us. In July 1943, however, the Nazis apparently pressured the Slovak army and we were all discharged. We returned the uniforms and the army supervisors left, but 410 of us stayed in our barracks at the brick factory, performing the same labor.

Our gentile coworkers would hear rumors that the S.S. is coming to pick us up, so we'd run off to the woods and hide. Then our gentile coworkers would come tell us it seems like everything is quiet, so we'd come back. This was going on for about sixteen or seventeen months.

Then on October 28, 1944, several thousand S.S. with machine guns and cannons came to capture 410 of us! They handcuffed us and we were thrown into trucks, five or six of us in one truck with ten or fifteen S.S. men!

AUSCHWITZ   We arrived in Auschwitz November 1, 1944. We were the last transport to Auschwitz.

We saw the chimneys and smelled the smell of burning flesh, and we knew what was going on because some people who had come back from Majdanek had told us that there would be a selection, and all the children and older people would be killed on the spot. So we were very surprised that, though we saw the big dogs and the yelling, they did not divide us up.

We waited two weeks. Then they lined us up, men to the right, women separately, children separately. "This is it," we thought. We went through the shower bath, and again we were afraid because we had heard about those so-called showers. Then we got uniforms. Two Jewish boys started giving us these tattoos, these numbers, and they were doing the same thing with the women and children. We were no longer people, we were numbers. I was B14083.

We were sent to dig rutabagas. The mud was to the knees, and we knew we wouldn't last long. Then a kapo comes in the barracks, a political prisoner with the red triangle, and he wants twenty Czechs. We had a conference. Shall we dare volunteer? We decided we can't lose much.

We didn't know what was going to happen. But at five the next morning the kapo and the S.S. picked us up and took us to the weaving factory, only about 100 steps away! There was an enormous warehouse full of pieces of plastic, and we were to distribute it to women who would weave it into ropes for the German navy. These women were *mussulmen*, persons who had lost the look of a human being. They were human skeletons.

The S.S. left. Our kapo, I can remember his name, Gottfried, and I can see his face, like today. It was a very cold winter, but I survived because I was inside that factory and because of him.

THE TRANSPORT   January 18 was the evacuation of Auschwitz. We were about 30,000 people marching to Gliwice. It was snowing bitterly. It was maybe sixty miles, but it took three days. People just sat down, and the S.S. pushed them into ditches and killed them. More than half the people in our group never made it to Gliwice.

Then, after two days in Gliwice, they asked all the Jews to come out. I didn't try to hide because I had the city of Jerusalem on my face, as we say. Some Jews, blonds who looked like non-Jews, did try to hide but the bloody Polacks, Polish prisoners, they called out to the S.S., "Here's a Jew!"

We wound up on a big train in open cars, about 200 in a car. There wasn't room to breathe! They gave one bread to each prisoner. We traveled seven days, all over Poland, Czechoslovakia. Half the people in our car died, and we had to throw them out. In Czechoslovakia people saw the cars going by and they threw in bread. We were scrambling like mad dogs, so hungry that some of us killed each other for a piece of bread!

We came to Mauthausen, but we were not allowed to get out because there was no more room in the camp. It took another seven days to come to Sachsenhausen. There was no food for those seven days. The only thing we had was the snow coming into our trains, except at Oranienburg, where we got some hot water, the first time we had anything in our mouths from the Germans in the fourteen days from the time we left Gliwice.

FORCED LABOR   There were thirty of us left alive, from a full car of at least 200. I was very, very hungry, very sick. After three or four days, we were divided into groups to go to work camps. I was sent to Flossenburg, to the stone quarries, but we were so weak we could no longer lift even a little stone! People were dying very quickly because we all got dysentery. In a bunk they would put in six people, and every morning there were one or two dead.

Then they sent us to a place where supposedly we were going to build an airfield. We were as capable of building airfields as I am capable of walking to the moon. But we went to the airport, about 300 of us. We built tents and we were sleeping there. We supposedly were pouring cement, but I don't think we did anything. Every day people died or were killed because they weren't moving fast enough. And then the American air force started coming and dropping bombs.

LIBERATION   Then we were marching again, and everybody who slowed down was shot. And then, on a Friday afternoon, April 27, we were resting not far from Dachau, and an S.S. man read a message: "All the prisoners are now freed, and should report to the American army." It was a sunny day. The wildflowers and the daffodils were out, and it was very bright. There was no jubilation because people were so weak that many of them just didn't have the strength to get up. But a few of us picked ourselves up. Instinct told us, "Move away, try to see what it feels like to be free."

Two other fellows and I, we walked slowly into the neighboring town in our striped, filthy prisoners' uniforms. A farmer told us we could rest in the haystack and brought us some boiled potatoes. We stole eggs and ate them raw.

The next morning the farmer told us the S.S. had been there asking for prisoners. He told us he would bring us food, but in case we were caught, not to say he'd been helping us.

We were in that haystack until May 2 when we saw tanks, Americans, They threw us chocolate and took us into town. We broke into a bakery where the bread was still half raw, but we started eating. I wound up in a hospital unconscious.

I was in the hospital for about two and a half months, very sick. American doctors brought me back to life. I remembered I had a brother in the United States, and his address. The day his first letter came, that's when I really woke up from that nightmare.

The Czech government sent trucks to bring us back home, and we didn't come back as "damned Jews," we came back as national heroes. There wasn't much housing or food, but the government gave us housing and double rations. We got free schooling and jobs, free tickets to all the theaters and to the symphony.

I found one survivor from the transport my mother and sister were on. She told me my mother was murdered by a drunken S.S., one sister vanished in Majdanek, one in Treblinka. My whole family was gone, at least 150 aunts, uncles, cousins. There wasn't a single survivor.

I was active in Jan Masaryk's party, which was on a collision course with the Socialist and Communist parties. I saw the Communists taking over the country, and rumors were that there would be a coup. I was working for the trade ministry and arranged to go to Canada in December 1947, to represent the Czech textile industries, to sell their products. The second day I was in Toronto, Masaryk was killed. I never went back.

My brother got me a visa, and I came to Minneapolis and tried to get a job in international trade. I went to all the big companies that had an international department—Cargill, 3M, General Mills, Pillsbury, Honeywell. Everybody was very nice. "Mr. Grosmann, it's wonderful. Wonderful experience. We'll call you." But nobody called. Then I went to an employment agency and they told me, "Ed, there isn't a single Jew working in these companies. You'll never get a job there. Forget it."

I enrolled in university night school, but I had to earn some money. Finally the Jewish Family Service got me a job at the Hasty Tasty restaurant, the graveyard shift. They asked me if I am a cook. I said yes. In fact, the only thing I knew how to cook was hot water. I was making sandwiches and hamburgers, and they promoted me the third night to make waffles. That was my downfall. I forgot to take the waffle out, smoked up the place, and they kicked me out.

From there I had a menial job at a company making shirts, and another being a receiving clerk. Then I met the president of the company I'm still with today, thirty-five years now. He gave me an opportunity to start an export department for them, and I am today a senior vice president. So America has been very good to me.

LOOKING BACK   I was brought up in a very religious home in a very religious community. I believed very strongly in God. In Auschwitz, I lost total belief in any supreme being. I didn't want to have anything to do with the God who let my little nephew be burned alive in Auschwitz. I told Him He should mind His own business and I was living my own life.

Then I met my future wife. I told her I would like to get married by a justice of the peace. She said, "No synagogue, no wedding." When we had our first baby, we had to name the baby in the synagogue. Before I knew it, I was woven into the fabric of religious and community life, and I don't regret it.

The most important thing to me, as a survivor, is the price I have paid to be a Jew. In the last moments of the war, when I weighed only eighty pounds and was very ill, what kept me going was that I wanted to see the downfall of the Nazi regime, to see that the Jewish people survive. I have a very big investment in the Jewish people.

A roundup of Jewish men in Czestochowa, Poland.

Orthodox Polish Jews tried to flee the advancing German army in 1939.

In 1945 survivors of the death march from Buchenwald to Dachau retraced their steps and dug up the remains of the hastily buried bodies of friends who had died along the way. They bought coffins and held a funeral service in Hof, near Bayreuth. Peter Gersh, who contributed this and other photos on this page, is seventh from left.

Ed Grosmann (*second from right*) with members of his Slovak army labor battalion, 1942.

Ed Grosmann (*left*) with his cousin,
Nathan Moshe Wald, Prague, 1945.
Wald and his wife survived, but
their four children did not.

CHARLOTTE HIRSCH
Transylvania

On Shabbat, guards were beating us more, giving us more work. On Yom Kippur we were
taken a long way to work and came back to
camp after dark, and our food was ugly, much
worse than other days.

*Charlotte Czitron was eighteen when World War II began. Her father managed
forests for a lumber company, and she grew up in a family that was warm, loving,
with lots of laughter. At Auschwitz Dr. Mengele selected Charlotte for life but sent
her mother and father to the gas chamber.*

Our city was Tirgu-Mures in Romanian and Marosvasarhely in Hungarian. I came from a very religious family, middle class, not rich, not poor.
We had nice dresses and a nice education. My father was tall, very good-
looking and a very good man. My mother always said she never wanted to
survive one minute without my father. They died together in Auschwitz.

My father used to go every evening to the synagogue, and one day he
came home and said, "Something very wrong is coming. There is a Polish
Jew here and he is saying we'll be taken to a ghetto and terrible things
happen there. They kill people." My mother said, "I don't want to hear
about it."

THE OCCUPATION   We collected clothing and money for the people in Poland. Then the Germans arrived, and next day we were ordered
to wear yellow stars. The Germans took all the people out of a large
apartment building, took from rich people, oriental rugs and silver and
crystal. Jewish girls had to clean the apartments, and the German soldiers who supervised, some would rape the girls and tell us, "If you say
one word, I kill all your family." We were so afraid.

My brother went to the Hungarian army in 1940, but after a couple
months was transferred to the work battalion. My other brother went to
work battalion, too. I was working as a dressmaker, making good money.
Then Jews were forbidden to work. Bucharest was under bombardment,
but my sister who lived there was risking her life going to the railroad
station to send us packages—two dozen pair silk stockings and other
things we could sell to buy food.

But then they didn't let Jewish people go to the market. They started
to take our bicycles, the radio, cars, everything. There was a knock on

our door, soldiers saying, "You have a sewing machine." I said, "Yes, I have." They took it and left. The ghetto consumed us.

Then one day our neighbor said, "Tomorrow morning we're going to be taken away." My mother said, "Go to sleep and don't think about tomorrow." We were so close to the border that if you walked just one hour you'd be in Romania. In twelve hours we could have been in Bucharest with my sister and survived. But my father said, "I'm not going. I don't want to be separate from my neighbors. What happens to everybody else will happen to me."

DEPORTATION   The morning of May 3 my mother was preparing lamb meat—we used to eat our main meal at one o'clock—and a neighbor came running and said, "Come look, come to the gate." I saw a long line of people with packages on the back, in the hand. So we quickly packed what we could, clothes, feather comforters, pillows, cooking pots. The Hungarian police—they had rooster feathers in their hats—came to take us to the brick burner outside town. The lamb was left cooking on the stove!

When we came in there was a basket, and we had to put in the wedding rings. All our other jewelry was taken already. It was not a building, only four posts and a leaky roof, only rocks and dogs' dirt, and it was raining in all the time. We put down our comforter in that dirty place and tried to sleep on it.

We could not wash regularly. There was no medication, no food. People who had more food, they gave it to the others, and everybody gave it to the children. Our nanny from when I was a child tried to bring food, but it never got through to us.

May 29 we were taken to the railroad station. The street was dead, nobody outside, but we saw people looking out the windows, very curious to see what's going on. We were standing in line all one day—old people, young, sick, pregnant, everybody crying. Everybody almost couldn't walk because they were carrying so many packages. It was so hot people were just one after the other fainting, and we couldn't help because we couldn't move out of the line. My father was like a statue, so tall and strong and very proud.

We were put in railroad cars, eighty people. The Germans push and beat and push, push, push. We had no food, no water, nothing. That was Thursday. Friday my mother started to cry because she cannot light Shabbat candles. She almost died then.

AUSCHWITZ   Sunday morning we arrived in Auschwitz. It was dark and fog. The car was very high up off the ground, and they beat us when we jumped down. We saw an officer, very tall, very good-looking, very imposing. I know his name was Mengele because I talked to him when I tried to save my mother.

Mengele says, "Right, left." My father could not be on the right side because he lost his hand, a war injury and then an infection. My mother was very pretty, and I put my red scarf on my mother's head so she would look young. But Mengele put the stick between us and sent her to the left. When he turned away I went to my mother, but he took me back to the right side.

Somebody said, "Look, there are the children, the babies." Very far away we saw silhouettes of women pushing baby carriages, but later we found out there were no babies in the carriages. They were sorting out valuable things to send to Germany.

A fat S.S. woman said, "Take off everything." I think of my mother with all these strange people naked, and the German soldiers watching, and I cry. I had long, black, beautiful hair and they cut it, not even. Then into the showers, many under one shower, very little water, and so cold. Everything happened so fast, no dress, no hair, no nothing, wet and cold like an animal.

I got a silk dress that was short, white and red, very thin. I picked up two shoes, both for one foot, one with a high heel and the other one flat. In August, like a miracle, another prisoner gave me a dress with long sleeves and a high collar. Otherwise I would have died there.

I was three months in Auschwitz. We had one meal in the morning after rollcall—a piece of old bread, a bit of marmalade, sometimes a piece of cheese crawling with worms, and coffee-colored liquid. We went to work digging trenches in the forest. My feet were freezing. I was beaten, hit twenty-five times, my nose broken, with broken ribs and a lung hemorrhage.

Then everyone was taken to Stutthof for the gas chamber. But there were too many before us, and they had no more gas, so we escaped death. From Stutthof I went to Bromberg, where I became a tailor for the S.S.

LIBERATION   In January 1945 the Russians were coming, so we began walking. We were walking seven days. The road was slippery, and the S.S. were shooting people, and all the time were bombings. And then one morning we get up and there are no Germans. The war was over for us.

Three of us, three girls, we were traveling January, February, until the end of March. Russian Jewish soldiers gave us food, but they could not give rides because it was still the war. We walked to Lublin, and after Lublin we found a train—no windows, cold. We traveled across Warsaw— flat, like nothing, from fighting and bombs.

Six months before, my town was freed, so my brothers were back. I was sick with headaches, pain. I didn't want to believe my parents wouldn't come back. I went to Bucharest to live with my sister and brother-in-law. I had everything, I became elegant again, I learned to live with the pain. But I still have pain every day.

I knew Alexander Hirsch from before the war, from Hashomer Hatzair. For six years we were dating. When I got home somebody says, "You don't have to wait for him, because he had typhus. He must have died." But after maybe two and one-half months in Bucharest, I said I feel like I have to go back to my home town. All his family was killed by the Germans, but Alex was there, and we got married. Later we went to Palestine, but I could not take the climate. In 1968 we came to the United States.

LOOKING BACK   We lived a normal life, and just like the snap of a finger we lost family, friends, everybody. Three times I stood in front of the gas chamber and lived. Not many can say this. We have to believe in God, only we must not forget.

DAVID JAGODA
Miechow, Poland

When I was liberated, we ate and ate and ate. No
feeling when it's enough, no taste like is it salty or is
it sweet, just the knowledge that I'm hungry, and maybe
tomorrow I won't have. We didn't know how to stop.

David Jagoda grew up in a small town, where his father owned a candy store. The Germans occupied his town in 1939. He still wonders what would have happened if each Jew could have killed one German.

Once when I went out with my girlfriend this guy went by, said "Jews," and kicked me a few times. You couldn't do anything because other guys were watching you.

After '31 we saw coming up Hitlerism, and we saw coming up Communism. We heard Hitler on the radio and we expected war. My mother wanted us to go to Russia. I didn't want to go because the parents, the kids, maybe we won't find each other. We were discussing this when the Nazis occupied our town September 4.

THE OCCUPATION   Economically it was not good because we had no work, but socially, we were better off. Everybody started grouping together, helping each other.

Right away, the Germans took a bunch of people to the church. The non-Jews they let go home, and then they shot thirty-five Jews, so we knew this is no play. I had an uncle, a barber, he minded his own business. They came in, took him and another guy and shot them. I said, "Why?" and a guy said to me, "David, there's no 'why.' Because he was Jewish, that's all." I have seen hundreds of those incidents.

We had a dentist, they wanted gold from him. As a dentist you had to have gold. Well, he didn't have any, and everybody had to come and watch while they hanged him. One day, two S.S. guys took a good friend of mine, she was in the ninth month pregnant, and two old guys, and everybody had to stand around in a close circle. The three of them had to kneel down and the S.S. shot them, so slowly, one by one. You should have seen those faces, waiting for her to be shot.

In 1942 they took us to the train to take us to Auschwitz, and there was a girl my sister's age, fifteen years old. She said to me, "David, what should I do?" I said, "Run away." There was a little hill, just to cross over, but Christian guys who were watching started yelling to the Germans that the Jewish girl ran away, and they went after her and shot her.

My father, my mother, my brothers and sisters, my uncles, all were shipped to Auschwitz. I was a mechanic, so they took me to the airport in Cracow to work, maintaining the cars. For six months we lived there, about 300 people, in Plaschau, a big labor camp on Jerusalemskaya.

LABOR CAMP   There was a commander named Goeth. One day Goeth came with two big dogs and told a guy from our city—a big, big guy—to undress. We were lined up, everybody, watching. Goeth gave orders to the two dogs, and they just tore him apart! Even now, a poodle dog going by, I'm afraid!

From there they sent me to a small camp which was very good. Did you hear of Oskar Schindler? He made pots and pans, and he was very nice to the Jews. We even had enough food. I was there maybe a year, until the summer of '43. This was when they sent me to Mauthausen.

MAUTHAUSEN   Everybody got clothes—a shirt and shoes and a pair of pants. They gave me a pair of ladies' shoes with high heels, too small, and I couldn't say nothing. One day, cold, snowing, they took away all the clothes, they're going to disinfect us. I fell asleep and when I woke up, I went to get the clothes. They beat me so I couldn't sit down for weeks!

In Mauthausen I worked in a mine digging rocks and carrying them from one place to the other. Then we were making airplanes. Everybody had a number on the chest and on the pants, a metal number. One day I lost my number, so they called me to headquarters. The S.S. man starts talking nice, so gentle, sweet, and then suddenly he takes a whip and starts hitting me over the head with the handle, so hard. If he wasn't talking so nice, I would have been alert, but it was such a surprise I didn't get my hands up to protect myself. I had to cut my cap open to fit my head, it was so swollen.

Once they started kicking some Hungarians, like a soccer game. They killed five guys, just kicking them.

We knew how the war was going. Guys would clean the Germans' houses and steal a newspaper, or read a little, or you could buy a paper with your piece of bread. On April 15 they took us to the woods. They didn't give us any food, any water. We heard the shelling and the S.S. were on edge, they were angry. They said, "You're all gonna be dead. We're gonna kill you."

LIBERATION   It's pretty hard to describe liberation. Suddenly you see people who don't kick you when they walk by. They're bringing food, as much as you want. You start thinking, is it a dream?

I was together with my brother, always. We were dreaming we're going to be liberated, but my brother said, "David, there's going to be a lot of people who see their freedom and won't be able to enjoy." He died a month after the war. His stomach couldn't take the food.

I started looking for my family, couldn't find anybody. I found my girl friend in Germany and we got married. I didn't want to stay in a D.P. camp, I had enough camp. We lived in Munchburg, a small community, very friendly. My wife was a photographer. In '47 we had a son.

All we knew about the United States was New York. Everybody wanted to stay in New York. But HIAS made it so 100 people go to Chicago, 100 people go to St. Paul. I didn't have any idea what St. Paul is, if it's a city or what! We still call ourselves newcomers, after thirty-five years.

LOOKING BACK   I have mixed feelings about being a survivor. Sometimes the mood is up, it's nice, I'm happy I survived. Sometimes, if your mood is down, you hate yourself, a feeling like I sneaked out. My whole family got killed. We didn't want to be apart, and suddenly you did part.

I sometimes feel guilty because I didn't do anything. They had the guns, and you were afraid. You thought, "Maybe I will survive," so a thousand guys let fifteen or twenty Germans take over.

HINDA KIBORT
Kovno, Lithuania

Frau Schmidt taught us to have real perspec-
tive. When we were humiliated, or cringing inside, or hurting, she said we should remember
who was the animal and who was the human
being: "The real animal is the one that humili-
ates another human being."

*Hinda Danziger's father was a designer in a shoe factory. She was nineteen when
the Germans marched in and announced, "The Jews are not human beings." She
watched S.S. guards shoot her mother.*

Because my parents came from Riga, they spoke Russian and German fluently. We children spoke Lithuanian, Yiddish, and German. I attended a private school where most of the teachers were imports from Germany, and starting from January 1933, when I was twelve, Jewish students were not allowed to participate in sports activities and were always pushed aside. By April we had to enroll in a Jewish school.

In June 1940 the Russians marched into Lithuania and the government was overthrown. Landowners and people who were in business were now "undesirable elements." My first experience with people being taken out of their homes in the middle of the night and sent away in freight cars was under the Soviets. The girl I roomed with at the university, her parents and sister were taken. We went the next afternoon and saw trains for miles and miles, people being shipped to Siberia.

When the Germans marched in in July 1941, school had let out for the summer, so our whole family was together, including my brother who was in the university and my little sister who was in tenth grade. We tried to leave the city, but it was just like you see in the documentaries—people with their little suitcases walking along highways and jumping into ditches because German planes were strafing, coming down very low, and people killed, and all this terror. German tanks overtook us, and we returned home.

THE OCCUPATION   We did not have time like the German Jews did, from '33 until the war broke out in '39, for step-by-step adjustments. For us, one day we were human, the next day we're subhuman. We had to wear yellow stars. Everybody could command us to do whatever they wanted. They would make you hop around in the middle of the street, or they made you lie down and stepped on you, or spit on you, or they tore at beards of devout Jews. And there was always an audience around to laugh.

They came in the middle of the night and arrested all the Jewish men, including my father. Unless one had an awful lot of money for bribes, there was only one way to get somebody out of jail, and that was if he was absolutely needed to run a business or a factory.

The very large shoe factory where my father worked was taken over by the German military, and they put a Lithuanian in as director. I went to that Lithuanian and asked if my father could be released. He grabbed me by the neck and threw me out.

I came home and announced that I wanted to go directly to the Germans. My mother and her friends thought I was crazy! I went to the headquarters building and waited and waited. Then the guard was changing, and I just opened the door and went in.

Inside stood a stocky man with gray hair, and I heard people addressing him as "Herr Commandant." So I said, "Herr Commandant, may I have a few minutes?" I spoke German like a German, with no accent, and he gave me five minutes! I told him what it was all about, and he wrote me a paper in red pen that said, "Danziger is to be released."

I ran home, and I shouted, "Papa is coming home!" You should have seen my mother and those other women whose husbands had been arrested! They put me on a chair, and one brought me water, and one stroked me. They thought I was out of my mind. But my father came home the next day.

THE GHETTO   In September all the Jews were enclosed in a ghetto. We lived together in little huts, sometimes two families to a room. There were no schools, no newspapers, no concerts, no theater. Officially, we didn't have any radios or books, but people brought in many books and they circulated. We also had a couple of radios and we could hear the BBC, so we were very much aware of what was going on with the war.

As long as we were strong and useful, we would survive. Everybody had to go to work except children under twelve and the elderly. There were workshops in the ghetto where they made earmuffs for the army, for instance, but mostly people went out to work in groups, with guards. A few tried to escape, but were caught.

We did not know yet about concentration camps.

In 1943 the war turned, and we could feel a terrible tension from the guards and from Germans we worked with on the outside. We could exchange clothing or jewelry for food, but this was extremely dangerous because every time a column came back from work, we were all searched. A baker, they found some bread and a few cigarettes in his pocket. He was hanged publicly, on a Sunday. There was a little orchard in the ghetto, a public place, and we Jews had to build a gallows there and a Jew had to hang him. We were all driven out by the guards and had to stand and watch this man being hanged.

November 5, 1943, was the day all the children were taken away. They brought in Romanian and Ukrainian S.S. to do it. All five of us in our family were employed in a factory adjacent to the ghetto, so we could see through the window what was happening. They took everybody out who stayed in the ghetto—all the children, all the elderly. When we came back after work we were a totally childless society! You can imagine parents coming home to—nothing. Everybody was absolutely shattered.

People were looking for answers, for omens. They turned to seances or to heaven to look for signs. And this was the day when we heard for the first time the word *Auschwitz*. There was a rumor that the children were taken there, but we didn't know the name so we translated it as *Der Schweiz*—Switzerland. We hoped that the trains were going to Switzerland, that the children would be hostages there.

THE TRANSPORT   On July 16, 1944, the rest of the ghetto were put on cattle trains, with only what we could carry. We had no bathrooms. There was a pail on one side that very soon was full. We were very crowded. The stench and the lack of water and the fear, the whole experience, is just beyond explanation.

At one time, when we were in open country, a guard opened the door and we sat on the side and let our feet down and got some fresh air. We even tried to sing. But then they closed it up, and we were all inside again.

LABOR CAMP   When we arrived at Stutthof our family was separated—the men to one side of the camp, women to the other. My mother and sister and I had to undress. There were S.S. guards around, men and women. In the middle of the room was a table and an S.S. man in a white coat. We came in in batches, totally naked.

I cannot describe how you feel in a situation like this. We were searched, totally, for jewelry, gold, even family pictures. We had to stand spread-eagle and spread out our fingers. They looked through the hair, they looked into the mouth, they looked in the ears, and then we had to lie down. They looked into every orifice of the body, right in front of everybody. We were in total shock.

From this room we were rushed through a room that said above the door "shower room." There were little openings in the ceiling and water was trickling through. In the next room were piles of clothing, rags, on the floor. You had to grab a skirt, a blouse, a dress, and exchange among yourselves to find what fit. The same thing with shoes. Some women got big men's shoes. I ended up with brown suede pumps with high heels and used a rock to break off the heels, so I could march and stand in line on roll calls.

After this we went into registration and they took down your profession, scholastic background, everything. We got black numbers on a white piece of cloth that had to be sewn on the sleeve. My mother and sister and I had numbers in the 54,000s. People from all over Europe— Hungarian women and Germans, Czechoslovakia, Belgium, you name it—they were there. Children, of course, were not there. When families came with children, the children were taken right away.

As prisoners of Stutthof we were taken to outside work camps. A thousand of us women were taken to dig antitank ditches, a very deep V-shaped ditch that went for miles and miles. The Germans had the idea that Russian tanks would fall into those ditches and not be able to come up again!

When we were done, 400 of us were taken by train deeper into Germany. We ended up in tents, fifty women to a tent. We had no water for washing and not even a latrine. If at night you wanted to go, you had to call a guard who would escort you to this little field, stand there watching while you were crouching down, and then escort you back.

We were covered with lice, and we became very sick and weak. But Frau Schmidt taught us to survive. She was a chemist, and she taught us what roots or grasses we could eat that weren't poisonous. She also said that to survive we have to keep our minds occupied and not think about the hunger and cold. She made us study every day!

Even now I remember Russian poetry she taught to us, by heart, when her turn came to be lecturer. My friend and I spoke about lectures we remembered from school. The one that was very hard on us was Lorna from Belgium, who always spoke about food. We called the day when it was her turn to speak, "the day Lorna cooked."

By the middle of December we had to stop working because the snow was very deep and everything was frozen. January 20, 1945, they made a selection. The strong women that could still work would be marched out, and the sick, those who couldn't walk or who had bent backs, or who were just skeletons and too weak to work, would be left behind. My mother was selected and my sister and I decided to stay behind with her.

We were left without food, with two armed guards. We thought the guards will burn the tents, with us in them. Then we heard there was a factory where they boiled people's bodies to manufacture soap. But the next day the guards put us in formation and marched us down the highway until we came to a small town.

We were put in the jail there. There we were, ninety-six women standing in a small jail cell, with no bathroom, pressed so close together we couldn't sit down, couldn't bend down. Pretty soon everybody was hysterical, screaming. Then slowly we quieted down.

In the morning when they opened the doors, we really spilled outside! They had recruited a bunch of Polish guards and they surrounded us totally, as if in a box. So there we were, ninety-six weak, emaciated women, marching down the highway with all these guards with rifles.

Then the German guards told us to run into the woods. The snow was so deep, up to our knees, and most of us were barefoot, frozen, our feet were blistered. We couldn't really run, but we spread out in a long line, with my mother and sister and I at the very end. I was near one guard, and all of a sudden I heard the sound of his rifle going "click." I still remember the feeling in the back of my spine, very strange and very scarey. Then the guards began to shoot.

There was a terrible panic, screams. People went really crazy. The three of us always hand-held with my mother in the middle, but now she let go of us and ran toward the guards, screaming not to shoot her children. They shot her, and my sister and I grabbed each other by the hand and ran into the woods.

We could hear screaming and shooting, and then it got very quiet. We were afraid to move. The guards wore those awesome-looking black uniforms with the skull and crossbones insignia, and every tree looked like another guard! A few women came out from behind the trees, and eventually, ten of us made it out to the highway.

With our last strength, we made it to a small Polish village about a mile away. We knocked on doors, but they didn't let us in, and they started to throw things at us. We went to the church, and the priest said he couldn't help us because the Germans were in charge.

We were so weak we just sat there on the church steps, and late in the evening the priest came with a man who told us to go hide in a barn that was empty. We did not get any other help, whatsoever, from that whole Polish village—not medical help, not a rag to cover ourselves, not even water. Nothing.

LIBERATION   The next morning there was a terrible battle right in front of the barn. We were so afraid. Then it got very quiet. We opened the door, and we saw Russian tanks. We were free!

The Russians put us into an empty farmhouse. They gave us Vaseline and some rags, all they had, to cover our wounds. Then they put us on trucks and took us to a town where we found a freight train and just jumped on it.

At the border Russian police took us off the train. They grilled us. "How did you survive? You must have cooperated with the Germans." It was terrible. But finally we got identity cards—in Russia, you are nobody without some kind of I.D.—and my sister and I decided to go to the small town where we had lived. We thought somebody might have survived.

In Vilna station a Jewish doctor said we were the first survivors he had seen. He told us, "Don't go to your small town. They'll kill you! There are no Jews left in small towns in Lithuania." When we said we were going on, he ran to the Russian officers and two of them took us off the train, so my sister and I stayed in Vilna. In October '45 we heard our brother and father had also survived.

To get out of the Soviet Union was impossible then, just as it is now. But the Zionist underground managed to get us documents that we were Polish citizens, and in 1946 we were allowed to "return" to Poland. Then we crossed the mountains on foot into Czechoslovakia and took a train to Germany.

I worked in Munich for the Central Committee of Liberated Jews, which administered all the Jewish D.P. camps in the area. I met my husband-to-be, who is from my home town. He had gone through Dachau. He came to Minneapolis in 1947, I came in 1951, and we were married here.

LOOKING BACK   I was a prisoner from age nineteen to twenty-three. I lost my mother and twenty-eight aunts, uncles and cousins—all killed. To be a survivor has meant to me to be a witness because being quiet would not be fair to the ones that did not survive.

There are people writing and saying the Holocaust never happened, it's a hoax, it's Jewish propaganda. We should keep talking about it, so the next generation won't grow up not knowing how a human being can turn into a beast, not knowing the danger in keeping quiet when you see something brewing. The onlooker, the bystander, is as much at fault as the perpetrator because he lets it happen. That is why I have this fear of what is called the "silent majority."

So when a non-Jewish friend or a student asks, "What can I do?" I say, when you see something anti-Semitic happen, get up and say, "This is wrong" or "I protest." Send a letter to the newspaper saying, "This should not happen in my community," and sign your name. Then maybe somebody else will be brave enough to come forward and say that he protests, too.

MANFRED KLEIN
Posen, Germany

Before '39 Hitler was quite willing to let the
Jews leave Germany. The hard thing was to en-
ter other countries. America wouldn't take any
Jews in; other countries didn't want Jews either.
Even after the war it took me five years to get
my visa.

*Posen and the territory around it became part of Poland after World War I, and
residents could choose whether to be Poles or Germans. The Klein family moved to
Breslau, in German territory. In 1938, however, the Nazis arrested Fred and his
father. They were Germans, but they were also Jews.*

There was always a slight anti-Semitism in Germany, but German Jews
were very assimilated. We thought of ourselves as German citizens of the
Jewish faith. In 1933, when the Hitler movement came, people were
afraid, but Germany was a democratic country and we said okay, he was
voted in, we will be able to vote him out. We were wrong.

You were very careful after '33 who you talked to. I had non-Jewish
friends, but you didn't talk with even friends. Among gentile persons
even parents didn't trust their own children, and vice versa. We were
allowed to have so many percent of Jewish children in certain schools,
and I had to fight my way in and out of school. I was fifteen.

I was a member of Zionist youth groups, a citywide leader. We had
to divulge the membership of our groups and let the Gestapo know
where our meetings were. The Gestapo was in police headquarters, up
on the fourth floor, and when you went in you never knew if you
would get out, so we met without letting them know. Jews weren't
permitted to go to university, so when I graduated I went into the
family business.

In July 1938 there was a big roundup of so-called criminals—Jews who
were married to gentiles, had a gentile girlfriend or boyfriend, things
like that. Then in November it all went "poof!" On *Kristallnacht* they
destroyed everything Jews had. Our business was destroyed, everything
smashed. Our bank accounts were closed, gold and silver and all valuables had to be handed over to the Nazis, and so on. They had a three-
day roundup, and my dad and I were arrested.

We were shipped to Buchenwald by passenger train under heavy
guard. Nobody resisted. If he did, he was dead.

BUCHENWALD   At the main gate to Buchenwald we had to run a gauntlet, about 100 yards between two rows of S.S. people having fun cursing us, hitting us with sticks, and trying to trip us. You didn't listen, you didn't look back, you were preoccupied in running and getting out of their way so you didn't get hit. I also had to protect my dad, who was sixty. I kept him in front of me to see that he didn't fall. Anyone who fell and was too weak or too old to get up was beaten to the ground.

We were 10,000 men crowded into five Nissen huts, like army barracks. Inside you had tiers five high, just enough room so you could crawl in. We had nothing to do all day. We got watery soup and blood sausage to eat, things like that. Orthodox Jews weren't supposed to eat the sausage, but the rabbis told them they should because preserving life comes first.

When people went to the infirmary they didn't come back, so our own doctors treated our people. One man had an appendix operation done during the night by a Jewish surgeon who was also a prisoner. He operated by candlelight, using a pen knife.

When you are looking at the tower with machine guns pointed at you, you know you can be killed. And for the slightest offense you were punished, or sometimes for no reason at all.

You were punished with what they called the *Sachsengrusse,* standing on your tiptoes for two or three hours with your hands behind your head. Other prisoners had to lie over a saddle mount and got fifty lashes, seventy-five lashes. One prisoner escaped and they captured him, so next day we had to watch the execution on the gallows. A lot committed suicide, died of heart attacks, things like that. Of 10,000 people, 2,000 died in the nine weeks we were in that camp.

LIBERATION   Ransom for our release was paid to the German government by confiscation of our property and by money raised in other countries, so in December they started letting us go. My father was in the first batch they let out, people over sixty, and people who were German soldiers in World War I and had the Iron Cross.

Then they started to release you if you had proof that you could leave the country. My mother bought me a permit to go to Sweden to be trained in farming, so I could go to Palestine. Five friends and I were all released together on January 13. We left the camp area by truck, then went to Berlin by train. The first thing we did, we all got drunk!

Unfortunately, I didn't really have a permit to go to Sweden; it was a fake. And you couldn't enter Palestine because the British wouldn't let Jews in. You could go to Shanghai for $200 in American money, but you couldn't buy American dollars with all the German dollars in the world.

All of us young people were going to the Jewish community center in Berlin, trying to find ways of emigrating to other countries. I met my future wife there in April, and we became engaged. Meanwhile, I had friends who went over the "green borders" through the forests into Czechoslovakia or Holland or France. But if they were caught by border guards or the police, they were handed over to the Gestapo.

Finally I got a permit to go to England as an agriculture student, and my fiancée got a nursing permit. July 17, 1939, we went to England. We were married in London in October, one month after war was declared.

I could communicate with my mother and father through Sweden by Red Cross notes, twenty-four words. For a while I got notes and letters back. Then in '43 my parents were taken to Auschwitz, to the gas chambers.

LOOKING BACK   In the concentration camp I became an atheist. I was angry at God. I wouldn't even enter the synagogue. But my wife wanted the synagogue, and slowly I softened up, when my son was born, and later on for my grandchildren.

From the Holocaust Israel learned that if you keep quiet, it doesn't make the tiger go away. You have to stand up and fight.

BEREK LATARUS
Lodz, Poland

They told my sisters to go away, to give the little
child to my mother. My two sisters didn't want
to leave her. One took from this side her arm,
and the other on this side, and the four of them
walked to the crematorium together.

Berek Latarus worked with his father in the family lumber business after graduating high school, buying firewood by the carload and selling it to bakeries and factories. He could have stayed behind as a laborer when the Germans liquidated the ghetto, but he chose to go with his family to Auschwitz. He is the only survivor.

When we heard the Germans were coming, everybody ran out in the street. We saw them on their motorcycles, with the dogs and everything, and it was kind of fun, an army comes in. Our parents said, "Ah, we know the Germans. They're going to be the same like it was in our war."

Really, average people were not afraid. They didn't know what was going on in the world. They were occupied with work, with children.

THE OCCUPATION   But right away the Germans burned the synagogue. Lodz had one of the most beautiful synagogues in the world, and they burned it to the ground. Then they took some Jewish people— women and men—and hanged them in the market by the feet with the head down, to show us we would have to be scared.

THE GHETTO   They made a ghetto, strangled you around with barbed wire. You couldn't go out, but you were afraid to escape, anyway. Where would you go? To the Germans? Everybody was working for the Germans in straw factories and shoe factories and clothing factories. I was delivering for the Germans, straw, food, fabrics to the clothing factories, in trucks and by horse and buggy. For the work you'd get stamps for groceries, maybe two or three pounds potatoes a week for a whole family, one loaf of bread, some horsemeat. You couldn't live on it, and you couldn't starve on it!

People who didn't work, you used to see them swollen from not eating, and they just died on the sidewalks. In the ghetto you knew everybody, so you knew friends who died. There used to be mass funerals.

There was a curfew, and rules where you could not assemble. On every Jewish holiday, the Germans sent people to concentration camps. The first that went were the educated people—doctors, lawyers. Then they went for the older people who were not able to work. In 1940 the Germans threw the children out of the windows onto trucks. I saw them do it.

In Poland people used to save gold and diamonds, that was their security. The Kripo, they knew which Jewish family had gold or diamonds. After my father died in 1942, I was three times in the Kripo. The one in charge used to be in the same business as my father, so he knew. I had to take everything my father had hidden and give it to him. Otherwise they would have killed me.

DEPORTATION   The day they liquidated the ghetto they told us to take whatever we can carry with us. And then we came to the boxcars, and they didn't let us take nothing. Chased us into the boxcars and closed the doors. We were riding with no food, no water, two or three days. One of the stations we stopped at, they opened the door for fresh air and some of the Polish people tried to give us water.

Nobody knew where people were sent. We thought they shipped them out to Germany or somewhere else in Poland, for work. Nobody knew about Auschwitz, or concentration camps, or the ovens.

AUSCHWITZ   In Auschwitz, the first thing, they separated women from men. Then you took off your clothes to take a shower, and when you walked out of the shower they gave you a pair of wooden shoes and the uniform with the stripes—pants and a short jacket.

In the barracks you were sleeping on a burlap sack with straw inside, on a bunk, until four or five o'clock in the morning. Then they woke you up so they could count you and select you for work. Our barracks was close to the crematorium, and we could smell that smoke from the chimneys.

In the morning they were supposed to give you coffee, but the kapo, he either liked you or he would just pour it on the floor and tell you to wipe it up. They gave you a piece of bread that's supposed to last you two or three days. If you ate it up, the other two days you starved for it, but when you didn't eat it, the next one stole it from you. I saw with my own eyes, sons stealing food from their own fathers. People don't realize what hunger means.

In one camp I was working in the kitchen so I had enough to eat, but in other camps I was like anybody else. One time I stole a bread and they took me to shoot me, but a non-Jewish guy from Cracow, he was my friend, and he ran and took me away from the Germans! This non-Jew was on good terms with the S.S., he used to smuggle them cigarettes, and we called him the "Jewish father" because he was sticking up for us all the time.

To survive you had to be lucky, keep yourself clean, stay well. We had just the one uniform, never washed, never cleaned, but you could wash with cold water sometimes. Some people who were sick, hungry, they got so depressed they didn't take care of themselves. People who got sick, you didn't see them any more. I never got sick.

To survive you also had to always look like you were working, like you were digging, or something. Some people couldn't work, and then you heard the guns. And you had to use your head. People who were smoking used to sell their soup for a cigarette. These people didn't survive. And some people were so religious they used to go during the day in a corner to pray. When somebody from the S.S. caught them praying, they were through, too.

THE TRANSPORT   From Auschwitz we were sent to Regensburg, locked in boxcars for days. There were people in the boxcars so hungry they couldn't control themselves. They would bite the flesh out from dead people, eat the flesh of other people who were already dead.

By Regensburg we worked on the railroad to clean up every morning from the Allied bombing. One day we saw planes coming. Our guards ran away, and the bombs fell where they hid. They got killed and we were free! I ran with two friends, and we were hiding in a cemetery. An old woman gave us food and clothes and told us, "Go away," but civilian Germans surrounded us, and took us back to camp.

Later our camp was walking for weeks to another part of Germany. I was still with people from my town, relatives, friends, people I grew up with. My three uncles, they were very strong guys, but they got sick and couldn't walk any more. They shot all three. Everybody was waiting for their turn. I really didn't think about surviving; I thought more that I was going to be dead.

We were walking through this little town, Laufen, in May 1945 when some farmers came running out on the highway, saying, "The war is over!"

LIBERATION   There was an army camp not far from there, and it became a D.P. camp. Then later we moved into a house, four of us guys. We opened a Jewish Center and I was president. HIAS helped us, and UNRRA.

People started leaving to look for relatives. I knew my own family went to the crematorium, but I looked for aunts and uncles, a relation. I couldn't find anybody. One of the guys I lived with, his sister came looking for him, and we got married in 1947. In 1948 our daughter was born. My brother-in-law and I opened a fabric store, buy from the factory and sell, from one town to another in Germany and Austria. My wife had a sister who came to the United States, so that's why we came.

LOOKING BACK   I was really bitter about the Germans after the war, but you change. You have good people, you have bad people, hate doesn't do any good. I believe in God now.

When my children were growing up, there were nights I couldn't sleep. I was still in Auschwitz and could still see everything. It was heart-breaking, and I used to cry. I really couldn't talk to my children about it, but my children and my grandchildren, they said to me, "Why don't you tell me?" Now I feel it should be talked about.

HENRY OERTELT
Berlin, Germany

Brown-shirted S.A. troops were marching
down the street, singing, "Once the blood of
Jews squirts off our knives, everything will go
twice as well." It was a very frightening thing
for a small Jewish child to listen to.

*After Henry Oertelt's father died, his mother worked as a seamstress to support her
two sons. Henry went to trade school at age fourteen to study furniture design and
was apprenticed to a furnituremaker.*

I grew up in a neighborhood that was predominantly gentile. I was the
only Jew on the soccer team at school, and soon after Hitler came to
power, I was made to know that I'm not welcome on the team any more.

When Hitler came it was not a sudden thing, it was growing since
1921, really, but everybody was frightened. People with money had a
chance to escape, but we were poor, and my mother's work diminished
more and more as Christian people were not allowed to have contact
with Jews.

Beginning in 1941 we were forced to wear the big yellow star with the
word *Jew* written across. The law prescribed that these had to be sewn on
in tight stitches, and an S.S. man, or one of the brown-shirted S.A., or
just a plain policeman would stop you, take a pencil out of their pocket,
and try to get with the pencil under and between the stitches. If they
could, you were taken right away to the Gestapo. Many people that
happened to, they were never seen again.

Being a teenager, I made a star out of tin, glued material over it,
soldered a pin in back, and stuck it into my jacket. I went with this thing
away from the house, and then I just took it off, hoping that nobody
stops me. I also did not obey the curfew law too much. I'm not trying to
show that I was brave. I was actually pretty stupid.

Jews were not allowed to have radios or record players, bicycles, cars,
pets. I remember when we had to turn in our pets, the old ladies walking
in the street carrying their birdcages, tears running down their cheeks.
In summer Jews were not allowed to be on the street after nine, in winter
curfew was at eight. No Jew was allowed to visit movies, theaters, restaurants, any public places. You could use public conveyances only to go to
and from work.

Berlin was not a small place—it was in those days four and a half
million people—so to get around was not easy. But young people want

fun, so the group that I belonged to, musicians and so on, would get together at one of our apartments on Saturday afternoon, make music, do all kinds of things, and stay overnight.

Jews were put on ration cards before anybody else. When the rest of the population was put on, Jews' food rations were cut lower. You had to buy clothes on rations, and it nearly took all year's ration points to buy a pair of socks. For Jewish laborers, half the wages went into Hitler's treasury, and out of the other half the taxes had to be paid, so there wasn't much left to live on.

In 1939 almost all Jews were taken out of their professions. Lawyers, doctors, businessmen, and in my case furnituremaker, were put on street work, shoveling dirt, rolling and carrying rocks. All we had was hand shovels and four-wheeled wagons we had to pull with ropes or leather straps.

Most people in Berlin lived in apartments, without even a yard to dig in, so they were very, very unhandy with tools. We were also a very odd-looking group. Next to me worked a tiny man, not so young any more, a very famous surgeon in Berlin. He came to work in the only clothes he had, a double-breasted, blue-striped suit. He couldn't even go out and buy himself a pair of work pants because of the rations. He was carrying rocks, with those tiny hands. It was a most comical sight, if it wasn't so sad.

School field trips would come by, and the teacher stops and points and talks, and the kids are giggling. Where you would normally see a crew of tough hard-hats, you see a bunch of really comical looking people like this little doctor, dragging wagons, and so forth. Hitler wanted to prove to the German population that Jews are actually sub-human, and these kids were being educated to kill something that is of no value.

For two years I did street work. Then in 1941 Hitler found himself short on skilled help, so he took people like me and the doctors and put them back into practice. I was put into a factory, with my own workshop, to make furniture for some big-wig Nazi.

DEPORTATION   Pick-up actions for concentration camps were increasing constantly, so when you went to bed at night, you almost anticipated you're not there in the morning. Sometimes they would come to factories, load the Jews onto trucks, and haul them away.

Apparently this big-shot I worked for had enough power to say, "Hey, I need this little Jew that makes furniture for me, so leave him alone." But in March 1943 the inevitable happened. About two in the morning we heard gun butts banging on the door, two S.S. men in their black uniforms, with a dog. You expect it but you still don't believe it, so when it really happens you run around crazy, throwing things into suitcases. You've got fifteen minutes, no more.

We were taken to a waiting truck and hauled off to a collection center, a burned-out synagogue. When there were enough people to put a transport together, we were brought to the train station. I was on my way, with my brother and my mother, to our first concentration camp.

THERESIENSTADT   In those days, Theresienstadt was one of the milder camps, controlled by Czech police who tried to stay their distance. Women were separated from men, but I could see my mother sometimes in the evening.

There were no gas chambers yet in Theresienstadt. They didn't need gas chambers because people died of starvation and all kinds of sickness. Lice, fleas, bedbugs all were having a feast on everybody, and there was no way you could get rid of them. People could not resist to scratch, and would die of infections.

The smell from the bakery lingered over the whole town, but it was a teaser. When our food was dished out, it was a piece of white bread three by three inches and a couple of inches high. Sauce with meat, you got maybe half an ounce, one spoonful, poured over that bread. Usually you got soup, dished out from huge barrels. You learned that the guys that dish out the soup, they wouldn't bother to stir the stuff, so if you were not one of the first in line, you had a chance of getting a nice hunk of sludge, not just water, in your bowl. People would dig in garbage bins to find a piece of rotten bread or vegetable.

After about a year in this place, my brother and I were ordered to the train station. Guards with gun butts, fists, and sticks shoved us into cattle wagons like sardines. This is the way I came to Birkenau, to Auschwitz.

AUSCHWITZ   Of course we were tattooed. It was then announced that there will be no more names used. If you are asked what your name is, you have to answer your number. Particularly in the beginning, you're standing for headcounts and you're getting nervous, and a guard comes toward you and taps you on the shoulder and you hear him say, "What is your name?" And in your nervousness, you blurt out your name. Well, by the time you get yourself off the ground because you had his boot in your belly or groin, you remember you've got to blurt out your number. So you look at your arm because you forgot your number, and that's when you got another kick, because you're supposed to remember.

Another favorite game of theirs was they would go to one of the prisoners, grab their cap, throw it out of the guard lines, and order the prisoner to retrieve it. Every prisoner knew that if they would step out of the guard lines, they would be shot. But you know if you don't obey orders to retrieve that cap, they beat you to a pulp and you die. So what are you going to do? The eternal belief comes through that there may be a glimmer of humanity in somebody's heart, and you step out of line to retrieve the cap. And you always were shot. These are two examples of how those guards, standing around guarding prisoners with nothing else to do, would start games to entertain themselves.

In Auschwitz I let it be known that I make furniture, and sure enough, some Nazi put up a workshop for me outside the camp.

FLOSSENBURG   From Auschwitz we went to Flossenburg. My brother and I, we talked to each other a lot to keep ourselves sane. Also, we recognized that our only chance for survival was working because they weeded out the sick people and hauled them away to the gas chambers. Our mother went that route. Then I got an infection, a swelling under the arm, big as a tennis ball. My brother was taken out to work camp, but I was hopelessly sick. I saw that I had no survival with this thing.

At the sick barracks were long lines of guys that had swellings on their bellies, their faces, huge growths. These people were weak, starved skeletons. I saw that if a doctor would ask a guy to put his foot on a stool, and the guy would falter, this doctor would take his fist and smash the guy in the face or the belly. Then he would take his knife and just slit the growth open, and pus spurted out, and that was it.

Finally my turn came. These guys were whining and shaking and asking for help, and I figured that the German militaristic thing is always to be stiff and straight and short-speaking. I was in terrible pain and weak, too, but I spoke in very short, militaristic words and stood straight, and the doctor's eyes opened wide, and he says, "We will give you anesthesia."

Well, it was a big operation, and I have a big scar. I stayed in the sick barracks, where they would send the very sick people to the gas chambers, but he always would pass me. I was the only one he was nice to.

LIBERATION   From Flossenburg we were put on a death march, and after about two and one-half days I was liberated by a contingent of Patton's Third Armored Division. I weighed eighty-two pounds.

The Americans in those armored vehicles opened the hatches and threw out food, the ration boxes American soldiers used. It was a wonderful thing, but also regrettable. We scrambled for them like crazy—cans of meat, fat, butter with oil swimming on top. Some of the guys would sit right down and tear the boxes open and stuff themselves with both hands. Many started to have dysentery, and it couldn't be stopped. They died from that food!

Fortunately, my brain was still working. I opened some saltine crackers and took a few of those, and I only took a little tiny piece of the chocolate. Then American medical teams came and took over, and the food boxes were taken away. I started a fight about my food box, so they put my name on it!

We were assigned to farmers' houses, and the farmers were ordered to take care of us. Then the war was over, and I started to walk to Berlin because we had said that if we survived, we would try to get back to Berlin. It was a 700-mile trek, and I was picked up by military vehicles, but a good stretch of it I walked.

The end of June I arrived in Berlin, but my brother didn't come. All the Jewish organizations, the walls were full with slips of paper, "I'm looking for so-and-so," "Anybody knows the fate of. . ." I put on notes, too, but nothing happened.

I got married to a girl I knew from before the war, a little girl who used to say "hi" to us teenagers. And then one day a fellow comes by and says, "My gosh, you're lucky. Your brother is in Munich." Knowing what physical shape I was in when we separated, my brother never even looked for me!

My brother stayed in Munich and went from there to America. The apartment we owned was in the French sector of Berlin, and the French did not allow anybody to leave except to go to France. France wasn't far enough away from Germany for me; I wanted to go to America, too. Finally, by buying false papers, we moved into the English sector the beginning of 1949 and came to the United States in 1950.

LOOKING BACK   In Auschwitz they separated the children, telling the parents, "You will have to work very hard, and you won't have time to take care of the children." Then the children were immediately killed. This is the Germans' biggest crime, the most terrible thing.

But a good number of Germans were helping Jews by risking their own lives. As a teenager, one thing that hurt me most, in the beginning, was to give up my record player and some special records. If you were out at night, you were constantly stopped and asked for identification, but this Christian friend sneaked to our house carrying his record player with records and a bag of food. We would play the music with blankets over our heads, so the neighbors wouldn't hear us, and then he would sneak out again. And when it came time for us to be sent to the concentration camp, he offered to hide us.

And that doctor that operated on me in Flossenburg, I was asked to be a witness against him, but I would have had to say the truth. He killed other people, but he probably saved my life.

Any totalitarian system—Nazism, communism—thrives on the dilemmas of people. Unemployment in Germany raged at about 40 percent when Hitler came to power. He promised he would create work and feed the people, and he did! War manufacturing was prohibited under the Treaty of Versailles, but people started to work and to eat, had money, and couldn't care less what Hitler was doing in other departments. It's like when you're feeding a hungry animal that strays to your door, it stays with you the rest of your life.

Charles and Gessya Danziger and family, Kovno, Lithuania, 1933.
Hinda (*right*) and her brother and sister survived.

Leo Kibort, after release from Dachau, 1945. He and Hinda Danziger met in Germany after the war and were married in the United States in 1951.

Hinda and Leo Kibort with their children (*left to right*), Sandra, Joni, and Charles, 1964. Photo taken in St. Louis Park, Minn.

Henry Oertelt (*right*) and a friend took off their yellow stars and went bicycling outside Berlin in 1941. If caught and recognized as Jews, they would have been sent to a concentration camp.

BEN ROSENZWEIG
Szuzkoczyn, Poland

After the war the Jews came back. The Polish
people stretch out the arms and say, "I'm so
glad you came home. I got everything you left
for me, I give you back." But some Polish people just looked for a Jew to kill. I couldn't believe this could happen in 1945.

*Ben Rosenzweig left his Polish village at age twelve to apprentice to a tailor, and
at fifteen he went to work in Katowice. In Buchenwald, he traded his tailoring
skills for food.*

THE OCCUPATION   When the Germans came in we had to go to
work, very hard work. We worked on the streets every day in the cold, no
gloves, pieces of rags over your feet.

My mother risked her life, took off her armband to go to a farmer,
about seven kilometers. She bought pots and pans cheap and traded
them to this farmer for flour, bread, potatoes. Most of the Polish people
would sell a Jew for ten pounds sugar, but the farmers, they were good
to you. They had a tough life, and they were afraid of the Germans, too.

Sunday morning, July 1942, somebody knocks at the door. My brother
and me, we hid under the bed, but they took us 300 miles to labor camp,
to work in an ammunition factory. An uncle of mine and his wife and
children tried to hide. Them they took out to the cemetery, made them
dig holes, and shot them all.

LABOR CAMP   They gave us clothes from the people that got killed
in the Warsaw ghetto. They were nothing but blood.

We did a lot of sabotage. You thought your life wasn't worth anything,
anyway. People used to say, "Where's God?" We said, "God is in the
United States. He doesn't want to see what's going on over in Europe."
But the Nazis were God!

A German guard would say to a guy, "Hey, why don't you walk down
there." So the guy starts walking, and the German takes out his pistol,
boom-boom, he's dead. For no reason! If you walk straight, maybe they
kill you. If you walk like crippled, wasn't good either. One German got
drunk, and he called everybody out from the factory, saying, "You, on
this side. You, out!" They took my brother, other people, and sent them
away to die. I had made friends with a kapo and we took a wagon, like we

deliver supper from one barracks to the other, and brought my brother back.

A train came through our camp and all our families were in that train. I see my mother now, with my five sisters and brothers, going to Treblinka to die. The youngest was a girl, four years old.

BUCHENWALD   In '44 we wound up in Buchenwald. This was the first concentration camp in Germany—1933. There were prisoners still there from the time Hitler came to power.

I was twenty-two, my brother nineteen. They shaved our heads and everything, put us on striped suits and gave us Holland shoes. We ate one piece of bread a day, and water soup. Bread you'd take a little piece and eat, a piece and eat, it should last you for a long time.

In Buchenwald we worked for no reason. Take some sand from here and put it there, mix water with the sand, make mud, take the mud and put it on the other side. Pull big stones, rocks, like horses. If you didn't make it, you were killed right there. Buchenwald was a slaughterhouse, for slaughtering people.

To survive in camps, you had to make yourself friends. I was a tailor, I said to those kapos, "If you need, I sew on a button." One kapo I said to him, "Hey, look at those shoes. You want me to fix your shoes?" With needle and thread, how can you fix a shoe? But I got myself a friend. So I got bread, and there were times I had two, three bowls of soup, not one.

One day I wanted to rest. I pretend I'm getting weak, I'm falling down, and I wind up in the hospital. They put me with another guy in one bed. They gave us a slice bread, I ate my slice, but he put his under the bed, fell asleep. In the morning he was dead, and I was laying all night with him! I got out right away from that hospital.

THE TRANSPORT   Then we got put in trains, cattle trains, for two weeks. It was so hot. I'm sitting with some guys talking, and while I'm talking to them, they're dead.

The Germans don't know where they're going, and they're scared. All they know is the Americans are coming closer. One German went into town, stole bread, and gave it to us. They start talking to us, "It wasn't our fault, we didn't start the war. I'm human like you. I was given orders."

LIBERATION   Finally we wind up in Theresienstadt. You should have seen me, no meat on my whole body, just bones. May 7, 1945, everybody started hollering and screaming. I look out the window, see the Russians are here! Everybody started running out, but I was too weak. A lot of people got killed for joy, hammering on the tanks.

My brother brought in food, and I started eating. I got sick, more sick. Then the Russians gave you like a diet, so then I start feeling good. After five, six weeks they say, "Everybody can go home."

I was back in Poland for two months. Everybody was afraid. Not far from my town, in Kielce, was a pogrom, Poles killed Jews. So from small towns we came to the big cities, where there was more Jewish people. I got a job as a tailor, found a cousin, another cousin. Nobody else.

I came to the United States in '49, married an American girl in 1955. I got two sons, one twenty-two, the other nineteen, in college. My brother lives eight blocks from me.

LOOKING BACK   I can be driving in the car, and what happened comes in my mind, and the tears come. How could this ever happen, something like this? And it can happen again, you know why? Because everybody has a gun, so they got to have somebody to fight. The Arab countries, they wouldn't have Israel, they would fight more with each other.

SEVA SCHEER
Piotrkow, Poland

Some people are lucky. They get sometimes, from a relative that left before the war, a picture of their parents, but we were such a close family we stayed all together. I am the only survivor, and I have nothing.

When Seva Silberstein was eight, her family moved to Lodz. Her father was a scholar who spent his time studying, so her mother ran the family grocery store until Seva's brother was old enough to take over. He and Seva developed a prosperous import business in coffee, tea, and cocoa.

My brother taught himself by corresponding to a school because my parents could not afford to send him to college. He was an accountant and he had a diploma, and before we started our wholesale business he was a bookkeeper in a mill.

At home we spoke mostly Yiddish, but outside we spoke Polish, and I took German in school. It helped during the war, my speaking German. I did a lot of translating because most Polish people spoke only Polish, and the Germans used to get furious if you could not understand them.

You always heard in Poland, "Jews, go to Palestine." If Poles met a young Jewish man in a dark street, they would give him a slap, do some harm to him. The Poles were very poor, mostly working people or farmers, and whatever bad happened, the Jew always was the scapegoat.

When the Germans came, I was on vacation at a very nice resort. I was having dinner in the big, beautiful dining room, and a young man comes in, saying, "It's a war! It's a war!" Everybody was talking about war for many, many years, so we didn't pay any attention, but he says, "There are notices about the war on all the buildings!" So I went out, and my God, there it was! Notices that there is a war, and everybody should stay close with their families and gather some food, and so on.

I was really frightened because I was so far away from my parents and my brother. I took my suitcase and went to the train depot, and by golly, then I believed it was a war. There were so many people you couldn't get on. I left the suitcase and just pushed myself in. On the way you could see military trains with soldiers sitting, horses running with the train, soldiers all over.

I don't know if it was corruption, but the Germans came in so fast, and there was not much the Polish army did about it. There were a lot of people in Poland who were born in Germany, but you never knew these people were Germans until the war came. They they just "grew" like mushrooms after a rain, and they were bad and mean, even worse than regular Germans from Germany.

THE OCCUPATION   The day we heard the Germans took over and they're marching in, we all ran out. They were walking in the middle of the street, the army, and we were all standing, Jews, Poles, everybody, standing on the sidewalks looking at them. I thought, "They don't look so bad. Maybe it won't be as bad as people say."

Jews tried to stick together, but it was hard. Wartime is a time that mostly you are by yourself, for yourself. We had no newspaper, no radio, but somebody put a radio together, and people would gather in a basement to listen, and one was watching if a German is coming.

It was forbidden to gather together lots of people, but we lived in a very big building, mostly Jews, and my father called together the whole building on Rosh Hashonah. They went to the basement and he blew the shofar. Then he went back to Piotrkow, planning to rent an apartment. We were to come there, the three of us, but they closed the ghetto and we could not get out, could not communicate. We never heard from him again.

THE GHETTO   We had a beautiful home, lovely furniture, but you could take only what you could carry. I had a girl friend that lived where the ghetto was, so we moved in, five families in this small apartment.

In the beginning there was a little work—like, for instance, I got a job in a factory where they were making leather coats for pilots, because my father was the bookkeeper. But the ghetto was corrupted, that factory was corrupted. The quiet, refined person who couldn't push himself, lost out. If you could holler a lot, open a big mouth, you'd be a big shot.

Getting a job meant getting soup every day. Otherwise you got a ration once a week, a little bit of bread, two or three tablespoons of sugar, maybe a small slice of margarine. People were swollen from hunger. You talked to the person, he looks perfect, almost fat, then half an hour later he was dead!

Where I lived was far to the bakery for that piece of bread. If you'd go out early in the morning when it's dark, they would shoot you, so I would stay overnight with a girl friend that lived in the same house where the bakery was. Sometimes when you came to the window, they closed it. Spend a whole night not sleeping, stand in line waiting, and when it came to me, no bread.

Fresh bread goes very quick. You eat it fast and you're still hungry. Old bread is better. Some people, whatever they got, they ate up right away. I always saved bread, sugar, thinking about tomorrow.

One day my brother woke up and couldn't walk. In normal times, you're sick, you go to a doctor. What do you do in a ghetto? All the Germans need is to see someone that cannot walk. Then, for sure, they take him away, and that's it! But I had saved a whole bread from the ration, and for a bread you could get things on the black market. With the bread I bought a very small bottle of vitamins, a miracle. My brother got up from bed and could walk again.

The Germans would come in the middle of the night, three gun shots, and you had to dress and be down in the street. They took my mother, and I tried to go with her. A German soldier pushed me away and said if I move he'll shoot me. My mother wanted to save my life, so she screamed that I should not go after her. Of course I could not sleep any more, and when it was morning, I walked to the hospital because I had an idea they took the people there.

I passed the market and saw seven Jews, hanging. Then I got to the hospital. The people they gathered during the night were there, but I could not go in. I saw people standing at the hospital windows, knocking, crying, pleading, but nobody could help.

I came home and lay down on our rollaway bed. For the day we had to take it up, so other people could go through to the room where they lived. My brother told me he cried, he hollered, he tried to feed me, but for two days I was lying on that bed, not moving, looking at the ceiling, just numb.

DEPORTATION   In '42 they took me and my brother. They said we should take anything we want because we are going to a work camp where families can be together and work together. We didn't believe it, and we were right.

They took us to a prison, but you had a diamond or something, you gave it to the warden, and we got out. It was very dark, and you had to walk through a little creek between the prison and the ghetto. We walked and walked and walked, and somehow came back. But then a Jewish policeman showed the Germans where we were hiding, in an attic.

One German had a whip and he hit my brother! Every time he hit him, I felt my heart going out, and I pleaded, I said, "Hit me!" When my brother could hardly walk they took us both.

We were two days and two nights, locked up, a cattle train. No toilet, so people had to go where they were standing or sitting. We couldn't wait to come to that promised place where we'll be able to work and get a ration, and we'll have a little room. But we came straight to Auschwitz.

AUSCHWITZ   Nobody in the ghetto heard of Auschwitz, and what I saw, I couldn't believe my own eyes. I said, "My God, we must be in Africa," because that's how the people looked to me. It was July, and here were women, girls, almost naked, with shaved heads, and faces dark from the sun.

We were separated, men and women, my brother and me. We were sleeping standing up, for days. Every night I prayed to God that he'd take my soul. Then there were notices that they need 500 girls for work. You cannot trust, but I said to myself, "Whatever happens, happens," and by some miracle, it really was a working camp, to make parts for airplanes.

MAUTHAUSEN   Girls had such bad, hard work there, but I was lucky. Before you put together the airplane, the parts are washed in naphtha and gasoline. It got to our lungs, and some girls got sick, but I was in the control department, and I had a little scale to weigh switches, screws.

We worked in a bunker underground. On top was a beautiful park where music was playing, so the enemy shouldn't know there is a factory. We got up around 4 A.M. and walked in the dark like soldiers, five in a row, to the factory, many kilometers, with German woman soldiers and big shepherd dogs on both sides. We came in the dark and we walked home in the dark, so you didn't have much time to sleep.

You got one soup a day, a piece of bread and a little sugar. But the barracks was fairly clean, and we had a bunk and a little blanket to cover yourself. After Auschwitz, that was heaven! We stayed there until the Germans started to lose, and then they took us to Bergen-Belsen.

BERGEN-BELSEN   You lay on boards, four in a bunk, no pillows, covers, nothing. I woke up one morning and the girl I slept with, she was dead, and I slept the whole night right by her side. I was terribly sick with typhus. I begged for a drop of water, but nobody helped me, they had to take care of themselves. I couldn't lift my head up, and I prayed again to God to take me.

And then a girl came in the barracks and started to holler, "The Germans are leaving!" I lifted my head as much as I could, and I saw the Germans taking off their white belts and their hats, and they're running!

LIBERATION   The Americans were so good, they tried so hard to help us, but it was not the right help. Many, many people died because we were so starved the stomach couldn't take it, the Spam, chicken soup, tomato soup. What we needed was a few spoons of Cream of Wheat.

I didn't eat. My teeth were all pyorrhea from vitamin deficiency, and I had tuberculosis. They sent me to a hospital in Sweden and nursed me back. I have the best memories of Sweden for those five years. I met my husband in Sweden—he's Polish but I met him there—and our first son was born in Sweden. But I didn't want to stay there. I wanted to be as far from Europe as possible.

My husband had a cousin in the United States. He sent the affidavit and we came in '51. HIAS helped us, and the Jewish Family Service took care of us for two weeks until my husband went to work. We came with $25 in the pocket, and it was very rough, but we made it.

LOOKING BACK   To be a survivor of the Holocaust means that your heart is broken. It might mend a little bit, but it could never be complete.

I still believe there are some good people in the world, and I believe in God. You have to, or you couldn't live. But I am the only survivor. My mother had four sisters and a brother, my uncles and aunts, lots of cousins. My brother was healthy, young, strong.

Jews and non-Jews, everyone that is a human being and has a heart, should know what happened. Never again should be a Hitler, or Nazism.

MAX SCHWARTZ
Krosniewice, Poland

> Your kids, they don't have grandparents like
> other kids, they don't have uncles. They start
> asking, and what can you say? Nobody can give
> me back my parents, my sister, my brother.

*As a teenager, Max Schwartz joined Zionist clubs and dreamed of being a pioneer
in Palestine. He learned how to be a carpenter, so he could help build the country.
He was twenty-one when the Nazis marched into Poland.*

My parents were working people. My father had a store—coal, he sold,
and wood. He was religious, went three times every day to pray. I was
never religious. I was a Zionist.

After Hitler came to power, Germans living in Poland would stand in
front of Jewish stores and tell gentiles not to buy by the Jews. One night
anti-Semites, boys our age, started to hit us. We went running to the
police, and the police came and they caught these kids but sent them
home.

On September 5, 1939, there was already bombs around our town.
Eight days later the Germans came in, cut off beards of Jews coming
home from the synagogue, and they took all the Torahs. They start to
take every Jew, twenty hours work a week. We shoveled snow, other
work. I was young and strong, I could work sixty hours, so I went for my
father, I went for my grandfather. My brother he went to Russia, but the
Russians sent him back.

In 1941 they took maybe 200 from my town to Goldau, a labor camp
not far from Poznan. From Goldau we went to Wanenheim by foot, then
by train to Auschwitz.

AUSCHWITZ   I was Number 141597. They separated us, who can
work, the other people they took to the gas chambers. My youngest
brother, they took him right away, my father and grandfather, too.
Friends said my mother and sister, they took them to Chelmno and killed
them there.

LABOR CAMP   I was in Auschwitz maybe four, five days, then I
went to Schweintochlowitz, a factory for ammunition. I put together
wood houses for the prisoners—build, build, build, bigger and bigger.
Because Germans worked with us, they want us to keep clean, so every

day we got to take a shower. Wasn't enough food, just bread in the morning and soup, but we were clean. The gentiles, they received packages from their parents, but we didn't have nobody to get packages from. In the night, you went out the window to steal food.

When I came from Schweintochlowitz to Buna, a friend was there, and my next youngest brother, Abraham. They made a roll call in the morning and in the evening to count you, and if you ran away they caught you, hung you. We were forced to see. On Sunday doctors checked us. If you still can work, they keep you. If no, they mark you down for the gas chamber. You never think about if you could survive, you just go on, day . . . day . . . day . . . day.

THE TRANSPORT   In January 1945 we knew the Russians already were close, so the guards got time to transport us to Buchenwald, by foot, by train, four days, five. It was open trains in winter, in snow, but we had some blankets, sat close to keep warm. People, Polish and in Czechoslovakia, they threw packages for us to eat.

April 7, 1945, they told us, "March!" At the Germany-Austria border they marched us in the woods, and we were thinking, "This is the last day. When we go in there, they kill us." But this was a camp, and we could hear the bombardment from the Americans, and the Germans ran away.

From Buchenwald 2,000 prisoners went out. At the end, we were only 158. One more day, nobody.

LIBERATION   In the night, American soldiers came and told us we're free. They came with a lot of food and the people start to eat! But if you were hungry for three, four years, and you start to eat too fast, you get sick. For the first four weeks I was sick, but doctors, American, they gave us good health.

I started to look if my brother is alive, stopping in every city and every town to ask. Then in a train was three or four people and we were talking, and one said, "I know Abraham Schwartz. He is living not far from this town." And he gave me the address for my brother!

My brother and I lived together in a small city near Bergen-Belsen. We had food from UNRRA. All the years, in all those camps, I didn't see one woman. Never. Not one! Then I met a Warsaw girl, a survivor too, and we got married in 1947. In 1948 my daughter was born.

In 1949 we left for Israel. I work eleven years, and then we came to Columbus, Ohio. My wife wanted to be with her brother, the only survivor.

LOOKING BACK   My two daughters and my son are in Israel, and you want to be with your kids, this is your investment in life. I'll go back there when I retire.

When our generation goes away, and the younger generation, we'll be history. There's not enough paper and not enough time to tell everything, but maybe a hundred years from now will come children, they will read this and ask, "Could it be true?"

FELICIA WEINGARTEN
Lodz, Poland

> In Bergen-Belsen we began to die. It was a slow process. One became thinner and thinner until one became a skeleton and died, either walking or sitting in the filthy barracks. I watched my mother dying.

Felicia Karo's father was a principal of a Jewish boys' high school. His family had lived in Poland since the sixteenth century. Felicia was thirteen years old when the war began.

Before the war there was no ghetto and one was free to live almost anywhere. I lived in a very nice residential area, where Jews were about 20 percent. I used to play with Polish children, and my father would find jobs for our Polish neighbors.

I was only a child, but you couldn't be Jewish and not be concerned about what was happening to the Jews of Germany. In 1938 Jews who had been born in Poland but lived in Germany were forcibly thrown over the Polish border. The Nazis just rounded them up, and some of them came in robes and house slippers! When war broke out, we naively thought maybe Poland would win because we were hoping England and France would come to the rescue. Poland fell in less than two weeks.

THE GHETTO   My father was arrested in October as a member of the Jewish intelligentsia. He came out the end of December and had to spend four weeks in a hospital, to recover from the beatings and the terrible food in prison. In the meantime, we were ghettoized.

My mother prepaid our rent three months, a bribe so we could take a few sticks of furniture and some possessions. Our furniture was very big and very heavy, and we were not permitted to hire a wagon, so we took two small beds and dragged them on a sled, and left the rest where it was. For three of us we had a tiny little room, no bigger than a bathroom. There was no heating fuel, so we lived in "ice palaces," and you had to hack through ice to wash yourself.

On April 12, 1940, my fourteenth birthday, they threw barbed wire around the ghetto and put armed guards around it.

There were two sets of laws, one for Poles and one for Jews. They were in the newspapers and posted all over town. Curfew for Poles was 7 P.M., for Jews 5 P.M. We had to wear a yellow armband, later changed to a yellow Star of David on the left breast, on the back, and on our apartments.

The German army was quartered in the nicer Jewish apartments, and they helped themselves to Jewish goods and Jewish people. Little by little we became robbed of everything we owned.

FORCED LABOR.   We were a highly skilled people in an industrial city, and they used us. Everybody from fourteen to fifty-five had to work twelve hours a day or night, in shifts. Then it was from age nine to sixty-five. And if one didn't work, one didn't get a ration card, so one was as good as dead.

The food ration was cooked and issued at work. It was a little bit of bread, and "soup" that was just lukewarm water, with maybe a bit of vegetable or potato floating in it. Very rarely were we issued a piece of meat, and almost never an egg or butter. It was no more than 500 calories, probably less.

We were ruled by the *Judenrat,* and we had Jewish bosses of the working force. If one had the right acquaintances, one could get a better job where there was a little food or labor was not that difficult.

At first I made decorations in a ladies' hat factory. Then I received a good job in a bakery, where I was given an extra bread ration. Later I worked in a kitchen, where I could eat a little and leave part of my ration for my parents, and I worked in a laundry. The Nazis didn't know it, but I also went to school secretly, even in the ghetto.

In the summer of 1944 there were about 70,000 of us still left, barely alive, in the ghetto. Parts of eastern Poland were under Russian control and we could hear the guns, but the Russians stopped their offensive and gave the S.S. time to clean out the Lodz ghetto.

DEPORTATION   In August and September 1944, from morning until late at night, soldiers, S.S., and special police went from house to house, flushing out whoever was hiding. Some people didn't hide because people were starving, and one received a loaf of bread if one went willingly. Some were caught right on the street. A classmate of mine didn't have a chance to even say goodbye to her mother. We were hiding in my father's office, but the office manager had a child who cried, and we were found.

They took us to the depot. The German commandant responsible for the ghetto (he was hanged by the Poles after the war), he opened his coat and said, "See, I have no guns. I've been your friend. We are going to resettle you to save you from the oncoming Red Army."

We dreaded this so-called resettlement. We knew that people who were sent away very rarely came back, and sometimes a transport would stop and the people, skeletons, were telling of horrible beatings and torture and hunger. But we had absolutely no idea of concentration camps.

They shoved us into cattle trains, and somebody found a piece of paper stuck between the slats, and he read it aloud. It said, "Brothers, save yourselves. Death awaits you." But it was too late.

AUSCHWITZ   We went through the selection for life and death, men and women separately. It went very quickly. The German officers would with the flicker of a finger send you to the right or the left.

I didn't know who went to the right and why, but I could see from the corner of my eye that these were women with children, sick people, grey-haired, crippled, or young women walking with middle-aged women. I was waved to the left. My mother was tall and handsome with dark hair, and she, too, was waved to the left.

We walked for miles to a bath installation. We were told to undress and line up, and give up our jewelry. I had a watch and a small diamond, my mother's engagement ring. I didn't want to give it to the S.S., so I threw it in a corner. They looked in our crevices, the mouth and elsewhere, to see if one didn't hide jewelry or money. They cut our hair. Then they shoved us into a bath hall, and cold water came out. Then we stood naked, shivering, and after several hours they issued striped uniforms or ragged, very torn civilian clothing.

We marched for several miles again to another part of the camp, and we were seated on the floor, packed like sardines. You'd open your knees and somebody would sit between your knees, until we formed fives. And the next five, next, to the left and to the right. When we started to be very tired from sitting in this position, we started to complain and cry, and scream and yell. Some young girls ran in and told us to stop. They said, "This is a death camp." I knew what death is, and I knew what camp is, and I still recall trying to understand what these words meant together.

There were constant beatings and "selections" weeding out those that were weak or emaciated, separating families, sisters, mothers, and daughters. On the fourth day, I found out that the ones they took went into the gas chambers.

LABOR CAMP   I stayed in Auschwitz only a week. Then there was a demand for Jewish labor, and we were sent to Germany to an airplane factory and then to a huge munitions factory in Bad-Kudova. German civilians lined up on the street and made fun of us. They called us "monkey people" and "rag people" because we were wearing ragged dresses and our heads were shaved.

The prisoners of war who worked in the factory, and the other slave laborers, who came from many parts of Nazi-occupied Europe, tried to cheer us up, and told us to hold out because the Germans are losing the war. The foreman even came with a notebook and asked my mother, "I'd appreciate very much if you would sign your name in this notebook, and say I never hit you, and I treated you with as much humanity as I could." And I realized, if a German foreman is that scared, the war must be close to an end.

I remember only twice an act of decency from the S.S. Once an S.S. woman was asking somebody, "Did you have children?" And the woman said, "Yes, I had a child, who was taken away from me in Auschwitz." The S.S. woman said, "I would never give up my child." The woman was afraid to tell her, "I didn't give her up, she was taken." She just cried, and the S.S. became very angry and made her work without a coat, and the woman was freezing. But about an hour later, another S.S. woman saw this poor woman's face, and her fingers frozen, and she removed her gloves and said to the woman, "You can keep them." Then she said very quietly, with tears in her eyes, "I have a son fighting on the eastern front in Russia, and I hope perhaps somebody will be kind to him, too."

BERGEN-BELSEN   On the death march to Belsen we walked through snow, away from the oncoming Russian army. I don't know how my mother made those three days. I think love drove her on. We could see blood on the snow, and she knew if she would sit down, I would stay with her, and they would shoot both of us.

In Bergen-Belsen, they did not distribute any food. There was very little drinking water, a lot of lice, no work. We began to die of disease and starvation. My mother and I became sick with typhus, burning up with fever. I had no water for my mother, and no medical care to save her.

LIBERATION   We came to Bergen-Belsen in February 1945, and on April 15 I was freed by the British. Physicians came in wearing gas masks because we stank. Women were still dying in their own excrement and lice. Mounds of bodies—among them, my mother—were everywhere.

Nobody had the strength to bury them. The British buried them with bulldozers.

I was dying of malnutrition. I could only walk a few steps, I could not talk above a whisper. I don't know how much longer I would have lived—a few days, a week.

A month and a half after I was freed, a young army medical man said, to my amazement, "Heart okay, lungs okay. You're okay." I was still very thin, and my left leg suddenly would buckle under me and I'd fall, but I got a job with the Jewish Relief because I knew Polish, German, Yiddish, enough English to fill out applications. I was nineteen years old.

We began to look for one another. Friends, a brother or sister or a cousin, very, very rarely a parent and child, survivors were finding one another. My father had six brothers and a sister, all married and with children. None survived. I visited the Jewish D.P. camps and found friends, met my future husband.

People began to marry, to make plans. Repatriation began for those that wanted to go back wherever they came from. Illegal *aliyah* began through Italy to Palestine. I came to the United States in April 1948.

LOOKING BACK   I was busy learning to speak English better, getting a job. My husband had been a medical student and he didn't know English, so he could not go back to medicine. It was a very slow struggle.

It took a long time for me to really understand what I have lived through, and how the German people could have done what they did, how the Nazis could sway a whole nation with clever promises, propaganda. And I realized the role that Christian anti-Semitism played in Nazism.

I also learned my father was right when he said we have to have a country of our own. The Nazis originally wanted to push us out, but there were no buyers, there was no place to go. If we had had an Israel, they would not have been able to kill us all.

My mother believed in God very deeply. When I witnessed the death around me, the abandonment that I felt, I was wondering, where was God? And after the war I was living with the picture of my mother dying, trying to imagine how my father died, and trying not to go crazy. I pushed the thought of religion and God as far away as I could. But when my second son was born I visited the synagogue, and it reminded me of the synagogue in Lodz that my parents belonged to.

Now I attend the synagogue. I love the Hebrew, which I learned as a child. I like the Jewish tradition and Jewish ethics, I like being a Jew. I was born one, I'll die one. I try to believe that God exists and that perhaps I've been blaming Him unjustly because men killed, not God.

I was not born a refugee. I was a loved child that had a family and belonged to a community. Wherever my husband and I travel, I look up other survivors—friends and acquaintances who remember me as a child, who knew my parents. I am not a nobody to them, who suddenly arrived in this country as a refugee. These few survivors represent to me my former self, and that is very precious to me. They also represent the remnant of my people and my culture—a very great culture, and a very old one.

I have been working in the Jewish community for many years. It makes me feel that the gift of survival which was granted so randomly—it was pure chance that one survived—that perhaps I have used to good purpose those years that were given to me.

FRED WILDAUER
Riga, Latvia

If the Germans had put all the engineers, all the
professors that worked on destruction of the
Jews to work on the war effort, if they would
have utilized the brains of the Jews they killed,
they could have won the war. Meitner, Oppen-
heimer, Einstein—Jewish people they gave
away—came here and developed the atomic
bomb for us!

On a single day in 1941, Fred Wildauer lost more than forty relatives. He and his younger brother survived because Fred's non-Jewish wife could bring them food to supplement their meager diet as slave labor and because they were mechanics. The Germans needed mechanics.

My parents were Orthodox Jews. My father sold ladies' and men's shirts, ties, stuff like that. My mother worked with him, and they struggled to make a living. I only went to school until I was fourteen, and then I got my first job—full-time, a mechanic in a knitting factory. When we came out of grammar school we could read and write perfectly, do arithmetic, were ready for life.

Latvia was a very small country. The longest distance was about a two hours' train ride! There were 90,000 Jews, 40,000 of them in Riga, enough for two Jewish political parties, and enough Jewish votes to send a member to Parliament. When I was in the army, there came a directive from the war ministry that we should have the day off on the Jewish holidays, so we can attend religious services. The commander was an anti-Semite, and he said the hell with it, so one of the Jews wrote to a leader of one of the Jewish parties, and the commander was demoted.

But a Jew could not get any rank above corporal. We never had a Jew running the streetcar. We didn't have a Jew in the police force. We didn't have a Jew at the telegraph company.

After Hitler came to power in Germany, my father lost his business. People would go into a Jewish store and say, "I don't like Jews, you can sell it cheaper," or "Why don't you go to Palestine?" They didn't let Jews have decent apartments. A Jew could not get a job, and Jews tried to employ Jews, but we were only allowed a certain percentage. The majority had to be Latvians.

I see myself right now, September 1939, sitting in a friend's apartment, and I see that radio standing in the corner, hear the announcement that war was declared.

The Russians came in June of 1940. They sent the German population back to Germany—people that lived there for ten generations, ministers, community leaders. All of a sudden the doors were open to us, and Jewish people were equal to the rest of the population. Of course the Latvians resented that, and when the Germans marched in in 1941, they were very willing to help the Germans do what they did to the Jews.

I had a married sister who had lived in Berlin. When things started to get tough in Germany, her husband lost his job, and my sister and her children came to Latvia. Her husband had no papers, and they sent him back. Then he crossed into Belgium. We received a Red Cross card, "On my way to Marseille, to go to America." He never got to America.

When Germany attacked Russia in June of 1941, we listened to war news from both sides. The Germans were reporting they shot down fifty planes and lost one, and the Russians were reporting they shot down fifty planes and lost one! My dad said, "If I had a choice, I would rather take the Germans than the Russians. After all, they're cultured people." But my sister said, "Dad, you don't know what you're talking about!" I still remember the way she said that.

THE OCCUPATION   The German army was pursuing the Russians, so Latvian collaborators formed "freedom fighters," with bright red-white-red bands on their sleeves. The very first night, they came to our house because we were about half a block away from the big building which had been the Latvian ministry of the interior and then the headquarters of the Russian GPU.

The police knocked on every door, took all the Jews of our apartment out, about twenty-five of us. We were taken to the headquarters building, where there were several Latvians and a high-ranking German officer. The toilets were overflowing, and they made us clean up the mess. Then one of the Latvian officers said, "Let's take them downstairs." Downstairs the Russians had built a vault they used for torture, with little cells about three feet wide. But the German officer said, "Can't take anybody down. Tomorrow morning the photographer's coming." They probably would have tortured us, killed us.

So we were sweeping the yard, and my older brother swept and swept, swept himself out the gate, and walked away. I followed him and my younger brother followed me, the same way.

The next morning I head for the factory where I work, and there's a couple Latvians standing by the headquarters building. They spot me right away, that I'm a Jew. "Where are you going?" "I have to go to work." "We'll show you some work!" But I said, "I have to open the factory, I have twenty girls waiting to get in," so they let me go.

The very same day in walks a German with a briefcase, and he said, "We want you to go on production twenty-four hours a day," stockings, underwear, things like that. My boss, a Jew, was shoved out and a Latvian named manager, but he got me a pass to go to work and not be arrested. With that piece of paper I was walking every day the gauntlet. I had to show it many times.

We had to register. We got *Jew* stamped into our passport. We were handed a star, and we had to put it on the chest and the back of our clothes. We were only allowed to shop in a Jewish area, so we had to walk across the city to buy groceries, and people would spit on you as you walked by.

THE GHETTO   They fenced in part of the city and told the Jewish committee to allot two square meters per person. Two or three families lived in one room with a curtain across. I bluffed my way into a little milk store and moved in there, together with my younger brother and my sister, who had two children. My parents found one room and a kitchen. They had five rooms of furniture, and the furniture remained in the yard. There were hundreds of apartments the same, and every morning they would go down and break up a piece of furniture and use it for kindling wood.

November 29, 1941, there were placards all over that the ghetto is going to be moved, and everybody is allowed to take twenty pounds along. Everybody put on the most valuable things they had. If they had diamonds or money or gold buried in the ground, they dug it out and sewed it into their clothes to take along.

People that worked in town, like we did, were not allowed back to our families, and we ended up nine men in one tiny little room. In the middle of the night I heard shots. I thought it was in town, maybe an uprising, Latvians against the Germans. I didn't realize Latvian guards were taking the Jews out of the ghetto in groups, into the woods. Later we heard that Russian prisoners had dug out trenches, and the Jewish people had to take off, in orderly German fashion, their shoes, their coats, their glasses, whatever they had on. In their underwear they went into those trenches and were shot there. Meanwhile, the Germans were ripping the clothing apart, looking for valuables.

I lost that night almost everybody in my family—parents, my two sisters, their children, aunts, uncles, cousins, just wiped out.

The Germans were slick about it. They couldn't get everybody out the first night, so to prevent people from running, a letter came to the ghetto a day or two later, saying, "We are all well. The quarters are better here . . ." and listing twenty or thirty names. Everybody found a name that could be an uncle, could be a friend. But these were 24,000 people, so twenty names is nothing! My wife came to see me at the university where I worked—like a student, she would walk through the halls—and that was the first time I broke down.

There were six of us who worked at the university as handymen. We fixed cars, bicycles, motorcycles, the electricity. The Germans got tired of hauling us back and forth, so they gave us a room, formerly a theater, and said, "You build yourselves some bunks." They gave us extra bread sometimes. My shoes wore out, so they took us to a clothing store and told me I should pick out my own pair of shoes. They told us at night, "You lock yourself in." They had a theory, "My Jews are good Jews."

We could have walked away and nobody would have known it for a while. But where would you go? A friend, two of them just walked one day away, and somebody hid them a couple of years, and both of them survived. But you didn't know how long the war would last, and maybe Germany will win!

LABOR CAMP   In late summer of '43 our unit was whittled down, sent to a camp outside Riga. There were a couple of thousand people there, people who were not even Jews—German communists and criminals, even a double murderer. To sleep you had just boards, no straw, nothing.

Again I was lucky. When I was at the university, they got a delousing unit built in Germany to test it, and the unit needed water, so they put it right next to the kitchen. The stoker and the cook asked if I could get them some tobacco. When we went to farms to work, my brother always brought back tobacco leaves and dried them in the barn, so I brought a whole bunch of those leaves to those guys. Now when I got to that camp, there was that cook, and he said, "If you need something, you come in the kitchen." To have a right to walk into the kitchen in a concentration camp is like having a ticket to the White House here in the United States! So every morning I went to the cook, and it was like shopping in a grocery market. I would pick up potatoes and peas and chunks of horsemeat, and I gave food every day to my brother.

Then he asked me if I already have a unit to work with. I said no, and he said, "You're going out with Umbrey." Umbrey was the stoker, the other guy who got the tobacco from me! We went out every day, several hundred prisoners, to work on gasoline storage tanks, putting a cement wall around each tank so if one blows up, they all won't go. It was a very tedious process, to shovel sand into the machine that makes cement. There were German craftsmen working with us, but the laborers were these poor Jews, and it was so cold, we had rags wrapped around our feet to keep warm.

Then Umbrey said, "You know anything about technical things?" I said yes. The next morning there was a blacksmith waiting, and he took me to work inside, in a little shed in a storage yard. They brought in seven, eight guys and I was like a foreman in a factory.

They would search us when we came back to camp, but there was a group of watchmakers, they would stand with their hands up, and gold in their hands! Men used to smuggle salami or bread under their jacket in the back because when they search you, they usually go right on the sides. But if they caught you, you're the next one to go to Auschwitz.

They had something they called the *Himmelfahrtskommando*. They were picking thirty people at roll call—people the leader didn't like or who committed a little crime, or older people. Or sometimes the commandant would just count down thirty men. I tell you, you sweated it out because none of them ever returned. One time he cut it off at the next guy, one away from me!

Luckily, I was only six weeks in that camp. Then the Russians were coming closer, and my younger brother and I decide we're going to run away. I had a truck to repair, something on the motor. I still don't know anything about trucks, but I told them there was something not right in the electrical system, and I said there's a guy in camp who really knows it well.

So here's this huge truck, real high, big wheels. I was sitting on one fender, my brother was on the other fender, and we looked at each other with, "Should we, or shouldn't we?" We were all alone, no guards, just to walk away. And all of a sudden we see through the gate the whole unit coming in. They're going to ship us out.

DEPORTATION   It was night, no moon, no lights. We still had time to go in the barracks, say we have to change clothes or something, and take off. But by that time we'd lost our guts.

They put us on barges, no supplies, nothing to eat for twenty-four hours, but I was lucky again. I lagged behind and got on the tugboat. I found myself a warm spot next to the smokestack, and we found food and ate.

STUTTHOF   Stutthof was a big camp—45,000 people subdivided into little camps with different food, different treatment. There was a German submarine commander, the whole Lithuanian government was in there, a Danish police force! The barracks for Jews were designed for 300 people, but they took in 1,500, and there was a woman's camp, partitioned off with wire.

The women knew they were going to have to go into a shower, get prison clothes, so they started to throw over sweaters and jackets to the men. But in the middle of the night a guard turned on the lights and ordered us to line up outside, and we had to run the gauntlet to do it. Polish guards were standing with big sticks, planks, hitting everybody that came out. Then we had to run back. This whole process repeated itself three or four times that night. Again I was lucky. I got a knock on the shoulder, but people were walking around with bloody heads and broken bones.

I saw for the first time there one of those crematoria. Every single day they took little groups of people down there, maybe ten or twelve of them, mostly women. The people knew where they were going, you could see it on their faces and the way they were walking. That smell was always hanging over the area.

There was organization among the prisoners—always is, immediately, a society. There was a Jewish boy, short but powerful, a boxer. A Polish prisoner walked up to him and says, "I see you got a watch. Why don't you give it to me?" This Jewish boy let the Pole have one, and the guy just flew through the air. The commandant immediately made the boxer boss over 2,000 other Jews.

It was foggy and wet, and to keep warm we would build "furnaces." Five or six guys would stand in a circle, calling other guys to stand on the outside, and pretty soon it would be like a huge beehive, hundreds of people standing in one mass, and inside was warm. Sometimes we would sing and start to sway, and we could stand for hours and hours that way. At night we would lay like sardines, in one direction, with the next guy's knees under your knees, and so on. You took off your shoes, rolled them in your jacket so nobody steals them, and used it as a pillow.

They had a little narrow track railroad where they brought in potatoes. We had to dump the cars, put them back on the tracks, push the train out, then put the potatoes in boxes and run across the road to a field where we buried the potatoes for winter. I used to eat raw potatoes right there, like an apple. The whole German population from the town walked by us when they went every day to the railroad station, so if there's anybody there that says they didn't know there was a concentration camp, they are liars!

My older brother didn't survive Stutthof. They decided one night there were too many of us, so they just took out his barracks, and they were gassed on the road in those infamous trucks.

FORCED LABOR   We were put on a train and they took us to Magdeburg. We got off in the middle of the night, and they brought us into a camp and we really thought we are in heaven because each of us got a blanket and civilian clothes. I happened to end up with a pair of pants that fairly fit me, and a winter jacket, and it was warm!

We worked twelve-hour shifts in a factory where you make shells. We hardly got any food there—thin soup, a slice of bread in the morning, a slice of bread on the way back. People in the camps usually ate fast their bowl of soup. Then they waited for extras, some of the guys with one foot ready, until the cook says, "Seconds!" Then they ran, killed themselves, and sometimes instead of giving soup, the cook would take the spoon and hit them over the head!

The last four or five months, it was a pitiful sight to see some guys. Couldn't put their shoes on because their feet were swollen. You couldn't see their eyes, because their whole head, everything was swollen. They were just full of liquid, all puffed up from starvation.

Hunger can do terrible things. I found a big can where they dumped food for the dog, and the dog could only reach part way into the can. There was a mold in there, but we cut it out with a knife, my brother and I, pulled out a couple of dog hairs, and we had a Sunday dinner.

There was one guy in camp, he slept right next to me. He was my size, my age, and somehow I saw myself in him. I was watching him because we didn't have any mirrors around. I saw how he was deteriorating, and then he was lying in bed all day long, and one day I came home and he was dead. I took his death more than I would take, today, my brother's death because I saw myself in him.

LIBERATION   April 12 of 1945 we were working on the outskirts of the city, and an American tank went by. Our guards took off, and we're free, but we didn't have any place to go. A guy going by says there are no guards at camp, so we went back, found something to eat, and my brother and I lay down to sleep in the S.S. guards' quarters.

In the middle of the night an announcement on the loudspeaker woke us up. The American tanks had pulled back, some of the guards came back, and we dumbbells were sitting in the camp! It was pitch black night and my brother and I, we pulled a board out of the fence, and another board. That noise a nail makes when it's being pried out, you know? It's terrible at night! But I thought, if I don't see them, they don't see me either. I stuck my shoulder through, and I was outside! Gives you an eerie feeling because inside, you're allowed, but outside, you're on the run! My brother followed me, and in about five minutes the rest of the guys were out, too.

We started to walk like soldiers, in step, toward where we thought the American lines were. But when it started to get light we decided we better get off the street before somebody sees us. We were in the bombed-out area of the city, and we climbed over the rubble and found a basement.

This is a place where a guy should get religion, because I think in the whole city of Magdeburg there wasn't a basement like this. The building was blown away by a bomb, but the basement was three compartments. One belonged to a painter, supplies and ladders and everything. The next one just had empty crates. The third one, everything was in there that a guy on the run should want! Canned stuff, asparagus, carrots, potatoes, matches, furniture. I made myself a bed in a huge wicker basket and my brother slept on a loveseat.

There's a German civilian there, afraid the Americans would kill all the Germans, so he brought us every day for seven days a bucket of water, sometimes a piece of bread. Then one day he didn't show up. I heard a lot of noise and I looked, and there was an American guy by a truck. A plain green uniform, and he looked like a gentile, but he said to me, *"Vis der Yid?"* (Are you Jewish?). I said yes, and he said, "Me, too." The first American soldier we saw! It was April 20, 1945—a beautiful day.

I wanted to find my wife. We had agreed that in case we survived the war we would write to a lady on the west bank of the Rhine river, a lady we both knew. My brother and I waited for an answer, but then we decided we're not going to wait. We walked across Germany for three weeks to get to that little village and found the lady had died!

The people there, they said they think my wife went to Solingen. I couldn't find her, and on the way out of town we saw a little printing store with a typewriter sheet in the window, government announcements. I went in and said, "I would like to put out a search ad." I wrote down my wife's name, Tamara Lilget, and he said, "I know her, she lives in the next street." And there I found my wife!

My uncle in the United States couldn't understand why we wanted to leave Europe, so I wrote to the soldier that liberated me. Jewish Family Service told his mother, "People don't do it for their relatives! You'll be responsible for them for five years!" But his mother had promised herself, "If my son comes back from the war unharmed, I would like to do something for somebody," so she sponsored us.

So that's how we came—my wife, my brother, and myself—to the United States. First we had a little grocery store, than I found myself a job to sell insurance and made a living.

LOOKING BACK   Sometimes, in spring, I am there, walking on that street, and I feel exactly that moment when I was liberated, how it was. In the middle of winter I sometimes walk out at night and I'm alone and it's quiet and I am back in the ghetto, the wind blowing, the dreary, hopeless feeling, and it comes to me right there, the memory—that night when I heard the shots, that night my family died.

Felicia Weingarten, Landsberg, 1947.

Felicia Weingarten, California, 1988.

Dora Zaidenweber was a member of a Zionist youth group in Radom before the war.
Only eight members in this 1938 photo survived.

Dora Eiger and Jules Zaidenweber met and fell in love in the Radom ghetto, 1941.

DORA ZAIDENWEBER
Radom, Poland

> The thought of death was with me for so long
> that it no longer scared me. All the emotion left
> in me was regret—sorrow that I, too, would end
> up on a pile of bodies, discarded like so much trash.

Dora Eiger's father was a community leader, a member of the executive committee of Poland's Zionist Labor Party. Dora was only fifteen when the Germans took Poland. At nineteen, she married Jules Zaidenweber in the Radom forced labor camp, where both were prisoners.

Radom was a town of 100,000, about 25 percent Jewish. It was a vibrant, active Jewish community. After World War I my father was planning on going to Palestine, but his father died and he was the oldest son, so he went to school and became an accountant. We had a large, very beautiful apartment, and my mother was an elegant lady.

We were in school six days a week. We had an awful lot of homework, but we had no television to distract us. We belonged to youth groups, went skating in winter, played tennis in summer. I was a gymnast and in track.

If a Jew insulted a Pole, he could be taken to court and severely punished for it, and there were young thugs who belonged to this organization which was violently anti-Semitic. But a neighbor girl might say to me, "You damn Christ killer!" and then ten minutes later, she'd come back and say, "You want to play?" So you don't live your life terrified all the time. Hitler was in Germany and we were in a different country, and it seemed that we lived in a civilized world.

When war broke out, I was looking up and seeing the anti-aircraft fire, the little silver bullets. German planes came in so low you could see the faces of the pilots, and the planes were spraying the area with machine gun fire. This is something you see in a movie, but you never think it would happen to you.

THE OCCUPATION   One week later, the Germans marched into town. A lot of orders were posted on walls. Everybody had to register to get an identification card and a ration card. Jewish I.D. cards were blue, and had the word *Jew* stamped on it. We had to start wearing an armband with the Star of David, which identified us as Jews.

German soldiers could just come into our apartments and take furniture, linens, and silver, and send it home. We had German officers billeted in our apartment, so you had to be very quiet, very careful what you were saying and doing. We had a live-in maid, but the German did not allow the maid to clean his room. I had to clean it.

To make a living, you either bartered or worked for the Germans. Radom was in Poland's "Iron Triangle," with a very large weapons factory and other munitions factories in neighboring towns. Another big industry was the leather tanning industry. The Germans were in great need of leather, and they had to keep the people who knew how to mix the chemicals for tanning. These factories may be the reason why there are many more survivors from Radom, percentagewise, than from other cities.

The tanneries were my father's clients, and accounting services still had to be done, so my father was working and was actually earning money. But there was a lot of poverty, a lot of sickness. The Jewish community had soup kitchens, and a lot of people wanted to put their children in the Jewish orphans' home, so the children would at least have some food.

THE GHETTO   The beginning of 1941 all Jews had to move into two ghettos, in areas of tenements and very poor-quality houses. Because my father was who he was, we and our neighbors got a house that had four rooms. It had an outhouse, and the water pump outside, but each family had one room, so it was really terrific compared to where people lived two and three families in one room.

That's when I met Jules, my husband, because his family moved next door. That summer our romance started blooming.

In June of 1941 the Allies had to run for their lives to England and the Germans sent the Russians running. We started developing a nihilistic attitude, sort of "to hell with it all," to live every day because it looked like there wasn't much left of our youth. This was it, the end of the war, and the Germans had won.

There was a curfew in the ghetto. You couldn't go out after eight o'clock, but we sneaked through backyards, and we partied and did a lot of laughing and talking and joking. Since schools were closed, groups of us met with teachers and continued with our classes, which was very dangerous.

On April 28, 1942, the knock on the door came at our house. A Gestapo man with a list in his hand asked if Isaiah Eiger lived in this house. My father hugged us and walked out with the Gestapo man.

We were just rudderless, floating. We had lost our protector. But then my mother gathered herself together, started making decisions. She had to feed us, so she started trading on the black market. A Polish woman who had been my uncle's housekeeper would purchase food, bring it to the wooden wall surrounding the ghetto, take money from my mother, and hand her the bundle. Then my mother would keep some for us and sell the rest to other people, making enough money to buy more.

On August 6 the Germans emptied out the small ghetto in Radom and they had some spare boxcars, so they came to our ghetto and rounded up another 2,000 people. They didn't get to us, but our whole family was gone, grandmother, great-grandmother, all the aunts, uncles, cousins. We didn't know what happened to the people in the boxcars. The word *gas chamber* had never even surfaced yet.

Those remaining were put to work as slave labor. Now we were six people in a tiny little room, maybe nine by fifteen, just filled with beds. The Germans staged raids in the daytime to flush out those who weren't at work. Twice they lined up people and just counted ten, and then executed every tenth person. I was weeding a huge field of lettuce and radishes and other vegetables twelve hours a day, and a soldier with a gun was standing there watching. I was assigned to mend rugs. I made covers for mattresses. I was a maid, a cook who didn't even know how to boil water. I did clean-up work after painters.

Jules and I got married on July 8, 1943. That was some kind of a wedding! The Jewish head of the labor camp was empowered to perform marriages, and Jules saved that marriage certificate by hiding it in his shoe.

Then we were sent to work at the weapons factory. I was in a women's barracks and Jules was in a men's barracks. I was the finisher, the polisher, in the woodworking shop. We were supposed to be working on shipping boxes for the guns, but a lot of Germans had us make fancy furniture for them. They would take the furniture to their home and bring me there to finish it. I could have walked out and just disappeared, but this friend of mine walked away, and her father was tortured to death.

DEPORTATION   One hot July day in 1944, we were marched out, 2,000 people guarded by S.S. with machine guns and dogs. A young boy tried to escape and they made him kneel in front of everybody and shot him point-blank with a handgun. People who lagged behind, we heard the shots. As the guards saw people who had a hard time walking, they invited them to get on horse-drawn wagons following us, and soon the wagons came back empty. It was a trail of blood and bodies.

The end of the third day, we arrived at Tomaszow and the women were taken to the local jail. We had no water, not much food, no toilets. After a week there, we were marched to railroad tracks, and there were the men! We cried, we embraced, and then we were separated again, and put in cattle boxcars. This looked like absolutely the end.

AUSCHWITZ   Sunday morning we arrived. The sky was as blue as can be. The sun was shining. As they opened the boxcars we saw the sign, "Arbeit Macht Frei." "Where are we?" we said. And somebody said, "Auschwitz."

Nobody needed to tell us what was going on in Auschwitz. The smell told us all, the horrible smell of burning human flesh. They were shouting orders. "Get undressed! Line up here!" They were shaving off people's hair. Have you ever seen a woman with her hair shaved off? It looks grotesque. The whole situation was so totally unreal, we were laughing, crying and laughing.

They told us to take our shoes with us. We were lucky because my mother had red shoes with heavy heels, and she had diamonds hidden in those heels, which later came in very, very handy.

One German officer was very tall, extremely handsome, wearing a monocle. He had a little stick under his arm, and he was wearing white gloves. There he stood, one finger pointing, to the right, or to the left. Those who were young and still in good shape were on one side. On the other side were women whose bodies were older, the skin hanging. The officer was Dr. Mengele.

Our group was shoved into a room that had shower heads. Water came out. Later I found out that the gas chamber on the other side also had shower heads. When we came out they handed us a dress, that's all.

Even in Auschwitz people settled down to a certain routine. There was always the chance that you'd get sick, that they would pick you for medical experiments, but in the meantime you had a routine to feel that you're still a human being. You'd think, "What's the use?" And you had to say, "I'm fighting. I resolve to be alive."

I was assigned to a sewing workshop, where I secretly made aprons and blouses for women who worked in the kitchen, to wear under the scratchy prison uniform. In return they gave me margarine, sugar, marmalade.

We had come to Auschwitz in August. In November the whole extermination process stopped. Transports were no longer arriving, they were leaving. In January the Germans blew up the crematoria and the gas chambers, and on the 18th of January we were marched out, thousands of women, in the snow.

THE TRANSPORT   In the three days on the march, we stopped in villages, where we were put up in barns. On one occasion, the people let some of us into their houses. Inside a warm house, can you imagine! And they gave us hot soup!

On the third day we were put in open boxcars. When the train stopped at Grossrosen, I impulsively said to one of the guards, "Could I get a drink of water?" He just kept walking, but later he came back and handed me a canteen of warm water with a slice of bread floating in it! It sort of restores your belief that some human beings are decent.

Next the train stopped in Buchenwald, where we were crowded into closed boxcars. For four days the train moved and stopped, and moved and stopped.

BERGEN-BELSEN   We got off in surroundings that were breathtakingly beautiful, a forest of pines with snow on the branches. There was a moon. We were marching again, and finally we came to a barbed wire fence and barracks with signs in French, Italian, Russian. It was a prisoner of war camp, empty. We were the first inhabitants of Bergen-Belsen, one of the most infamous of the end-of-the-war camps.

Daily, thousands of people were arriving. Each day we were given a slice of bread and a cup of soup made of rutabagas and water. Then the bread was cut out. Once I had some potato peels to eat, and I really just relished this marvelous food.

Lice started in the straw we slept on, and people were dying of typhus. By the end of March, only eight weeks since we arrived, half the 35,000 prisoners were dead already, of starvation or disease.

I became very, very sick with typhus. I tried to pretend I wasn't sick, to go to rollcall every day, but one day I just folded, and they took me to the "hospital" to die. My mother still had the diamonds in her shoes, and she went to the woman in charge, and that's where one diamond ring went. That's how I came out alive from that death-trap "hospital."

LIBERATION   April 15, 1945, the sun was shining on this indescribably horrible hell of a camp. We were shadowy skeletons. We heard rumors that Allied forces were on German soil, but when I heard a commotion I didn't even raise my head. Then I heard a voice coming over the loudspeaker, not in German but in Polish, the most beautiful words, "We have come to free you. This is the Polish Brigade of the British Army."

They gave us freshly baked bread, and soup with pieces of meat and fat in it. Some people actually died from eating it! Then they started giving us very bland, cereal-type food, what our stomachs could tolerate. I weighed about fifty pounds when I was liberated. In three months I doubled my weight.

UNRRA officials asked us to decide where we wanted to go. Mother was with me, but we didn't know if anybody else was alive. Then one morning in July I was walking to town, and I saw a figure in the distance.

The step looked familiar. It was Jules! Jules and my brother, David, were liberated together, and my father was liberated in Theresienstadt by the Russians. We were so fortunate!

Jules and I started making our way to Heidelberg, where some Radomers were. The Americans put us in a castle, incredibly beautiful. Then our whole group was transported to Stuttgart and put in apartments which had been cleared of Germans.

We'd lost five years. Jules wanted to study electrical engineering, so I started working for UNRRA because somebody had to earn money. We didn't have to pay rent or buy food, and the Joint Distribution Committee sent us used clothing, but to go to a theater occasionally, a restaurant, you had to have some money.

Then in 1948 we decided that I needed an education, too. I was the only Jewish person in the department of economics, out of some 200 students, but I spoke German very fluently, so they didn't know I was Jewish until summer, when they saw the number tattooed on my arm. Then the young men, all Germans, immediately started telling me they fought in France, Belgium, Holland, Norway. Nobody was ever in Poland!

Jules's mother went to Israel, and we really wanted to go to Israel, too. But my mother died, and my father and David left for the United States, and suddenly I realized that if I went to Israel, I might never see my father and David again.

The first winter in Minneapolis in 1950, I thought I was in Siberia! I got a job and I was admitted to graduate school in economics at the university. People reached out in certain ways, but they had relatives, friends already. Our social activities were among ourselves. Also, nobody wanted to talk about the Holocaust, and we had a real need to talk about it, to bear witness.

LOOKING BACK   Some say, "Why not just forget it and live a normal life?" There is no normal life after the Holocaust.

I speak to students and adult groups about the Holocaust, about people who would treat other human beings this way, how any group can become a victim, how the rest of the world turned away and pretended it wasn't happening. They didn't want to get involved. And therein is really the lesson of the Holocaust.

The question of resistance always comes up because Americans' notion of heroism always has to do with resistance, with violence. I point out that there was armed resistance in many ghettos and camps, but those who carried it out invariably died. Simple survival in those extermination camps was also an act of resistance, every minute.

JULES ZAIDENWEBER
Radom, Poland

We were slave labor. They didn't have to pay us.
They gave us a little watery soup and a piece of dark
bread. If a horse died, they'd cut up the meat and put
it in the soup. If they found some smelly herring,
they would use that herring juice in the soup. And
if we die, so what? They will have other slaves.

As the Germans advanced on Radom, nineteen-year-old Jules Zaidenweber and his friends escaped, wandered through eastern Poland for weeks, and eventually wound up in Lvov, under Russian occupation. He went home again when refugees in Lvov were being deported to work in Russian coal mines.

Jewish life in Radom was very active. There was a Yiddish newspaper, Yiddish theatre, Zionist and non-Zionist organizations, dozens of small synagogues. On the High Holidays we would go to our own family synagogue, donated by my great-grandfather. Poland being a Catholic country, they had religion classes in school three times a week, taught by a priest. We would have released time instead or a Jewish teacher who taught us Jewish subjects.

Jews were about 10 percent of the Polish population—3,000,000 Jews or more—but there was anti-Semitism everywhere. A Jew in Poland could not get certain jobs, even if he had a better education than the Pole had. A Jew could not become a judge or a notary public. Jews were in business, the police would harass them. Jews were not permitted to live in certain areas of the city, and you would be beaten up if you went there. You would be walking down the street, and you would be insulted.

When Hitler came to power in Germany in 1933, you could sense an increase of anti-Semitic behavior, even in the Polish parliament, where there were Jewish representatives. There was a small pogrom not far from our town, in Przytyk. Polish peasants attacked the Jews, the Jews fought back, and the Jews were tried in Radom in the circuit court.

The war started on September 1, 1939. September 2, nothing happened. September 3, without any warning, we heard bombs falling very close to us. Rumors started that the Germans would arrest all the young Jews. With tears in their eyes, the parents said, "Go! Save yourself!"

So we decided to go east, ahead of the Germans. You'd say to a friend, "I'm going tonight. Are you going, too?" There was no leader, no plan, nothing. Wednesday late afternoon we left home, saying, "We'll come back in two weeks because the war will stop by that time."

We didn't have hiking boots, equipment, or anything. We traveled on country roads, a huge mass of people. Some had horses and buggies. Most, including me, walked. People who had cars were honking, screaming, "Get out of the way!" They ran out of gas, stalled. The Germans would come down with their airplanes and shoot at us, and we would hit the dirt.

We got to Lublin on Saturday, in the middle of the night. Lublin was in flames. A few days later the Germans came, the victors, marching, with their bands playing, down the main street.

I stayed in Lublin, where my relatives lived, about two weeks. Then my friends and I decided it was safer to escape to the area occupied by the Russians. We went to Kowel, where the Jewish community put up soup kitchens for refugees, but there was no place to stay, so we went south toward the big city of Lvov.

Conditions in Lvov were not very good either, but at least you didn't have to be afraid of the Germans. The Russians allowed some young people who had credentials, including me, to move into a student dormitory and prepare to take the test to be admitted to the Lvov Institute of Technology.

I didn't have any money to buy food or clothing because when I ran away I thought we went for a short time. To earn some money, we would stand in line early in the morning at the liqueur factory. They would sell you one bottle per person, and then you would go out and sell the bottle, and make a few *zlotys*.

The Russians started sending refugees away to work in Russia. Also, as time went on, the less I knew about my family. There was no mail, no telephone—only the grapevine and people accidentally meeting others from their home town. I heard that in November a train was going to transport refugees from Lvov to the German occupied part of Poland, and it was to be a "free day" to allow Poles—mainly military and goverment personnel and their families who had been evacuated—to go back home.

So I came home to Radom the 9th of November and found my parents and sister OK. But the Germans were arresting people, so we had to hide, locking the doors. Everybody was scared. I stayed maybe a week, and then, at my parents' urging, I left again with a friend of my father's, through the German-Russian line, back to Lvov.

I moved into an apartment with my uncle and two cousins from Radom. December came, and January. The apartment had no heat. You would leave a cup of water on the table, and you would wake up in the morning and it was solid ice! In February we heard people were being sent deep into Russia, to coal mines in the Donets Basin. So again, a group of us decided to go back.

This time we did not have an open border with a train. We had to go in the dark to a place on a river, and some local person gave us a little map, how to get across. We had to be on the German side before eight o'clock curfew, or they shoot. It was snow to my chest and very, very cold. I had to pull out my legs from the snow, step by step. I was hot, sweating. But finally all of us came to the German side. A woman let us sleep in her barn and gave us hot milk. The next day we rented a horse and buggy for part of our long trip, and little by little we made it back to Radom.

THE OCCUPATION   I got a job as a clerk in the "housing department" of the Jewish community administration. If a German liked a Jewish apartment, the German would take it. If he was "nice," he would wait until tomorrow, or three days, or maybe even a week. Meanwhile, I had to find another apartment for the Jewish family. You could not rent an apartment because there were a lot of Polish refugees in town, so you assigned a room, two rooms, depending on the number of people in the family.

THE GHETTO   Then the Germans decreed that by April 15, 1941, every Jew had to move into a ghetto. We lived in the Large Ghetto, maybe 25,000 people, around the two large synagogues, where the majority of Jews already lived. The Small Ghetto was about 10,000. The Germans didn't want to monkey around with ghettos in every little *shtetl*, so they emptied out Jews from the small towns and villages around Radom and sent them to our ghettos.

So you lived with strangers, different kinds of people, a whole family or more in one room. You were lucky if you found a good room, with nice people you could get along with. There was little food, maybe no heat. The ghetto was boarded up, but Poles would come to the fence with, let's say, a bread that cost one *zloty*. They'd ask for two *zlotys*, jewelry, other things.

The night of August 5, 1942, the first big deportation took place. They surrounded the Small Ghetto with S.S. troopers, Polish police, Ukrainian guards. The Ukrainians loved Jewish blood, and they were very good executioners, good helpers to the Germans. Five percent of the people were shot right there, 85 percent were taken to trains, and about 1,000 young people capable of work were marched to the Large Ghetto.

I was dragged out of bed about 4 A.M. to help clean up the Small Ghetto. We carried the bodies to carriages and pushed the carriages to a mass grave, two huge trenches. Layers of bodies, undressed men and women together, were covered with lime and topped with dirt.

Two weeks later they did the same thing with the Large Ghetto. That was when my family went—my father, my grandfather, uncles and aunts, cousins. My sister worked for the German administration of Jewish properties. The leader got to like his Jews, protected them, but he got cold feet and brought all his Jews out himself for deportation.

About 90 percent of the Jews now were gone. They took three, four little streets, the worst area, and they stopped calling it *ghetto* and renamed it the Jewish Forced Labor Camp.

In July of '43 Dora and I got married there. The chances of staying together were better if we were married. There were rumors that we might be exchanged for Germans in Palestine.

Meanwhile, we felt that if we could get work in the gun factory in Radom, maybe we could preserve ourselves. I had a gentile friend; we graduated high school together. He was a medical student, but he couldn't study because the Polish universities were shut down, so he worked for the plant doctor. He arranged for me to work in the electrical department, and my wife, he arranged for her, too. You had to "grease"—pay bribes— if you could do it. We moved to the camp near the weapons factory, behind barbed wire fences and guarded by S.S. troops.

DEPORTATION   The end of July 1944 the Russians had started their big offensive after their victory at Stalingrad. The Germans were retreating everywhere, but the S.S. found it important to take us along. We marched over 100 kilometers in three days, men and women, to a place called Tomaszow. It was very hot. A lot of people passed out, a lot were shot.

We stayed in Tomaszow a week, and then they took us to Auschwitz in cattle cars. There they took all the women, the old men, and the sick, off the train. They sent the rest of us to a concentration camp called Vaihingen, south of Stuttgart.

LABOR CAMP   There was nobody else in that camp. We got the striped uniforms, the "formal" concentration camp garb. A leader was designated for each barracks. We had people supervising sending people out to work and we had a medical staff, including a few Jewish doctors. They started bringing in non-Jews and different nationalities— French, Poles, Ukrainians, Dutch, Norwegian, and Danish. Some were intellectuals—a judge and lawyers, very high officials— and some were people from the resistance.

I was in Vaihingen nine months. Every morning we would get up at 5:30 and line up for counting. After that we ate breakfast, a piece of bread, a little hot water mixed with some rutabaga, and so-called coffee—black water. Then we would go out to work guarded by S.S. troops. Other prisoners would bring us "soup" for lunch—more rutabaga water. In the evening we would come back, line up, and count off. If somebody made a mistake counting, he would get hit in his face. And then again we'd get our ration of bread.

This was not a strict regime camp like Dachau. If I had a friend in a different barracks, I could go over and see him in the evening when we got back from work. People were meeting secretly to pray. I even fasted on Yom Kippur. I worked that day, and I didn't pray much, but I didn't eat. It was very easy to not eat! On Passover there were people who would trade their pieces of bread for pieces of rutabaga or raw potato, to avoid eating bread.

We tried to keep as clean as possible. It was cold water and raw soap, take off the shirt, wash it and yourself, dry it, put it on again. A change of underwear, maybe, once in several weeks.

So this was not the typical ruthless camp. However, if you didn't take off your hat before an S.S. man, you got slapped. If you did take off your hat, they said, "Are you my friend, that you are greeting me?" and you got slapped. People did die, a lot of people, of typhus, dysentery, other sickness, just weakness, a mental breakdown, whatever. But there was no systematic killing, no mass murder, no gas chamber, no crematorium. Toward the end, especially, old German army officers and retired army people were recruited for guards, and they were less inhuman.

In Vaihingen I worked in a metallurgical factory, and later where they were building an underground factory. Germans worked there, too, and you could talk to them. There was a prison shop—shoemakers, tailors, barbers, who worked for the German guards. When a German needed to repair something or wanted to bring you a piece of bread, he would sometimes wrap it in yesterday's newspaper. Or he would come in, read the paper, and "forget" it. Even later, in Dachau, somebody brought in a Nazi party paper that said Roosevelt was dead.

The papers said the Germans were in "victorious retreat," but we knew if they are retreating, it's not very victorious. We could sense that the war was coming to an end soon.

On Christmas Eve of 1944 the lights suddenly went out in camp—a blackout. We could hear planes flying overhead, wave after wave after wave of planes, and we knew they were bombing nearby. One time we heard the Germans were chasing British paratroopers that had landed near us. In early April we were working outside the camp, and we were shot up by American planes with machine guns.

A few days later, on April 7, the German guards ran and took us with them! They left maybe two-thirds of the camp there, people not healthy enough to march fourteen kilometers to the railroad station, but they took about 500 of us, 90 percent Jews, and shipped us to Dachau.

DACHAU   In Dachau we had to take off all our clothing, throw it into the pile. The only thing we could carry with us were our shoes. I wanted to keep mine because from the day when an S.S. officer at Vaihingen slapped me on the face for having a bulge in my pocket—a few pictures—I wrapped the pictures in heavy paper and put them in my shoe, and I walked on them. Those were the only pictures I had of my parents, my family, my wife. I didn't even know if my wife was still alive.

They gave me a big suit, and some big guy probably got my small suit. They assigned us to barracks 22. We were not tattooed because the only place where they tattooed was in Auschwitz. And that was it.

There was no work. All we could do all day long was walk back and forth in the courtyard or just sit on the bunk. Some volunteered to push the cart with the dead bodies. Every morning there would be ten, fifteen bodies, and they would pile them on and pull the cart to the crematorium. Maybe they got an extra piece of bread, I don't know. I didn't volunteer.

On the 27th of April the American army was coming close. The Germans took out about 2,000 Jews, just Jews, and marched us to a railroad trestle and gave us olive green Russian army overcoats. They left us with the striped suits, but they gave us those warm coats, plus a Finnish paper sleeping bag wrapped up with a string, very nice and neat, and a Red Cross box the size of a shoe box.

Unbelievably, they put us on a passenger train. The rumor was, the war is at an end, and they are trying to exchange us, make a deal. It was Saturday, April 28, 1945, and we were standing in a drenching rain in this Alpine railroad station. Then we heard the news that the war is over, and the Germans are giving up, and we are going to be free. Well, people just went crazy. Even the Germans were jumping, kissing each other! It was unbelievable!

But it turned out it was a false message from a resistance radio station, and when these S.S. troopers, these bastards, found it wasn't true, they started beating on us mercilessly with their rifle butts. Then they walked us into the mountains and left us in some barns for the night. The next morning they put us on a mountain train and carted us to an area where in front of us were mountains, in back the road, on the side a mountain stream, and the guards were on the other side, so we were wedged in. Night came, and again we went to sleep, but in the middle of the night we heard noises and woke up and found the guards had disappeared!

LIBERATION   We decided that meant the Americans are close, so we organized a group of Radomer, about thirty of us, to march on the highway to meet them. It didn't take long until we were stopped by an S.S. and an army officer. They could see the striped pants and the jackets, but we had those big green coats, so they were not sure who we were. We said the guards told us to go north. It wasn't true, but it was a good story! The army officer said, "This is the front line. Get up in the mountains, off the road."

All day we hid in a shepherd's hut. Cannonballs were flying over our heads, and every so often a German army straggler would walk along and look into the hut. They were loaded with ammunition and grenades, and we were afraid that one was going to drop a grenade right in the middle of us.

When it got dark, the shooting stopped. The next morning, May 1, we heard trucks, heavy vehicles, rumbling by on the highway. We sent scouts, crawling on all fours, down to the road. They came back running, screaming, "Americans! Americans!" We found the strength to run, too, down to the road. The Americans started throwing candy, chocolate, all kinds of things, and we were screaming, "American, American! Long live America!" We were liberated!

Now you think this is the end. But we started marching again. We were weak, but the strength came to us because we were free! We walked maybe eight kilometers to Garmisch, in the rain. I found a rucksack, chocolate—I hadn't seen chocolate for six years—and a shirt, and other things I could use. The Americans told us they would put us up in some barracks, but we said no more barracks for us. My brother-in-law and I, and some others, about six of us, found a place behind a laundry. We slept on the floor, but this was probably the sweetest floor that I have ever slept on. It was our first day of liberation.

The American Jewish army chaplains organized a registry for survivors. Lists were sent all over Germany, and in July we found my wife's name and her mother's name, and where they were. I was working for an American officers' mess, and I got military fatigues, and a letter "To Whom It May Concern" saying to help me with transportation and food, and I took off to get my wife. I rode on coal trains, stopped army trucks. It took me six days to make the 600 miles to Diepholz. As I walked from the main road to the D.P. camp, I saw far away two young women on the road, walking in my direction. My heart started to pound, and sure enough, there was my wife! Can you imagine our meeting?

Now we had to think about our future. At first we were thinking of going to Palestine, but we wanted to catch up on our missed-out education. Germany was my least favorite place, but the Jewish D.P. camp in Stuttgart was very nice, and in February of '46 I started to study electrical engineering at the Institute of Technology. German was a foreign language, and I was out of school more than six years, but one of the benefits we got as survivors was that we didn't have to pay, and little by little I got into it, and I could handle it.

When I finished in 1950, we emigrated to the United States to join my wife's father and her brother, who came in 1949. My mother, who miraculously also survived, remarried and settled in Israel.

LOOKING BACK   After the war, people didn't want to listen to you talk about the Holocaust. But in the last few years people started asking questions, started listening. I feel a certain mission we survivors have, to tell the story, not for pity or sympathy, but so people will be aware, so nothing like this will happen again.

You hear about survivors, you speak about survivors, it sounds as if there are hundreds of thousands of them. But actually there are not. I'm one of very few.

So here I am, alive. I'm enjoying life, and my children. But why was I destined to be alive, and not my father, my sister, my grandparents, all my cousins, uncles and aunts, and just plain strangers? Nobody really knows why.

PART 2

*Survivors Who Were
Not in Concentration Camps*

Some Jews survived the Holocaust because they were hidden by non-Jews, who risked their own lives to save friends, or, sometimes, by total strangers. Some fought with the partisans or the resistance. Some hid in cellars or closets or forest bunkers, sometimes for years. Some escaped to other countries. Some had skills the Germans needed for the war effort and were assigned to labor camps or factory work. And some passed as non-Jews. Here are the stories of twenty-three such survivors and of two Polish Catholic women who were members of the Polish underground.

HENRY ABRAMOWICZ
Lodz, Poland

> I don't talk to my family about the past. There's
> no point of talking. An American cannot under-
> stand it. The only person who can understand is
> one who was there. I try to tell my kids other
> things, like not to be cowards. My son, he's eigh-
> teen; he wouldn't let anybody beat him up.

*Henry Abramowicz's father owned a large shoe company and was vice president of
the Jewish businessmen's association in Lodz. When Poland surrendered to the
Germans, Henry was nine years old. By bribing border guards, the Abramowicz
family escaped to Russia.*

In Lodz we had 300,000 Jewish people and the whole town had maybe
500,000 population. I went to a Jewish public school where the principal
was gentile and maybe 70 percent of the teachers, but when we had what
they called "religion," this was a Jewish teacher.

Jewish people were in Poland second-class citizens, like in the army
you could be a sergeant but not a general or a colonel. Nevertheless, we
felt pretty patriotic, and when the war started my father was mobilized.
Everybody thought Poland's going to win, but the Polish army were on
horses and the Germans came on half-tracks, motorized. There was no
contest.

On Shabbos morning, September 10, we saw German tanks and artillery moving along the street. This German drove by and he said, "You
are Jews?" We said yes. He said, "A bad time is coming to you." But I was
only nine years old and I didn't worry. In October, about midnight one
night, we heard a big noise, probably dynamite. It shook the whole
neighborhood, and then we could see our synagogue was burning. But
nobody could foresee that this was the first stage of destroying all the
Jews!

Poland was divided. The Russians took half and the Germans took
half. My father was a prisoner of war in Russia, but the Russian people
kept the Poles and they told the Jews "Go!" So he came back about the
first of December, walking and hitchhiking all the way from Bialystok,
maybe 200 miles.

The Germans took anybody who was anybody, the leaders, right away.
So when my father came, my mother told him, "We're leaving." We had
a big store with hundreds and hundreds of pairs of shoes, worth a lot of
money, but my mother and father left everything! My uncle was really a

bright man, an inventor, and my father begged him to go too. But my uncle made jokes, said anybody who is going is crazy. He didn't think he had to go. He didn't survive.

Our parents settled in Warsaw, where father did business and knew people. Just before Christmas, my sisters hired a horse and buggy and took us to Warsaw, too. About a week after, the border between Lodz and Warsaw was closed, so we were lucky.

When things got bad in Warsaw my father went to Bialystok and sent people to bring us over. We went on a train, and by horse and buggy, and on foot and by boat, papering every hand to smuggle us through, 200 or 300 *zlotys* a head. It was a business for them, smuggling Jews.

In Bialystok there were a lot of people like us. We were called *bieznik*— displaced people, runners. I still had the Star of David on my shoulder, and Russian soldiers said, "What is that?"

Then, in June, about four o'clock in the morning, NKVD people came and put us in cattle trains and sent us to Siberia. And this is what really saved our lives. When the Germans started the war with Russia in 1941, it took them about two days and they were in Bialystok, but we were so far in Russia they didn't get to us.

We lived there in one room, all six of us. We had a little wood stove, but the water would freeze in the house. We didn't have enough winter clothes but we had featherbeds so we could sleep. Milk was never available, meat only on holidays, but we went fishing and we would catch ducks. We could even have a little garden, potatoes. I went to school and learned Russian.

Then there was a Polish government-in-exile organized in Russia, so after fourteen months we were allowed to leave Siberia. We were twenty Jewish families in a little town on the Volga river.

My father joined the Russian army. When the war ended, we all left together. We went to a little town, it used to be Germany, but after the war it was Poland. I met people from our town, a friend of mine who told me about things he saw. We stayed six months, but then we went to Germany, the Russian occupied area. They gave us apartments where Germans lived before. I never went back to Lodz.

I studied at the university in Giessen and graduated as a veterinarian. Then I studied medicine for three years in Munich, but my father and mother went to New York in 1952, and when my quota came up in 1954 I left without finishing school. My father came from being a big businessman to work in a factory, but he didn't complain. I came to a job with the federal government in Minnesota in 1960.

I met my wife here. One of my daughters wants to be a doctor, my son wants to be a veterinarian. I have another son and two daughters. The littlest one is the age I was when the Germans took Poland.

SAM ACKOS
Athens, Greece

> The greatest author of the world can never de-
> scribe the truth of this Holocaust. There is no
> pen sharp enough to write exactly what hap-
> pened, no mind big enough to believe the
> things that took place. Long life to America!

*Sam Ackos was only twelve when his father was taken away by the Germans in
1944, and he became the head of his family, shining Nazis' shoes and trading on
the black market for food for his mother and four little sisters.*

We didn't have department stores. My father was a wheeler and dealer
guy—go to a warehouse and buy blankets, put them on his shoulder or
pushcart, and go to the neighborhoods to sell to the ladies. Also he was a
goldsmith—buying, selling, gold and copper and silver.

We respected and loved God. I attended all the high holidays, to keep
our customs alive and our religion. But gentiles were our friends, colleagues, classmates, neighbors. Religion had not much to do in the neighborhood and in the world of business, except at Passover, when it was
also Easter and the crucifixion, the Good Friday. Greek mothers would
frighten little boys and girls that if they're not good, they would give
them to the Jews, and we would prick them with pins and needles, to take
their blood for the Passover bread!

October 28, 1940, the Italians attacked the Greeks. Everybody and his
brother went to fight for the freedom of our country, and Mussolini had
to ask Hitler for help. In April the Nazis marched into Greece, and
everything turned upside down. The last thing Greek radio said was,
"Everybody has to fight against the Nazis, even if it costs his life. Long
life to Greece!" Then the Nazis took over the radio, and everything else.

In no more than two months, everything had disappeared from
Greece. Our father had saved gold we were selling on the black market
to buy food. One pound of beans and three pounds of bread would last
the six of us three days. People would sacrifice their houses for five
pounds of beans. We lost more people from starvation than we lost from
bullets.

There wasn't such a thing as a ghetto or forced labor in Greece. There
was no wearing yellow stars, nothing like that. Anybody over fifteen had
to have an I.D. with his name, residence, occupation, religion, but in
every neighborhood precinct one or two would risk their own lives to

give the Jews false I.D.s, claiming the Jew was a Greek Orthodox with a different name.

We hid radios inside of wells, and in the afternoon we were getting them out to listen to London BBC. The penalty for listening to BBC was immediately death, so we used to send boys three or four blocks, so when the German electronic cars were coming to catch where the radio's coming from, a boy would come running and whistling, and we would put the radio back in the well.

We heard Winston Churchill say, "Greek people, if you damage one screw out of the great German machine, you lead us one step toward victory." So kids were doing everything and anything to damage the conquerors. We used to steal fuel, blow tires. That you hated them, that was sabotage right there.

My mother's sister had a non-Jewish friend, a very well-to-do lady who had a house in a suburb of Athens. In '43, when we heard the Jews of Salonika were put in concentration camps, my father then went with the partisans and we were hiding in that lady's house, in a small basement room. She told the neighbors we were distant relatives, and our small village in the northern part of Greece was all burned up from the Nazis. Then my father came home, and we came back in our house again.

Toward 1944 the great Nazi snake was dying. The Nazi general in charge of Athens promised through the archbishop that he would not harm the Jewish people if every Saturday the men would present themselves in the synagogue for an hour. For several weeks the Jews were mustering at the synagogue, but March 25, 1944, was a tragic story.

I was helping my family by selling cigarettes on the black market, and one place I could make a little business was at the gathering of the Greek Jews in the synagogue. That Saturday the doors of the synagogue closed, with all the heads of the Jewish families inside. The Germans gave me a good kick, and said, "Get out!" I ran home and told what happened.

My mother's two brothers were at the synagogue, and one brother's wife and her two kids wanted to go with her husband. Mother's idea was to take us all and follow her husband, too, but I objected strongly.

They put the Jews in trucks and took them outside Athens, to a small concentration camp. Then word spread that the Nazis took the records of the synagogue, so they knew where every Jewish house is located, and they are confiscating whatever they could and want to take everybody into the camp. So again we walked the ten miles to our gentile friend for shelter.

I was shining Nazis' shoes in Constitution Square, in exchange for a little food. My mother and I were also wheeling and dealing on the black market, with small gold coins my father made during the good days. To buy food you had to go way out to the small villages. Ten miles, fifteen miles, the farther you're going, the more the Nazis will not go there. A small farmer, they were afraid to come to Athens, but they had corn or barley or beans or butter they were willing to sell, for gold. My father had left gold, and through gold you could survive.

After the war, we heard they kept the Jews in the camp for a couple days and then loaded them into trains to Auschwitz, Buchenwald, Dachau. According to survivors who came back from Auschwitz, my father was part of the plot to blow up the crematoriums there. One said they saw him selected onto the right for work, another said they saw him selected onto the left for the gas chambers. We didn't know what was truth and not truth, but he did not come home. Father was very strong, very brave, so mother thought Nazi bullets would not be strong enough to kill him. She refused to believe to her last day that her husband was dead.

The day the war ended, every Greek got into the streets, hollering, "Long life to the Allies! Long life to Greece!" The Nazi German flag came down from the Acropolis, and the Greek flag went up. Soldiers from New Zealand, England, America, France, and also from the Greek army that was fighting in Egypt, they all arrived in Greece, and King Paul arrived, and the whole entire country was full of flags. The radios were playing patriotic songs. We were hugging and kissing, and everybody was in such joy that the hunger, the thirst, the loss of the beloveds, all faded away for a while because the bright light of freedom was shining in the streets of Athens.

Organizations came from all over, the United States mostly, to help people come back on their feet. Food starts coming in, clothes start coming in, business starts building up. Our home was confiscated by a collaborator from the Nazis, and we could not prove he was a collaborator, so from four rooms we end up with only one, plus the cellar under it, and forced to be neighbors to the collaborator.

My dad had owned a taxicab, which was very unique at that time. The Nazis were confiscating anything with wheels, so my father took the cab apart. The wheels he gave to a friend to put in a basement, and the torso of the cab was with another friend who was a manufacturer of bamboo and straw things, and covered the cab with bamboo and straw, so nobody would see it.

To make a living after the war, my mother and I, we took the cab out and put it back together. I was too young for a license, so we had people to drive the cab, one in the day and one in the night.

Israel was reborn at that time, and Greece was one of the main links from which you could travel to Israel by sea. But a gentleman who knew father praised America so much, and he said that in America my four sisters would not need a dowry to get qualified husbands, so my mother knew that the only place in the world her kids can be happy was America. And that's why we're here.

We sold our taxicab to pay part of the transportation, and the Joint Distribution Committee paid the rest. We could stay in New York and live like Greeks, like living in our old neighborhood in a different part of the world, but mother didn't want that. We came to Minnesota to live like Americans.

Sam Ackos has four younger sisters. When the war ended, Evelyn was eight and Mary was six. Their memories are of hunger, hiding, and pretending to be Christians, a tall, loving father who disappeared, and life in an orphanage after the war. They came to the United States as teenagers, to live in a strange new country and learn a strange new language.

MARY ACKOS CALOF

It was not "in" to be ethnic thirty years ago. You forever were different, and to this day I'm still different.

When we went into hiding, we put all our belongings in storage with neighbors, and when we came back they would not give it back to us. My mother told us the court people said, "Why do you Jews make trouble? They should've killed you all." So I always had a very strong feeling of being scared that people knew I was Jewish, even after the war.

My mother's emotional state, on finding out she was alone, left with five children, was very difficult. There was an orphanage that was supposed to give parents the chance to put their homes and lives together, with not as much responsibility, so my mother put her two youngest, Evelyn and me, in the orphanage.

There must have been about thirty-five boy and girls. Evie's a very feisty person, and she would keep running away. I was very accepting, but I was very miserable. I spent the first three months in the infirmary isolated from the other kids, because I was sick with anemia. My mother used to come to visit, all loaded down with food I needed to eat, like raw eggs, and I would cry when she left. I was there two years, until they disbanded it.

I was twelve when we came here, and the community sent us to camp. I didn't know English, and I hated camp. Then in school I was the biggest, tallest person in third grade, but they kept shifting me every couple of months, and the next year I was a ninth grader.

My mother never worked during her marriage, but here she worked as a seamstress. She never complained, but she never really made the transition to America. She was forever looking toward Greece.

EVELYN ACKOS ETTINGER

After I became a U.S. citizen, I went back to Greece to visit. The pull back to my native land remains as strong today.

My father was a go-getter. He had a jewelry stand in the square in Athens, and I remember going in my mother's room and seeing on top of the dresser a stack of money. So even with the Germans there, we had buckets of food in the basement, potatoes, wheat. Dad was giving it to people across the street who had no food.

I was seven when my father was taken. Word had gotten out that something terrible was taking place at the synagogue. Aunt Tula and Aunt Esther took their children to the synagogue—beautiful blonde little children, one less than a year old. They said they would go wherever their husbands were going.

My mother went to the synagogue, but my dad made her go back and told her to take us to this friend, a Christian woman of very aristocratic background. She put her life on the line to save us.

In that area there were many Jewish families being hidden, even though we were two blocks away from a German camp. Nothing was really normal, so people could accept that we were relatives from a northern village. But I had to go to church with my mother and pretend to cross myself.

I had been in the gymnasium three months when mother asked us whether we wanted to come to America. I was the only one that said no. When we got here, they put me in high school, cold, just threw us right in.

After the war, mother would not celebrate any holidays, she refused. We used to go to the synagogue without her.

I think back about how we all handled the war, and what we did as children at the time, and I see how we face life today. Why did I make such a ruckus in the orphanage that mother had no choice but to take me home? Why was Mary so accepting? I think one tends to be what one is born, and deal with life that way.

FELICIA BROH
Breslau, Germany

The Nazis painted "Not For Jews," even on benches where you wait for the bus. But still we didn't believe that it will come worse. We were German!

Felicia Pinchas grew up in Berlin and married Max Broh, a metals dealer. After Kristallnacht *they wanted to escape from Germany, but they didn't have enough money to pay bribes for visas.*

It started already in 1925 the organization of Hitler or maybe earlier even. They had meetings, and we were a little bit scared. Then in the 1930s they started to close Jewish stores and painted signs on restaurants, "Forbidden for Jews."

An employee at my husband's company, my husband put him on top as the boss to cover that the company was Jewish. In 1938, because they picked up already the men for the concentration camp, my husband's friend said to him, "Go to my mother's house and stay there until it gets a little bit calm."

The mother hid my husband for a week in her apartment, and always when I heard steps outside my apartment, I was nervous and told my son to be quiet. He was eight years old.

We didn't know what to do. Shall we stay? Shall we go? There were no restrictions on Jewish people leaving, but so many people looked for any kind of place, it was hard to get in. We couldn't go to America because of the quota. We tried Bolivia but couldn't afford it. Then cousins told us two couples booked for China couldn't go and to go right away to the travel agency. We left all our things, but we were lucky. April 20, 1939, we took the train from Berlin to Italy, and a boat to Shanghai.

In Shanghai was mostly Russian Jews who came when the revolution was. In empty schools they built bunk beds for us, sometimes thirty people in one room. We lived there a few weeks until we found a house to share—one room, one family.

We were 10,000 Jews in Shanghai. We had good times, we had bad times. Women, they got jobs easier than men. I worked in a kindergarten for Jewish kids and cooked for all the children. My husband was in a Chinese factory in the metals business. It was not easy, but we saved our lives.

I bought an affidavit for my parents, and we went day by day to the harbor in Shanghai, but they didn't come and didn't come. Then we got a Red Cross *brief* from Warsaw that my father died suddenly, and my mother got sent to a camp in Poland. We never knew what happened after that.

About 1945 the Americans were bombing Shanghai. As soon as we heard airplanes or the siren, we rushed to the air raid shelter. If we couldn't make it, we ducked to the floor. The Americans didn't know that where the Japenese had hidden things like oil and gas was also a living quarter of our Jewish people, and a lot were killed.

After the war ended, we were talking about getting out of China. When you are there for such a long time, you almost lose your hope. But some people in America, people we didn't even know, they gave us this affidavit to come here. They made us promise we wouldn't even thank them! We came by boat to California in 1947.

My brother-in-law was in Buchenwald, but the Hilfsverein got him out and gave him a ticket to Bolivia. A sister of my husband heard that the Nazis will pick her up, and she took her own life. My mother, my aunts, all the cousins, my whole family got killed. The rest of my husband's family, too.

You hear German people say, "We never were Nazis." But where did the Nazis come from? We have here the same, people hating Jews. The hate goes on, I don't know why.

PAULETTE FINK
Paris, France

My husband said, "We are not going to run
away. We are going to stay here and fight." We
had almost five years of French underground.
Then my husband was caught and tortured for
over twelve hours before he died.

*Paulette Weill's husband was a wealthy businessman. Her father had been a spy
for France during World War I, and she and her husband joined the resistance
when France fell. After the war, she set up orphanages for Jewish children and
helped smuggle refugees into Palestine.*

My mother had absolutely no religious training, and as far as our home
was concerned, we had no tradition, but my husband was the grandson
of the chief rabbi of Paris. He had a fantastic pride as a Jew and a
fantastic desire to be respected as a Jew.

I never had any feeling of anti-Semitism, never heard that I was "different." I had as many non-Jewish friends as Jewish. Then I was in
Germany the end of '32, and at the swimming pool a sign at the door
said, "No Dogs, No Jews." A couple we knew arrived from Vienna in '37,
and I remember her telling us the Nazis were giving the Jewish girls
toothbrushes and making them clean the yard of the military barracks.
I'm not sure how much we believed. Besides, that was Germany, Austria.
What could happen to us in France?

My parents had rented a house on the southern coast of Brittany, and
that's where the war caught us. When the Germans came through the
Belgian border and were in Paris in seven days, we were in shock. My
husband was a lieutenant in the army, and he was taken prisoner. I was
on the front line as a Red Cross nurse, and I didn't know where he was.
But he escaped four times from a prisoner-of-war camp and finally
made it the fourth time.

We were under Marshal Pétain in Vichy, so-called Free France. He
sold out to the Germans, betrayed his countrymen. One of Pétain's big
lies was that if you were French for more than five generations, you've
got nothing to risk by declaring yourself. So we all went and declared
ourselves at the police station. We were never compelled to wear the Star
of David like they did in the occupied zone, but we were trapped.

The resistance started when General de Gaulle talked on the BBC
from London, saying we had to fight, sabotage, infiltrate, do everything

we can to stop the German war machine. We could very easily have joined my parents in Morocco, but for my husband, de Gaulle was a God.

The leaders discover themselves. My husband, who was proprietor of a big chain of five-and-ten-cent stores, took one of his stores for head-quarters. He found in his store tons of dried beans, lentils, green peas, and put an ad in the paper, "Monday morning, food will be distributed. Free." On Monday thousands were queueing up, but ration cards had been started, and the authorities arrested him!

I was terribly scared. I knew Marshal Pétain—I met him at my sister's wedding—and I went to him, and he said, "What can I do for you, my child?" I told him point-blank, "You can give the order to release my husband." He said, "My poor child, I am so sorry. If only you wouldn't be Jewish." In Vichy we had a few men who were working a double game, so I was able to find somebody. He was very cold, very suspicious, but he finally called the fortress and said, "Here is Marshal Pétain's office. So-and-so ordered to release so-and-so." And that night my husband was out!

We had no trains, no cars, no gas. For a little while I had a car; they put an enormous tank in the back, and you were burning wood to ignite the car. But then we were bicycling everywhere we were going. I was my husband's message carrier. I bicycled once over 200 kilometers!

My husband's store had yards and yards of a kind of blue jeans material, really mattress ticking, and if I gave a farmer enough to make a suit, he would give some butter and eggs and milk. The only thing was not to be arrested on the road going back, because if the Germans found you with even half a pound of potatoes, they put you in jail!

My husband organized a quartermaster corps to provide food, blankets, shirts and pants, tents, everything, to the resistance. We were getting money from Algiers to help the mother and children when the husband was gone. We were also getting bandages and always American cigarettes.

We had a friend who got picked up because he was having a cup of coffee at the bistro and he left an American cigarette butt in the ashtray. Another friend and his brother, they were in an apartment and they had two entrances, an obvious entrance with the number on the door, and a back entrance nobody could find. He had planned for years this whole thing of running the other way. Then somebody knocked and impulsively he went to the door. And that was the end for him. It's the things you never expect, you never think about. It's like everything you did was hanging by a thread.

All of us had the fear of being denounced. All we needed was to be recognized by one guy from the French *milice*, that was trained by the Gestapo.

We lived in many places. One was this gorgeous castle near Grenoble that had been abandoned. Thank God for the fireplace. All fourteen of us would be there by that fireplace, keeping warm, my two little daughters doing schoolwork, everybody doing something.

I don't remember the many names I carried in the resistance. To change identification cards was very tricky, not just "pick a name." We had an entire network of people finding who was in a mental hospital or had just died—all far away from where we lived, of course. We'd get the entire pedigree of that person, so that if the Germans caught you, you knew the answers.

Each of us also had an underground name. Whenever they were calling on the radio for "Walnut Tree," for example, you'd know it was you. We had to be very careful because the Germans were coming with electronic devices on their car and picking up the people who were taking the message.

Sometimes you were getting a parachute drop, parts of machine guns, and then you never got the second part because the Germans got the message before you did. We also picked up paratroopers—Canadians and Americans who were carriers of messages—and were hiding them.

We had an entire network of volunteers who were saving children. France was full of Jewish refugees from Poland, Hungary, Romania. The big trick of the Germans was to leave the children at the railroad station when they were packing the parents in railroad cars to take them to the camps. They knew these little children would be lost because they knew nobody, didn't speak French. They spoke Yiddish, and none of us understood them.

We kept a record of all the kids we had. Their names, their parents' names if we knew them, where they were hidden. I don't remember having any children smaller than about two years old because the mothers would usually keep the baby in their arms.

We were passing the children from one to the other, a chain with many links—priests and nuns, monasteries and convents, Catholic schools, some on farms to work as farmhands with no pay. The Catholics were fabulous, the Protestants too. At Chambon, Pastor Trocmé and his people, you could always be helped by them.

After D-Day, after the sixth of June 1944, de Gaulle, Eisenhower, everyone was saying to us in the resistance, "Go out now, work in the open, do as much harm to the Germans as you can possibly do." My husband did, and he got caught.

A friend came with the bad news. I immediately went into the garage to pick up my bicycle and said, "I'm going." And he said, "You cannot go where he is, it's not possible. Every mile is the Germans." So I didn't go, then. When we were liberated August 14, I took the kids and went there.

He was killed June 24 and buried under "unknown" because he was carrying so many false names, they didn't know his real name.

They wanted me to identify him, but I refused to look. He was tortured for over twelve hours, and I didn't want to keep that in my mind.

When the war ended, to see the Germans sitting at the café that morning, and in the afternoon, the Americans, it was unbelievable. But the main thing to us was that we got K-rations. I'm sure today I wouldn't even open one of those cans of Spam, it was awful, but it was so good! Later, when I heard in America the people tell me, "Those poor German children who starved during the war, you have to pity them, too," I said, "Starved? How could they? They stole everything from every country they occupied!"

I got involved with children's homes. I was the only one who spoke English fluently, so I went to see the head of the Jewish Joint Distribution Committee. I told him we know of hundreds of Jewish children that we can get back. We can requisition homes from the government. But we need money. He looked at me and said, "Well, Madame, prove what you can do and we'll help."

I made debts everywhere. Every grocery store, I said, "I'll pay at the end of the month," and they didn't want to let those children starve. We "requisitioned" a big house, and by hook and crook we found cots and mattresses. We raided a furniture warehouse one night and stole one of the J.D.C. trucks to carry the stuff! We had done much worse than that in the resistance!

But when the social workers told those kids that their name was Goldberg and not Smith, and they were Jewish, the kids spat at their faces. They didn't believe they were Jewish, they didn't want to be Jewish. So we kidnapped them, we really did. We got an old Jewish woman who taught the kids Yiddish songs. We wanted them to feel some *Yiddishkeit*, and none of us could do that. And little by little, the kids gave up their reticence.

That their parents would never come back, that we couldn't convey to them. It was impossible. Some refused to go to school, refused to get out of the house, because if the parents would come and look for them, they wouldn't find them. All the children were checked in at a center in Paris—name, address, parents' name, where they would be in case somebody looked for them.

After a while we had eleven houses, 1,500 kids. At the end of '45 I went to the Joint and said, "I can't go on. Americans send me shoes, but only sixty pairs for a hundred kids. Which children will get the shoes?" So he looked at me and said, "You go to America and see what you can do."

I came for three months, with my daughter Nadine. She was nine years old, and when we went into the dining room on the ship, she looks at the enormous platter of cold cuts and cheeses and fruits, and she starts to cry. We didn't have ration cards, and she couldn't believe there was such a thing as getting food you didn't have a coupon for. I covered forty-two states, making speeches, and I got the money.

One night in Paris, it's about two in the morning, and there's a knock at the door. I open my window. I see men. On the arm they have "Palestine Brigade." I have no idea who they are. They have almost 200 refugees and they want to leave them with me overnight. They have in their trucks a double bottom full of arms, and they want to go to Marseille, unload their guns, and come back to take the people to an illegal boat they're expecting.

We had two children's homes at that time on the outskirts of Paris. The other had been notified these people were coming, but they came to me by mistake. What do I do? I say yes.

When the guys came back, they took me with them. We found the place on the beach, and we put those people in inflated rubber boats, ten at one time, with one strong man to hold the rope. The rope was a link between the beach and the boat, two or three miles away. It was pitch black, no moon and no stars, and the people were holding that rope and just going into the complete darkness, in January, in that bitterly cold water.

I worked with Brichah from Italy, from Austria. We emptied the D.P. camps long before we were given permission. These were survivors, and the British were monsters, pushed the people with the butts of their rifles, put them in camps, kept them out of Palestine. But when you had lived through the occupation, what could the British do to you, after the Germans?

Then the state of Israel was created, and there was no more illegal immigration. But I went back and forth to America for eight years, for the spring fundraising campaign for the United Jewish Appeal, for Israel. Sometimes I was speaking three times in a day, a breakfast meeting, a luncheon, and a dinner, and in between, television and radio, and an interview with the paper. I just never stopped talking, and we got the money.

I brought my children to the United States in 1951, put them in school. At last they were able to lead a normal life. I couldn't see how I could settle here, but I married an American, and we did. It's almost an impossibility for me and my children to be on German soil, when I know how they tortured my husband, and what they did to all the people they had in their grip. They have a word in German, *schadenfreude*, and it means "the joy of doing harm." And that's the Germans. They're so sentimental, when they play Wagner, they can't breathe, they're so emotionally taken. And then they can do the things they did. Where do you find the idea of taking the skin of people to make lampshades? Of using people's bodies to make soap?

I have always felt that if we have been spared, we have a duty in talking about it, to show what hate leads to. In South Africa they teach people to hate the blacks, and this, too, is a holocaust.

The Oppert family, 1942. Yves (*second from left*) and his wife, Paulette (*third from left*), fought in the French resistance. Yves was killed in 1944. The rest of his family survived the war, including his daughters, Francelyne (*left*), and Nadine (*third from right, front row*).

Paulette Weill (Oppert) Fink with daughters Francelyne Lurie (*left*)
and Nadine Bicher, 1988.

In 1983 Richard and Francelyne Lurie and their six children traveled to Israel to
celebrate Adam Lurie's Bar Mitzvah at Masada, Israel's historic mountain fortress.
Adam's grandparents, Yves and Paulette Oppert, fought with the French resistance.

EDITH GOODMAN
Krischatik, Romania

They came one morning and told us they are
taking us away to work on a farm. We took pillows and clothes and pots and pans. My sister
and I had little knapsacks of dresses and things,
and I remember I cried. I was ten years old.

*Edith Fuhrmann's father was a prosperous sugar-beet farmer and cattle rancher
and her mother owned a grocery store. Through luck and their ability to adapt to
new circumstances, the Fuhrmanns saved themselves as first Russians, then Hungarians, then Germans occupied their country.*

In 1939 in the war between Poland and Germany, bombs fell in our
little town and six or eight people got killed. In 1940 Russian officers and
soldiers came to our house and my parents gave them food.

We thought life would go on as before, and besides, my father didn't
want to leave everything we had. But in 1941 it was decided for us. They
gathered up the Jews, and we went to the next town. We stayed in
farmhouses for a week, and then we were lucky. A Romanian official
who was in charge borrowed money from my father when he first came
to our district to farm, and my father never made him return it. My
mother reminded him about that loan, and when they were counting out
names for deportation he said, "You're going to stay here and work."
Then he told my father to leave. He said, "I don't care where, just go!"

My father got a horse and buggy and we went to the next town,
Zastavna. Jewish families took us in, but that same Romanian officer
came with guards, and all the Jews were taken to a border village. We
were told to go across the border and never turn back, or we would be
shot. Polish militia on the other side were refusing to let people in, but
our guards got drunk, and by the time they took us to the border the
Polish guards went home, so we got across safely.

We were a group of about thirty people walking all day, a hot July day.
My little sister was so thirsty, and she just bent down and drank some
water on the road. A nice Polish peasant saw her, and saddled his horse
and wagon and loaded up the kids and drove us into a little town.

All the whole summer in 1941 we went from one place to another. In
September we came to Edintz, and they put about 13,000 Jewish people
on an empty field under the sky, to sleep on straw. My mother and her
cousin would sneak out through the barbed wire and steal potatoes and

make soup. My father made acquaintance with a baker and would take bread from him and sell it, to earn bread for us.

Then my father bribed a guard and got us out into the town. A nice woman took us in, and my father started buying old clothes and selling them. The woman made us little girls' dresses out of ticking. My father got a coat for my brother, who was eight, so he could go outside to play with the other children, but it was a girl's coat and my brother wouldn't wear it!

Then my father met a man who said in a little town called Chernovtsy, in Russia, there were some Jews and a ghetto. That was where we lived out the war. My father even hired a *melamed* to come to our home, to teach my brother and me Hebrew. They gave him four kilos of flour a week. That meant more than money because it meant he had bread!

When the war ended, the Jews in Chernovtsy started to leave. We were afraid to go back to our little town because we heard that when Jewish people went back, the neighbors killed them. Besides, my father didn't want to move again. He was tired.

But then some horses died at his job, and my father was arrested. The police wanted him to be an informer. They finally let him go, but for months he wouldn't leave the house, and then we went back to Romania.

I married Max Goodman in Radauti in 1949. My father knew Max's father from before, and I knew his sister. I was eighteen, and Max was twenty-six.

Max had family in the United States, so he sent a postcard and right away we got a letter from a cousin, "You can work for me and if you won't like working for me you can find something else." To us that seemed very stange. There was no such thing in Romania whether you like a job or you don't!

My sister was in Israel, and my parents and my brother went to Paris. I didn't speak one word English, and when we came here I cried every night, and told my husband, "Let's go back to Europe or to Israel." A new beginning is very hard.

MAX GOODMAN
Radauti, Romania

There was a river nearby and people used to go
very early in the morning to take baths. The
river was outside the ghetto and people were
killed there if they were caught. Killed because
they went to take a bath!

*Although his Hasidic ancestors had come to Radauti in 1718, Max Goodman's
family were still considered "foreigners" because they were Jews. His father was a
grain merchant and dealer in agricultural products. Max was sixteen when the
war began.*

We were friendly with our gentile neighbors, but separate, never close.
In school Jewish students were always apart. Already in the 1930s the
trend was more and more to blame the Jews for everything. Newspapers,
the Iron Guard, their theme was that the Jews have to leave the country.

Radauti was close to the Polish border. After war broke out in Poland
the refugees came into Romania. A committee of citizens went house to
house and asked who would accept Polish people for a short stay. We
had a big house, so two Polish army officers came, but they saw the
mezuzah and refused to come in.

By 1940 part of Romania was occupied by Russia, and the Jews were
blamed for betraying Romania! Now we had Jewish refugees staying in
our home because all the Jews in villages had to go to the cities.

Life carried on, with every day new anti-Jewish regulations. Romanian
police would take a hundred Jews and keep them just in case. They said
if Jews will attack gentiles, hostages will be executed. They came to my
home and picked me up, but they'd change hostages maybe every two
weeks, so I came home okay. Then my father was thrown from a moving
train by the Iron Guard, and six months later he died.

In 1941 the Germans' war against Russia broke out, with Romania a
full-fledged ally of the Berlin-Rome axis. October 1941 it was announced
in the newspaper that all Jews in Radauti have to present themselves to
the railroad station to be resettled in the "territories of the east," where
Romania had occupied part of Russia.

We went, my grandparents, my mother, my sister and I, taking just
what we could carry on our backs. We were pushed into cattle wagons
and traveled a couple of days into Transnistria, then by foot about fifty
miles.

In Dzurin for sixteen people we had a room about eight by ten feet, a kitchen about half that size, and another little room. A sack with some straw was my bed for three and one-half years. There was a hospital with Jewish doctors, ten beds, but they used to keep 100 people there. We almost all had typhoid fever. Most of the doctors died taking care of sick people.

In that whole city of 4,000 there was just one water pump. I was so thirsty I drank muddy water from the river. From this I got dysentery, and I got so weak I couldn't even move from my bed. Then a relative came with some brandy made out of sugar beets, hot barley bread, pieces of fried animal fat, and after two or three days I got healthier.

I found work in a slaughterhouse, so our family had enough meat. In the morning when we used to open the doors to clean, we would throw out little pieces of meat, pieces of bone, skin, and 200 or 300 people would fight like dogs over these remnants.

Once a week, for two hours, Jews were allowed into an open market-place to barter with peasants, bread in exchange for a pair of socks, fifty pounds of flour for a suit.

People who could take along only what they could carry, took the best they had, but it was not enough. From 200,000 Jews deported into Transnistria in 1941, 150,000 died of starvation by 1943. If the Russians would have waited until fall of 1944, they wouldn't have found one person alive. In the morning you would see people lying in the street who died overnight. They would just put them in the street, and a pushcart used to pick up these people and take them to their graves.

In 1944 we began to see German troops retreating, going west day and night. Suddenly in March there was nobody, and then the Russians came in. A Jewish captain in the Russian army came with the first Russians into our ghetto and found his father there!

The population when we got home was very friendly. Romania formed a democratic government in 1945, and there was freedom the way we call freedom today.

Then in 1948 the Communists came to power and started to introduce their type of "freedom." There were Communist leaders who were Jews, but little by little the Jews were pushed out. The Communists introduced identity cards for everybody, and you had to declare your nationality. You could have said, "Okay, I'm not a Jew any more. I see myself now as a Romanian national." But most of Romania's Jews didn't change.

I went to school and started earning some money, so I could leave. But in 1951, when we thought maybe now is the time to go, they closed the borders. They let people go, and then they stopped, and then they let them go again, and then stopped again. In some cities they would give permits, in some they wouldn't. It was just like Russia. I didn't get my exit papers until 1958. Seven years!

MAX GROSBLAT
Dubno, Poland

I was nineteen when the Germans came. I
wanted to get out but there was no place to go.
Then I stole two rifles and joined the partisans.
Not all the Jewish people went to death like
sheep. Some of us were fighting.

Max Grosblat was the son of deeply religious Jews and thought about becoming a
rabbi, or a cantor. Instead, he became "Fearless Mischka" of the partisans.

My ancestors, they came from Germany and settled in Poland when the
Crusaders started after the Jewish people. Dubno was in the Polish
Ukraine, famous for its apple and pear orchards, a lot of poultry, eggs. It
was a town of about 70,000 people, 10,000 Jewish.

Everybody Jewish learned Yiddish, Hebrew, Polish. I also spoke Ukrainian. My dad was a tailor and spoke to his customers in their own
languages—German, Ukrainian, Polish, Russian, Czech. He'd take your
size and make a suit from scratch, so. Some didn't have money to pay so
they traded farm products for their tailored clothes.

Most of our customers were gentiles. We did not talk politics with
gentile people; we talked about a suit or pants or a jacket, business. We
also knew we have to stay away from the church after Sunday services
because when they came out they were looking for Jews to start a fight.
But my friends and I were a bunch of rough Jewish guys who never
stepped away from a fight.

I was seventeen when the war started and the Russians took our part
of Poland. The Russian system is if you want to buy groceries or whatever, it's all government owned. When I was only nineteen, I was running one of their stores all by myself.

Polish citizens expelled from Germany came to our town and told us
the Germans destroyed some Jewish businesses, broke windows, but we
didn't hear of anybody getting killed. People were expecting rough
times, but nobody expected the Holocaust!

When the Germans came in on June 24, 1941, right away they ordered
all Jewish people to move south of the city, near the river. They gave us
about three blocks wide from north to south, and seven blocks long from
east to west. We already lived where the ghetto was, but now there were
three families in our four-room house. I was working for the police,
cutting wood, but we didn't have enough for heating the house, so I was

breaking up fences to bring wood home, and my family were selling everything to get food.

Then the ghetto was divided. My father didn't work, and they told us to move on the other side. The guy I worked for couldn't tell me that if you move on the side with the ones who don't work, you won't live long, but he said, "You stay where you are." Three months later, they took those families out of the city about five kilometers, 3,000 people, and shot them!

I was working in a garage where on one side we were sawing wood, and on the other side police were collecting weapons the Russians threw away when they were running from the German army. I took two rifles, a long one and a cut-off short one. I had a two-wheeler to take sawdust home, so I put the two rifles in the bottom, put some rags around, filled it up with sawdust and wheeled it home.

I dug out a place and hid the rifles, but some people saw me, other Jews. Word got around and someone told me, "We're organizing. Get in touch if you want to join."

Then a lot of Ukrainian policemen and S.S. people came into town, and we decided it was time to leave. On the other side of town was a factory making sausages, and Jewish people used to work there. We went in a group, with Jewish policemen escorting us through the town, like they're marching us to work. Then when we had to turn right to the factory, we turned left! That was October 3. October 5 they liquidated the ghetto.

We were a group of fifty, mostly young guys nineteen, twenty years old. A Ukrainian took my rifles out of the ghetto to the woods. The woods were divided into sections, and we were assigned section 15 and told I would get my rifles back there. But when we came into the woods, nobody knew where section 15 was.

So we were just a group of people without any leader, without contacts, without weapons, without anything. Some of the people had gold pieces, and we would go to villages to buy food, or go out in the fields and take potatoes or cabbage or carrots. Then a man who was getting two pounds of sugar if he finds a Jew, showed the Germans where we were. Some of us had gone to dig a winter shelter, and we heard shots and came back, and found two of our people dead.

We decided to leave that area. But first I went to the village, and I was telling a peasant about my two rifles, and it turned out that the man I gave the rifles to, he was in the other room! So I got back my sawed-off shotgun and some bullets.

Ukrainians trying to steal whatever they could were giving the Polish population trouble, so we guarded the Polish people in these villages and stayed in their houses. Word got around to Russian partisans that there's a Jewish group here that has weapons, so they sent somebody to ask if we want to join up.

There were very few Jews in the partisans, and they killed a lot of Jews themselves. One fellow went to see his mother, and Ukrainians took his rifle away. When he came back without the rifle, his own comrades locked him in a barn and burned the barn! Another Jewish fellow who didn't want to admit he was Jewish, they played a Jewish tune on the record player, and he was humming the tune, so they shot him. Germans you could fool, but the Ukrainians, you couldn't fool them, even if you had papers saying gentile!

I almost got it, too. They gave me horses to take care of, and I didn't know to put ropes on the front feet so they wouldn't escape. I just put them in the pasture, and when we were supposed to start out, the horses were gone! But one fellow knew me from when I was managing that store, and he told them, "He's a businessman. What does he know about horses?" That saved me.

When I joined in February 1943, there were about 200 people in that partisan group. By April 1944, there were 2,000, and I was part of the general staff. They knew they could depend on me because I was not afraid. I didn't care if I got killed. I was in there to kill as many as I could, to take revenge.

We blew up bridges, and when German trains were going to the front with ammunition and weapons, we put dynamite under the tracks. You had to hide and pull a string to ignite it. Nobody wanted that job, so I did it. And when they wanted to find out if Germans are in an area, they would send me out for reconnaisance. They called me Mischka the Fearless.

For supplies we had an airfield. At night we used to make fires on four corners of the field, and planes used to come down and bring automatic weapons, explosives, things like that. We were in contact with Moscow by radio.

When the war ended we hitchhiked home. Back home there was nothing. Our house was demolished, rubbish. I was the oldest of five children, and the only one left was my sister. My mother and father, three brothers, uncles, aunts, cousins—there was nobody left. Across the street we had Polish friends, gentiles, and I stayed with them. I found out my father lived about three months after the liquidation, hiding out. Then he went to peasants he used to know in a village, but he never made it.

Not all Germans were Nazis or murderers. One I worked for used to bring me a loaf of bread hidden in his uniform. And there was one German-Austrian, he took a risk and came and warned the Jews before the liquidation. He was driving in the streets of the ghetto on his motorcycle and hollering, "This is going to be the end of you! Jews, get out!"

I met my wife in the partisans. We got married July 12, 1945, and

December we came to Berlin and then to the American zone, a D.P. camp. I was taking up auto mechanics and they offered me a job as an instructor. We had one room, with a kitchen set up in the bathroom. Somebody had to go to the bathroom you have to leave your cooking! Three years we lived like that. We came here in 1949.

I had a feeling even as a kid that I got to fight for my rights, to fight when nobody else will. You should fight for what you believe in.

HENRY HARVEY
Warsaw, Poland

> Imagine how you would feel if tomorrow morning two armed people walk into your house and tell you, "You have ten minutes, Pack your belongings and come with us." You don't argue with a gun.

Henry Gurman's father was a wealthy manufacturer. When war broke out Henry was fifteen. The Gurmans fled to Lvov, then were deported to a Russian labor camp. He fought against the Germans as a member of the Polish army-in-exile.

I grew up in the shadow of Hitler. Warsaw was one-third Jewish and there were Jewish political parties, Jewish newspapers, Jewish cultural activities. But I was the only Jew in my class in elementary school, and the kids didn't call me by my name, they called me "Jew." When they saw my report card, they would say, "Oh, the Jew-boy got an 'A'," and when they spotted a "C" they were like applauding, cheering.

Warsaw was bombed on the first morning of the war, 5 A.M. on September 1, and every day after that. On the sixth day we left—my father, my mother, and myself. We had a car and we got an allotment of gasoline, something like twenty liters, because my father manufactured military insignia. Three-quarters of the way to Pinsk we ran out of gas, so we bought a horse and cart and traveled southeast to avoid the main highway, which was being bombed by German planes. We were staying overnight in peasant's homes.

In January we ran again, this time to Lvov. We were refugees, homeless people, and the Russian authorities in Lvov asked us, "Do you want to become a Soviet citizen?" And we said, "No, we want to go home to Warsaw." We were so naive. My mother, especially, indulged in denial of

all the problems. We would say, "Gosh, the Germans are going to perse-
cute us." And she would say, "*Ach!* We survived World War I. All these
stories are exaggerated." But the Russians saved us from the Holocaust
anyway.

I was scheduled to receive my high school diploma on June 30, and
they came to get us on June 28, an officer and a soldier with a list of
names. My mother started crying, got a little hysterical. We were classi-
fied as a "socially dangerous element" because we were Polish and deported on freight trains, deep into Russia.

We were on the train about two weeks, going east, then west. We
ended up thirty kilometers from Yoshkar-Ola, in a labor camp. There
were about 350 in the camp, 80 percent Jewish. We did not have Russian
internal passports, but we were allowed to go into town because everyone
knew we were the Polacks from this camp two miles up the road.

We became lumberjacks. Our barracks was wood, with a stove we had
to feed constantly. Our family had one small room for ourselves. Food
was dark Russian bread of very poor quality, potatoes, milk we could buy
from peasants. The government store was usually out of everything. We
had religious services, figured out when was Rosh Hashonah, when was
Yom Kippur, when was Passover.

We were reading the Russian press, so we knew what was going on in
the rest of the world. When the Germans invaded Russia, overnight the
Germans became "bad guys," the British and Americans became "good
guys," and we became "semigood guys," because there was a Polish
government-in-exile in London. They freed us from the camps, and I
went to work in a metal fabricating cooperative, making parts for skis for
the military.

In 1943 I volunteered for the Polish army under the command of the
Lublin committee, forerunner of the Polish Communist government. I
was in that army for two and one-half years, first in officers' school and
then in combat in the eastern Ukraine, through Poland, and into Germany. But when we got close to the American lines they pulled us back.
They didn't really trust us.

When the war ended, I got a uniform from a friendly Soviet officer,
and some false papers, and traveled to East Berlin. When I got there I
dumped my uniform and burned my papers. Meanwhile, my parents
also came. To get permission to cross into the Allied zone, we registered
under a different name, as German Jews from West Germany, and it
worked!

We were in a D.P. camp eight months. I had a married sister who had
gone to New York in 1939 to see the World's Fair, and they were on the
ship coming home when war broke out. Their ship was turned back, so
they, too, survived the Holocaust. They were able to bring us over with

one of the first waves of immigrants, and we landed in New York August 30, 1946.

The Holocaust did not start as a Holocaust. It started with insensitivity of the German population toward scapegoating. Hitler used the Jews as a scapegoat for the economic ills of Germany in the 1930s, and for defeat of the German armies in World War I. He said, "We didn't lose in battle, the Jews and Communists stabbed us in the back." The average German didn't really believe it, but he was indifferent and that led to the Holocaust.

FELIX KAMINSKY
Sendjeszow, Poland

Can you imagine to be one of eight children and not to have nobody? I ask the rabbi, if there's a God, why didn't He send a miracle? Why was He waiting that 6,000,000 Jews were killed? Why didn't He do a miracle about 2,000,000? There's no answer.

Felix Kaminsky wanted to emigrate to Palestine but was drafted into the Polish army in 1936. During the war, he was slave labor at the airport near Cracow until he was assigned to work for Oskar Schindler.

One-third of Sendjeszow was Jewish, about 100 families. My father was buying and selling grain with gentiles, but even when I was a small boy, was anti-Semitism. Before Easter they used to throw things at you. And when we came as army recruits, Jewish boys used to have the best scores on tests, but the captain said to us, "I'm not able to take you to officers' school." Why? We are Jews.

I was in Hashomer Hatzair and went to an *achsherah*, so I could go to Palestine. But in 1936 I was called for the Polish army for eighteen months, and when I came back, my *kibbutz* wasn't any more. They all emigrated to Palestine.

I went back in the army in 1939, against Hitler. I was a special shooter on the front line, with a hundred-pound pack on my shoulders and a big gun. When we lost, the captain said everyone should go on his own. A Polack friend and me, we took two horses and a buggy, and a priest gave us two old priests' uniforms to disguise. We found a barn to sleep, but it was freezing, and the farmer said come in the kitchen. We went in the kitchen, and while we were asleep this farmer stole the horses. So we traveled by trains, four or five days, the 200 miles to go home.

Right away the Germans organized a *Judenrat,* responsible that we should go every morning to work. Women, young girls, they took to Cracow to work on the airport. I worked on railroad tracks cutting steel wires. One day the German guard was playing around, spinning a wire around his head, and it went in my eye. A Jewish policeman went with me to the hospital, where two Jewish doctors took out my eye. I used to wear a black patch.

At the first selection, in 1941, I took a handkerchief and started wiping my eye, as if maybe something was in it, so they wouldn't see the black patch. The Germans put the young, healthy people on wagons. Then they told the old people to run, and they shot them in the back—my family, the rabbi, over a hundred people. Polack farmers came with wagons and buried them in the forest.

My niece worked for a German guy at the airport in Cracow, raising tomatoes. She told me where a hole in the fence is, so when the Germans came for another selection, they took to the gas chamber my sister who was eight months pregnant, and my other sisters, but I ran away to Cracow and went through this hole. The boss registered me to work, so I was a free man.

But I still had a hole where the right eye should be. Then I read in the paper a German doctor was coming who could put in an artificial eye. So I took a risk. Kaminsky, it's a Polish name, so I took off my Star of David and went to the hospital. I came in with my boots on like the Polacks, and I'm talking Polish to him, so he was thinking I'm a Polack, so he made me an artificial eye right away.

I was working in the airport about a year, and then came two big trucks and loaded on eighty of us. The driver said, "We're going to Our Father," so we thought they're gonna shoot us. But we come in this factory and see this tall, beautiful man—Oskar Schindler. The factory was making pots and pans and later mess kits for the army. I was feeding the pigs and raising geese, and if Schindler found out there's a horse broke a leg, he bought the horse for us to eat, too.

Once he had a party for German big shots, and one was drunk and wanted to shoot some Jews. Schindler came to us in the kitchen and said, "Run away, leave everything, run!" He walked on two sides—for the Germans and for the Jews.

In '45 we heard the Russians are coming closer, and Schindler wanted to move to Czechoslovakia. He went to Himmler with a list of 400 women, 700 men, and said he has to have the same Jews because they have experience for this kind of work. The other Jews in Cracow went to

Grossrosen, but we went to Brinitz, where I worked in the kitchen until liberation.

When the Russians came, Schindler told us take the materials from the factory because the Russians are going to take it anyway. I filled up a big truck and went back to Cracow, sold the material, got money. I saw this girl holding two little pans, walking to the committee for a little bit to eat. I knew her because my parents, they used to have orchards, and her family would come in summer in the orchard. We got married January 27, 1946.

We wanted to emigrate to the United States, but you couldn't go from Poland, so we smuggled into Germany through Czechoslovakia. This was February, and we went in water and in the forest through snow. Eventually we got to Munich. I had a little store selling cigarettes, American coffee, this and that, and the Jewish Committee got me an apartment by a German, a Nazi. I didn't even pay anything.

In '51 we came to New York. The second day I got a job in a factory, making pocketbooks and wallets. My brother-in-law, he told the Joint he knows about cows, horses, so they sent him to work in the stockyards. Then he bought a farm, and in 1958 we bought this trailer park, 120 units.

I wouldn't go back to Poland. That's bloody, bloody land for me.

GISELA KONOPKA
Berlin, Germany

> In the resistance there was no glory, no reward.
> Even distributing leaflets was death. I stood in
> my solitary cell and said, "The worst thing is that
> nobody will know that I was even a decent person."

When the Nazis came to power in 1932, Gisela Peiper was a college student. Almost immediately, she joined the anti-Nazi underground. She and her husband escaped to France, and then in 1941 to the United States. She is internationally known for her research and writing on adolescent psychology.

During the First World War, when my father was in the army, a woman came running into our store and said that the baby who was the Christ child in the Christmas tableau was sick and could she borrow our little

Ruth, my baby sister. My mother said, "Certainly!" It was beautiful, my sister lying in the crib with all the angels around her, and they all loved my mother and loved us.

But when the war ended in 1918, anti-Semitism really started. Swastikas were painted on the streets, and we would scratch them off with our pocket knives. I was eight years old when one of the girls in my class drew a swastika on the blackboard. The kids said, "Gisela, you have to go and protest." But there was one Jewish teacher, and she was very afraid and told me not to make trouble. I started to cry and went home, and my father said to me, "Gisela, you'd better learn that Jews are there for suffering."

By 1932 I was studying to be a teacher. Now the Nazis would march through the streets, carrying spades. They were not allowed to carry weapons, but if you would say something against them, the spades would fall on your back.

I am definitely a product of the Weimar Republic, a time of great excitement, social conscience. We thought all adults were stupid and wished we could do away with them! We distributed leaflets against the Nazis, but even some Jews said, "Oh, it won't be so bad" or "At least we'll get rid of the labor unions." My God, we read *Mein Kampf!*

By 1933 Jewish professors had already been dismissed, and the day before my final exams, the Nazis searched my room and threw out every book. During the exam, a Nazi in uniform sat at the table. I vomited, but I passed my examinations, superior.

Paul Konopka and I were very much in love, but he was not Jewish, so we were not permitted to get married. Then a person asked, would we be willing to do underground work.

People here do not understand the word *totalitarian,* the horror of a society saturated with fear. There is incredible terror, no communication with anybody you hadn't known before, so it is very important that people know there is a resistance. Nothing was in the newspapers, only how wonderful the *Fuhrer* is, so we distributed leaflets, pasted slogans on walls. We were in groups, at most five people you knew and could trust, Jews and non-Jews together.

The first people the Nazis arrested were the famous Socialists, famous Communists. They were beaten, humiliated, made to scrub the streets with toothbrushes. Then in Hamburg in 1936 there was that ring of the bell in the night, for me.

I was at that time one of the major contacts to others. I swallowed their names very fast, without water, and in marched three young storm troopers. I pretended I was very surprised. They were tearing apart everything in my room, especially the books. Then they said, "You come with us!" They stopped at another place for a young woman of the same underground group, so I knew somebody had given names.

The first night they put us into what I would call a standing coffin, really a box. It was dark. I couldn't sit, I could only stand. I heard men scream, "Let me out, let me out! I'll tell you what you want." But I have a very good imagination, and I was on a meadow, the sun was flooding it. And later, when a young S.S. was standing in front of me and it was a flood of dirty words, I thought, "I'm wearing a raincoat, and it's just running off me."

The Hamburg prison was filled with political prisoners. I was there a very short time, but six weeks is an eternity, if you think you will be in solitary all your life. I lived through it by being able to say hundreds of poems to myself, to read whole pages of books without having the books.

One old jailer gave us hot soup, and there was one woman who did things to make life a little easier for us. But Christmas night I heard them pulling out one person after another and beating them mercilessly. Once in front of me walked a woman whose hands hung in a totally distorted way. I could see that the hands were broken. One day I heard a lot of shouting and looked out a peephole and saw with my own eyes a man literally hunted to death, like an animal. They made him run, then jump, run, lie down, jump, throw himself down, jump up, until blood spurted out of the mouth and he was dead.

Then one day they called me in and said, "You can go home," and shook my hand and said, "*Auf wiedersehen.*" They had told me at the last interrogation, "You will never get out of here," so I knew what they wanted. They wanted me to meet others who would then be caught.

I went back to Berlin. My father had died. I got my mother out of the country, to my sister in Palestine. And in my life are miracles. I walk in a street and see a young woman I know, Jewish, who looks beautifully suntanned. I say, "Where have you been?" She says, "Karlsbad, in Czechoslovakia."

I knew that, like me, she had no passport, and I said, "How did you get out?" She said there is a doctor at the Czech embassy who writes out a certificate that you are sick, and they let you go! He looked at me with big, sad eyes, and he wrote how desperately ill I was. Not a cent he asked, and I never knew his name.

I lived in Czechoslovakia about a week, mostly on hot water. Then the decision was made that I would fight the Nazis in Austria. Another woman is doing the same thing, so we move in together. Then this friend was caught, and we both were put into a horrible prison in Vienna, dirty, filthy. But it was police, not Nazis, and finally they let me go.

One day an old woman, crying, handed me a leaflet that the Germans are coming. That night the Vienna sky was filled with smoke, everybody burning material that was dangerous, and German planes were circling, circling, circling. I went to say good-bye to the Jewish people where I had earned a living, taking care of the children. The furniture was already demolished by Austrian Nazis.

I had seen bad things in Germany, but in Austria the Nazis were drunk with victory. The knew now they had the world! I was in a strange, almost shocklike state. I walked through the city and I thought, "If I ever come out, I want to tell what it was like."

Then I got a false passport and got on a train to France. Paul was in Paris, poverty-stricken and eaten by vermin, but alive. I was a maid, then a governess, then a refugee committee gave me a job. Then the idiot French arrested all the German refugees, their best friends, including Paul. And then it was bedlam, bombs falling, and the Germans were coming.

I squeezed in a train moving south, to Montauban. Montauban was like a miracle. Catholics, Protestants, the entire city opened their homes, gave us false papers, rations, all the things you needed. I was very sure I had lost Paul for all eternity, and then he saw somebody who knew where I was, and we were reunited. Paul became a woodcutter and we lived in a stable. We ate blackberries and suet and bread, and farmers gave us milk.

The life of a refugee is especially horrible if you were used to being important, part of the underground. We wanted to stay there and fight, but everybody said, "There have to be witnesses," and so, between the Unitarian Service Committee in Marseille and the Jewish Socialist Labor Committee in New York, we came to New York in 1941.

The committee arranged for us to go to Pittsburgh, so I could go to school to study social work. We went on a bus with six dollars between us. Paul was an ironworker and a welder, and then he went in the American army for three years, back in Europe, while I studied and gave a lot of speeches about the Nazis. In '47 I came to the University of Minnesota to teach. Paul then worked as an engineer at General Mills. It's not only since women's liberation that the husband comes along!

People still try to understand why what happened in Germany could happen in a country that had produced Schiller and Goethe and Beethoven.

There was terrible inflation and enormously high unemployment, and it's wonderful to have someone to blame, like the intellectuals, the Socialists and Communists, and the Jews. There were Germans who were good people, who fought the Nazis and died, but if the lie is big enough, and you make good propaganda, most people accept it. And then you give the power to the murderers, the sadists.

The child says, "I am going to school," and the mother says, "You can't go to school, they'll spit at you." The child says, "I'll spit back," and the mother says, "You can't because you are a Jew." This is the way one teaches children to be afraid. What we can learn is never to raise children to blind obedience and never to hate a group or a race.

Gisela Konopka's 1988 autobiography, *Courage and Love,* includes her activities as a member of the German resistance during the 1930s.
Photo by Paula Keller

JAMES LOEWENSON
Berlin, Germany

Our bus was filled with Jews trying to escape. A
French policeman went from one to the other
of these terrified people who didn't look like
Frenchmen, couldn't speak French, didn't dare
breathe. He looked at their brand-new, forged
identification papers, saying each time, "Merci,"
and saluting. When he finished, he waved the
driver on. Everybody was crying.

*Born in Posen, James Loewenson moved with his family to Berlin after World
War I, when he was twelve. When Hitler came to power, the Nazis began calling
his father to the police station every day because he was a Socialist. In 1933 his
father committed suicide.*

My family had lived in Posen for generations. The oldest son of the
family was always a jeweler. My father took over the jewelry store, but
when Posen became part of Poland after the First World War, he went to
Berlin and was a jeweler there, with a store in the center of the city.

As a boy, maybe fifteen years old, I already belonged to a youth
organization, the *Kamaraden.* Every Sunday we went out in the woods
singing and marching. When I was nineteen, I became an apprentice in a
library, had a room in a workers' neighborhood, and joined a union.

One day I saw trucks with Nazis in the street where I lived. They came
in my house and took people out—not Jews, but Communists. My family
decided I will leave Germany right away. It was May of 1934.

I went with an uncle for vacation with his family to Prague. He went
back after two weeks, but I didn't. I got a job in a publishing business,
thought I was a free man. But when you take a room you have to go to
the police and declare where you are, and they put me in prison! Herz-
felde, from where I worked—he was a Communist—he paid a bribe and
got me out, but the police gave me one week to leave the country.

I didn't want anything German any more, so I went to Zurich. But they
didn't like Jews without money, and they were afraid of Germany. After
three months the Swiss police brought me to the French border and told
me, "Don't come back, or else . . ."

I had no visa for France, but the French accepted every foreigner.
When I get out of the train, there was a Jewish man who showed me
Paris, gave me something to eat, gave me an address of a committee that
trained people to get a job.

When war was declared—I talk now about 1939—the French called it the "funny war," war but no war, no shooting. Then all foreigners, Jews and non-Jews, had to come to the police with a blanket, with food. They put us in a sports arena outside Paris for three days, and from there we were sent to camps. But these were good camps, plenty to eat, and always wine, and my girl friend knew somebody high up, so one day a French army officer came and took me back to Paris. I was a free man again.

Then real war began, and foreigners were sent to the south of France. When the Germans overran France, they left a little part near Toulouse, near the Swiss border, called Free France. The French gave us a paper: "He is a friend of France. Help him."

In Montauban there were hundreds of foreigners. My girl friend and I married. We had a room in the house of the mayor, and I gave his little boys German lessons, until he sent his maid to tell me that tomorrow morning all refugees will be arrested.

We warned friends, gathered our things, and took the train in the direction of Switzerland. About fifty kilometers before the Swiss border, we took a bus filled mostly with Jews from Poland who had lived in France or Belgium and were trying now, like me, to escape. They didn't speak, they only whispered.

After a while the bus was stopped by the French police. One of them came aboard and looked at their forged identification papers, then waved the driver on. This policeman, who had orders to arrest these Jews, let them go free, in plain view of his colleagues. He risked his liberty and his life for us.

I thought the moment I'm in Switzerland, I will be free. But when we came to the border a Swiss gendarme arrested us! He said, "We keep only old people and very young children, but not you. The boat is full." So we went to one of the little French towns. There were hundreds of foreigners there, and nobody knew what to do.

For money, many French tried to bring people over to Switzerland. I gave one my wedding ring, and we came by boat over the big lake to Geneva, maybe ten people, and now a miracle happened. The Swiss churches forced their government to open the border to refugees.

My wife was expecting a baby, and these weeks were too much for her. She died and the baby died, too. I was half out of my mind, and the police said, "He's German, so let him be in the German part," and transferred me to a camp near Zurich. There I met Swiss people who tried to make life for refugees a little bit easier. I got a job offer to become an apprentice in a book bindery, so the police gave me permission to leave the camp.

By September of '44, Paris had been liberated. I wanted to marry again, but I refused to be declared German. I called myself, "Jewish refugee of German origin," and Swiss authorities wouldn't give my girl friend permission to marry a foreigner who had no nationality. We decided to go to France. We found an apartment and I found a job. The end of 1953 we came to the United States.

Two days after our arrival, somebody sent me to the Jewish Family and Children's Service. I couldn't speak English, but the next morning I had a job!

I have two sons who know very little of my story. I can't talk about the Holocaust, I don't want to hear about it, read about it. I just don't have the strength. I would break down and cry.

KURT LOEWENTHAL
Gelsenkirchen, Germany

> We have not been in death camps, but we lived
> under the terrible threat, day after day. Our
> friends and our family were arrested and de-
> ported, and then we heard nothing more. My wife
> and I still ask ourselves, how come we are alive?

Kurt Loewenthal was a prosperous candy wholesaler when Nazi restrictions against doing business with Jews forced him into bankruptcy. He fled to Belgium and then to France. Although his parents, both brothers, and a sister were killed by the Germans, he returned to Germany after the war. Then he decided the Germans hadn't changed, and emigrated to the United States.

Until the rise of the Third Reich, German Jews had been in good positions as doctors, lawyers, and business people. But I remember in school they always said that in the First World War the German army was not defeated, it was the Jews' fault Germany lost! They loved to talk about fighting and wars, as if this was the highest thing there is.

Conditions got worse and worse in the 1930s. Jews could not go to any theatre, to any sports. My gentile friends were not anti-Semitic, they were not Nazis, but they were afraid! We lost almost all our customers, and the few who remained came after dark. My youngest brother was beaten half to death on *Kristallnacht*. Finally I had enough of the slogans, the persecutions, so I snuck over the frontier into Belgium.

I was called before a commission and asked why I left Germany. I tried to tell them, but one member stood up and said, "I have been in Germany and I have seen the Jews are still doing good business." So they didn't give me permission to stay.

I didn't have any money. I could have taken some with me, but I didn't dare because that was punishable quite severely if you were caught. Refugees were supported by the Joint Distribution Committee, with meal tickets to small Jewish restaurants and rooms in rundown hotels. Several times I was arrested because I didn't have valid papers. I stayed half a year, and then I went over the frontier clandestinely, to France.

In Paris was a big Jewish center, and thousands of refugees were there. Our mood was pretty low. Everybody was hoping that Hitler would just disappear. Instead, Germany declared war on France. We were told to go to the Stadium des Colombes. We were there a week, thousands of us. We were not mistreated, but nothing was organized. It was an open stadium and some straw on the ground—no blankets, nothing.

Finally we were shipped to a camp in Villeurbanne. There were barracks, shacks, and some refugees built houses for themselves. They fed us, but the food was absolutely lousy. Some Jewish people had money and were able to buy food in stores near the camp, but the people who did not have money, they were suffering malnutrition.

The French called it the "funny war," with the French in the Maginot Line and the Germans in the Siegfried Line, and nothing happening. We made fun of it, too, until the Germans decided to attack. France was overrun in six weeks.

As the cannons were coming closer and closer, the French were running and I thought I'd better run with them, so I took off, hitchhiking, sleeping in farmers' houses, in barnyards. After maybe a week I came to Montpelier.

Every town and city in France had a representative or a Jewish committee where refugees were helped. In Montpelier I met my future wife at the committee. She was a dentist in Belgium until the Germans came. We went to a small city near Montpelier and got married at City Hall on January 18, 1941. We didn't have anybody, just the two of us and the old couple where we lived. For pity, the butcher sold us one steak, and that was the wedding dinner.

Italy had occupied the southern part of France, and we felt secure among the Italian occupation forces, but in October 1942 the Germans occupied the entire country. Our son was only a week old, but we went to Grenoble by train. My brother and my wife's brother were also in Grenoble. Then they were arrested and deported so we went to the Vercors, a mountain range nearby.

We changed villages all the time. One time we were living near Oradour sur Glane when the entire population was wiped out in reprisal because the resistance blew up a German convoy. We had false papers saying "born in Alsace," but the French authorities inquired in Alsace whether there is someone by our name and there wasn't. French gendarmes came, about ten guys with shotguns, and asked to see our papers, but the captain was a resistance fighter, and he let us go.

Many times the French authorities, on order from the Vichy government, were told to assemble so many Jewish people and send them to "work camps." They didn't tell the truth. They sent them to Poland to the extermination camps. One time we escaped because I happened to know one of the policemen, and he said, "Don't sleep in your house this night."

We had a big map. The BBC told us what was going on with the war, and almost every day we crossed off another city liberated from the Germans. Finally all the cities, and France, had been liberated, and I will never forget this day of jubilation!

I still couldn't get a French work permit, so I decided, well, I don't like the Germans, but maybe I could take over my business again. Our daughter was born in Paris in 1945, so with two kids we went home to Germany.

I was told by neighbors that my father and mother, and my sister with her children, were "relocated." The Germans put them in cattle wagons and sent them to die in the ovens. My brother who was with me in Grenoble and arrested, I never heard from him again. My younger brother was in Buchenwald and survived, but all the sufferings he went through, he died after the war.

I saw that the Germans had not changed a bit. Most just didn't believe they had done anything wrong. Nobody was an anti-Semite, nobody was a Nazi, they were saying they were just forced into it. In 1951 we had a chance to come to the United States, and here we are.

MARK MANDEL
Warsaw, Poland

We looked like the Poles, and we spoke Polish,
my sisters and I. People couldn't identify us as
being Jews. This was why we survived.

Moshe Mandelbaum was only nine years old when the Germans came to Poland. To survive, he and his sisters begged, stole, smuggled, and traded gasoline, coal, cigarettes, and other items. After the war he went to Palestine and in 1948 he fought in Israel's War for Independence.

My father was a shoemaker with nine people to feed. I had six sisters— I was the only boy—and one sister worked as a seamstress, another as a store clerk. They helped out, but we knew hunger. He was a self-taught person, very much involved in politics, and I remember people gathering around him discussing events of the time, like the civil war in Spain.

It was unusual for Jews in Warsaw to live in a gentile neighborhood, but my father took this particular apartment because it was a storefront in a big apartment complex, a whole block. The gentile boys always used to attack us.

September 1939 we had the first air raid in Warsaw. We lived near railroad tracks, and my father felt this is going to be bombed next, so we moved in with my aunt. For about a week it was quiet, so my fifteen-year-old sister and I went back to our apartment to clean it up, so the family can move back. In the afternoon there was an air raid again. My father saw smoke billowing from the direction where we lived and ran to save us. To me and my sister, nothing happened, but he got killed in the air raid.

We took care of my mother. We were all capable children, resourceful, very aggressive. To this day I can't believe the things I did at the age of nine, ten, eleven.

At the railroad station, gasoline was spilling out of some tankers, and we took home gallons of it and sold it. We had it in our one room, where we lived, a big open tub filled with gasoline! We went to the railroad yards, and my sister jumped on a moving coal car and was throwing coal out for my other sisters and me to pick up, so we got coal to heat and to sell. A guy was carrying a big sack of peanuts in shells, and my sister grabbed it and dragged it home. We bought cigarettes wholesale, and we'd sell them. When the Germans marched into Warsaw they were passing out bread and you were supposed to get only one bread, but my sister got three.

We looked like Aryans and pretended we were gentiles, but people knew we were Jews. Early in 1940 there was a directive from the Germans that all Jews living in this area must vacate. We found an apartment in a Jewish area, our first Jewish neighborhood. This was the start of the ghetto.

We had a nice large apartment, but we were rationed, deprived more and more of material things and food. A lot of people burned their furniture to keep warm. We were smuggling, going through the wire barriers to the gentile side, buying stuff and bringing it back into the ghetto.

There was no transportation in the ghetto except a streetcar through two blocks. I used to go into the streetcar on the Christian side with my merchandise, and as the streetcar was going the two blocks in the ghetto, I jumped off. And many times my sister was riding the streetcar with a suitcase of merchandise—flour, sugar, different things—and I would jump on the streetcar, she'd hand me the suitcase, and I'd jump off!

One night I was out smuggling and got stuck on the Christian side after curfew. I was wearing knickers and I had them full of caramel candies, to be sold in the ghetto. I was only eleven, but I spent that whole night alone in a burned, bombed-out building.

Another time I got caught by a Polish policeman. They threw me in a jail with a bunch of drunks, but the next morning they let me go because I spoke Polish like they did, and they thought I was a gentile.

I saw a German guarding the gate to the ghetto, and a Jew was walking by, innocent, not bothering anybody, and the guard shot him, just like that. Then a cart went by, and they threw him on just like merchandise, discarded. I saw the Germans load up a whole bunch of old people, sick people, on the streetcar, take them to the cemetery, line them up and cut them down with machine guns. I saw it with my own eyes, looking out our attic window.

The Germans were systematically all this time taking Jews out to Treblinka death camp. They promised people they're going to give them a pound of jam and a bread if they'll come to the station to be "relocated." We never fell for it, but my mother's sister did, with her little girl, five years old. She was never seen again.

The ghetto was getting smaller and smaller. Etta, Mindel and I did the dealing and the smuggling, and we decided we're going to go to the town where my parents come from, Deblin. My youngest sister, five years old, had died of a kidney infection. I took my sister Ann over to the gentile side and put her up with friends—Polish Christians who knew we were

Jewish. The following day we went to bring my mother and my other two sisters, Masha and Riva, and take the train to Deblin.

But my mother told us to go ahead, with Riva. "I'll come, I'll follow you," she said. Well, I'm still waiting for my mother and my sister Masha.

So now we were left alone, four sisters and myself. We were with our gentile friends in Warsaw, but it was getting uncomfortable because some people knew we were Jewish and were blackmailing us.

Then the Germans decided to eliminate most of the Jews who were left. I got caught with a bunch being marched like cattle to the train for Treblinka. My sister Etta was walking on the sidewalk as a Christian, saying, "Let him go, he's not Jewish." And I was telling the Germans, "I'm gentile, I'm gentile! I'm not Jewish! Let me go, please!" Finally they let me go, and I ran with my sister.

We bought railroad tickets and went to Deblin, not knowing that Deblin was already completely *Judenfrei*, except for a labor camp next to the railroad station. My uncle and one of my cousins were in that camp, so we smuggled ourselves in!

But in the camp they were weeding out the Jews, too, taking them away. I sat in the toilet the whole night, and my sisters were laying in a dumpster outside the camp. After midnight I came out and my uncle wasn't there, he'd been taken away. My cousin was gone too.

My sisters climbed out of that dumpster and came into the camp, and we became laborers. I was assigned to a bunker to preserve potatoes. The Germans dug huge holes with bulldozers and put the potatoes in. Then we put on straw and then dirt, and then more potatoes and straw and dirt. My sisters worked in the greenhouse.

I was still a tough little kid. I stole a big aluminum pipe from a plane that crashed near camp and gave the pipe to a sheet metal man, so he could make cooking pots. I got one for free, and the rest he sold. I went around picking up cigarette butts and saved the tobacco to sell to people who smoked. I learned German, and during my breaks I cleaned the Germans' houses, fixed things, polished their shoes. So we got money and we bought bread.

Really, we were not hungry. There was a huge public kitchen, and everybody could go and cook. We smuggled potatoes and stuff, and my little sister Riva was cooking supper for us when we came home from work.

We thought we were the only Jews left in this world.

Then the Russians started advancing, and the Germans decided to load the 600 people in this camp on railroad cattle cars, but with open doors, not cooped up. The guards sat in there with us. We went to Czestochowa, and as we were unloaded, they took what we had away from us. Riva was only twelve, but she was holding somebody's child. She was ordered to drop the child and sent into the camp with the laborers. The other children her age, and younger, were taken away and killed. Again, we were lucky.

We lived there for six months, producing bullets for the German army, but the Russians kept advancing, and on January 16 the Germans marched us into a huge warehouse to load us onto trains. Then I saw airplanes flying and bombing, and the Germans ran to hide. Hours went by and the railroad cars were still waiting for us to be loaded, but the Germans didn't come. The next day we were liberated by the Russians.

We went into the house of the German leader and burned it. We raided the warehouse and found bread and two cans of honey. My one sister and I and her boyfriend started hitchhiking away from the front. We saw Germans killed, burning, tanks running over them. My sister almost got killed by a drunken Russian thinking she was a very attractive girl. We hitched a ride in a truck, and the truck fell into this huge ditch the Germans dug to stop the Russian tanks. All the experiences we were going through, it was as though somebody was watching over us.

We slept in Polish farms, being very careful not to tell the Polish people we were Jews. Then we came to a railroad station where we had a feeling that other people there might be Jewish, too. The password was *Am cho,* from the Hebrew words for "our nation." We'd ask "*Am cho?*" and if a person said yes, we knew he was Jewish. We found out my mother's cousin was alive in Lublin, so we took the train there and went to my cousin's house.

My other three sisters who were still alive came to Lublin, too. Three of us went to a Jewish orphanage where we were fed, got new clothes, started school. Then I found out some children from that orphanage were meeting secretly with a Zionist organization trying to recruit children to go to Palestine. I joined and went with the group to Feldafing, and we were taught Zionist ideas, and Hebrew writing and reading. My two older sisters married, but my two younger sisters and I, our goal was to go to Palestine.

In April '46 the British government allowed a thousand surviving children from concentration camps to go to Palestine. I was selected! I came to my sister and told her, "Guess what! You're going to find me with a shovel on my shoulder, building Palestine!"

I was assigned to a *kibbutz* named Kfar Nahum. Half a day we went to school, half a day we worked. I chose construction because I wanted the feeling that I build the country with my toil and my sweat. I also joined the Haganah at the age of seventeen. We were training with rifles, and early one morning as the sun rose we gave the oath to be a member of Haganah. It was a very proud moment, knowing that we put our lives on the line for Palestine.

In 1948 I fought in the War for Independence. When we had to go to battle they'd ask you who to notify if you got killed, and I was real sad because my sisters came to the United States and I didn't have anybody in Israel. On February 3, 1955, I was granted a visa to come here.

Many times I have an inner guilt feeling. For 2,000 years the Jewish people dreamed of returning to their land, and I'm sitting here. I try to make it up by giving money, but it's not enough. I really should be in Israel.

In our minds we were always hoping we're going to see our mother, or our sisters, or my cousin or uncle. Until this day, although I know it's never going to happen, I always hope we're going to see a face we'll recognize as one of my relatives!

ALLEN MASTBAUM
Dubienka, Poland

You sit inside that bunker. If somebody finds
you, you're gonna die. Every second, every minute, for two years, you think about death, you talk
about death. You can't imagine what this is like.

When the Germans occupied Poland in 1939, Allen Mastbaum was sent to Belzec as slave labor. Later, en route to Sobibor, he and hundreds of fellow prisoners broke through the sides of the wooden cattle cars and tried to escape. Most were shot, but Mastbaum survived and hid in a bunker for two years, until the war ended.

In 1938 we heard in Germany they started the attack on Jewish people. But all the old people remembered 1914, the First World War. "When the Germans came," my father said, "the Germans didn't touch nobody, just put you to work, but they didn't kill." That's why everybody didn't run away. But that was a king, Franz Josef. This was Hitler.

In 1939 the Germans crossed the border and the Russians came in, over the River Bug, and then the Russians moved back and the Germans occupied.

Right away they took about ten people, the best people from downtown, and started a *Judenrat*. The Germans tell the *Judenrat* what to do. For instance they want a million dollars, they say to the *Judenrat*, "One week, you have to give a million dollars, otherwise 10,000 Jews will be shot." The *Judenrat* had to come and collect the money.

In the ghetto were apartment buildings, maybe a hundred Jewish families. The Germans came and there was a big truck by the windows, and they threw the children through the windows, into the truck! The mothers couldn't take it. They jumped, too. I saw it with my own eyes.

In 1940 they took about 300 young people from our town to Belzec, a place where they repaired trains, a mill to grind wheat for flour, and a factory where you bring wood and they cut boards. There were 20,000 people in Belzec.

They gave you a little piece of bread and black coffee in the morning. At noon you got a little bit of soup, with a bone from a horse. People in town, the *Judenrat*, brought us packages of food every week.

When they took us to work we saw the Russians across the border. One German, he'd take your cap and throw it to the Russians. You'd run to pick it up, and he'd say, "You're running to the Russians, across the border," and he'd shoot you. They shot twenty, thirty people that way, until the Jewish people got a little smarter.

We were there one year. Then war broke out with the Russians, and they put us on a train to Sobibor, a death camp. We were in a wood cattle car, day and night, people dying on the floor. About five kilometers before Sobibor, the train stopped. We knocked out a wall in the cattle car, and people started jumping out. On the train roof it was Gestapo with machine guns, and they start shooting. There were maybe a thousand people lying dead, where the Gestapo shot them, when the train started moving.

I touched myself all over, and I'm not hit! I said to myself, "I'm alive!" and I crawled out from under the dead people. You want to live, it makes you very strong, and I ran to Chelm, where there were still Jews, still a ghetto. The *Judenrat* gave me a work card.

I was in Chelm until 1942, in a kitchen peeling potatoes. Then I heard that tomorrow they're going to take all the Jews to be shot. I took off at midnight and found some people to take me in a horse and wagon to my brother, about twenty kilometers from Chelm. I said to my brother, "The Gestapo, they're gonna kill everybody, so let's go out to the woods."

My brother had there a gentile friend who fought with him side by side in the Polish army. The gentile had a big farm near the woods, and my brother paid him, and he helped us dig a bunker. We worked all night and all day, dug the hole, cut trees, put leaves and grass on top.

November 28, 1942, we went into the bunker. We were there almost two years, my brother, my sister, her little girl four years old, and me.

We went for water, clear water, from a creek. My brother had money, gold pieces, so every week the gentile brought loaves of bread, butter, and we'd pay him. That gentile drank up the money because he was so afraid. His son-in-law didn't like Jews, and if the son-in-law told the Germans the gentile helped us, they'd kill him, kill the whole family.

Then my brother went to where he had a lot of things hidden, and a gentile brought the Gestapo and they shot him. I went with my brother, but I stayed outside, and I could see everything. I ran back to the bunker and told my sister what happened.

Summer 1944 the Russians came. I was afraid a tank would fall into the bunker and kill us, so I stayed outside and watched from behind a bush. We could see flames from the city, and the Germans running away.

We came out of the bunker, barefoot, in rags. In town the Polish children ran after us, laughing, making fun, hollering, "Jews still alive! Jews still alive!" A couple of Jews got shot, so we saw this is not the place for us.

We went to Woldenburg, in the Russian zone. In Woldenburg everything was expensive, in Chelm everything was cheap, so I would buy five kilos butter in Chelm, then sell it in Woldenburg. I was on the train when this Polish organization took about thirty Jews off the train and killed them. A Polish policeman didn't recognize I'm a Jew and asks me if maybe I saw Jews. I said I didn't know! He shot a Jewish woman, and her little girl, maybe seven years old, starts crying, "Mother! Mother!" So he shot the little girl, too.

This was 1946. At Lublin the government took me and the other two Jews left on the train to a Jewish organization, found us a place to sleep, gave us to eat. Then I went back to Woldenburg.

I said to my wife, "No more Poland! They shoot Jews." We went to Ulm, a D.P. camp, thousands of people. We were living in one room, but it was not too bad. The Joint and UNRRA gave us clothes, food to eat. I bought coffee in the PX, sold it to the German people, had a good business.

I know I have two uncles in America, my father's brothers. The names I know but not the address. I put on the envelope just "Jewish Organization, New York." After four weeks I receive a letter, a package, clothes, from my uncles in St. Paul, Minnesota. We came here, and after one week I filled out an application to Whirlpool Corporation, and I worked there nineteen years.

When I was in the bunker, the only thing was to be alive, to build back my family, to sit and eat by a table. But maybe tomorrow you die, so why wait in this bunker, hiding like an animal? Go out, get shot, much better right away.

I hate very much the Germans, because they killed sixty-four people from my family—parents, brothers and sisters and children, cousins. Six million Jews, they shot them, starved them, burned them, and nobody answers for nothing. I question, where's God?

HELEN MASTBAUM
Skalat, Poland

Just bad dreams are left me, nothing else. I hear
my husband screaming and yelling, and I wake him up
and say, "What happened?" And he says, "They pulled
me by my hair, they want to kill me!" It's already
forty-three years, and the Germans are still part of us.

From age twenty, Hinda Kornweitz worked for the German occupiers as a tailor's assistant. When the last Jews in Skalat were killed and the ghetto burned in 1943, she hid in the woods with other refugees until they were liberated by the Russians in 1944.

My father had a little store—pails, dishes, like a hardware store. We were religious people. We didn't understand too much about anti-Semitism, but when we used to go into the park, Polish kids would throw stones at us.

We were close to the Russian border. In 1939 we were very happy that Russians occupied us because we heard rumors that Germany will kill the Jewish people. Then the Nazis came. The first day they took 600 men and they never came back—600 Jewish men, young and old, all killed.

My brothers were both in the Soviet Army, and my father hid in the cellar. A German officer came and opened my closet and saw men's suits. He wouldn't believe it's my brothers. He started beating me and I started screaming and yelling, and then one soldier, he stopped them.

They took me and my sister to work in the field. My father came out of his bunker, and they took him to work in the kitchen because he spoke a little German.

We had a *Judenrat* because the Germans didn't want to speak to private Jewish people. They came to the *Judenrat* and would say, "You have to give us this day so many people to work," or "We need at this time so many furs." Then the *Judenrat* collected from us furs, silver, gold. And white sheets, because the Germans needed them at the front, to hide things when it was snow.

In 1942 they made a ghetto in our city. A gentile family, a shoemaker, took our house, and we went to live in their place, sixteen people in a very small house. I lived with my younger sister and my father's sister with her kids, until they were all killed. Clothes, furniture, everything, we sold to survive. We sold a bedroom set for ten pounds potatoes, a little flour, chicken.

One morning the ghetto was surrounded with S.S., shouting, "*Raus, raus!*" I was always having miracles, always hid when they made this kind of search, and they never could see me, never could find me. We hid in the attic, and after three, four days we hear people talking, voices we knew, saying they took this family away, they took that family away.

So we came down. Then it was back to work in the fields again for a couple weeks until a neighbor, he worked for the Germans, he was a tailor, and he said, "I have a daughter. Maybe she will help me in my shop." And they believed I'm his daughter and gave me a card so I can help him.

About three or four months I did this. Then one day I heard shooting, and I looked out the window and I saw everything's on fire in the ghetto. I ran out through the back door, and ran and ran and ran, and hid in a stable in the hay.

Finally I had to go out to find food. I went to my father in the labor camp in Skalat. It was all wires all around, but I crawled under and came to my father's cabin. I was hiding and my father used to bring me food. Then one day he says to me they would search this place, and he took me to a gentile woman who had a bunker in the kitchen. I was hidden by her for two weeks.

Then she came to say they killed my father, and they're going to finish all the people in the camp, so the city will be completely *Judenfrei*. When it got dark, the gentile woman gave me water and a piece of bread, and I started walking. Then I heard somebody behind me, a Jewish man and a woman, so we were already three of us.

For a whole week we hid in the fields by day and walked in the night, until we came to the woods. In the woods we heard voices, and it was people we knew! We made a bunker. It's hard to say this, but we stole. We dug potatoes, picked corn, beets. At night we made a fire to bake potatoes. One group was five, one three, one seven. We helped each other.

We were in the woods nine months, until March 1944. For twelve days we were surrounded by fighting. We could hear Russians, we could hear Germans. We were afraid a tank will come and crush us in our bunker, so we took turns watching. Then one day we heard a lot of Russians speaking, and we came out. It was March 14.

We started walking to the city. Everything was bombed, and Russian soldiers and German soldiers lay dead in the streets. The gentile woman who lived in my house was surprised to see Jewish people still living. I said I'd like to see my house, stay overnight. She made me sleep on the floor, treated me very bad.

Polish people were very mean to us. They would chop off a Jew's head to buy a pound of sugar! I was afraid. Then I was sick in the hospital, two, three months. When I was well, I went to the police, and they made that woman give me back my house.

There were maybe a hundred Jews left. I took a survivor family to stay with me, four people. They paid a little bit rent, and I found a job in a restaurant. Then I got sick again. My brother wrote from Russia and asked who survived. I wrote him back I was awfully sick, I couldn't walk, I didn't know what to do. He sent me money and told me I should leave this place because it was horrible to live with so many bad memories.

I went to Gliwice, met my husband there in 1945. We got out from Poland to a D.P. camp. UNRRA kept us there, gave us food. We started writing letters to some family here, and my husband's uncle sent us papers.

ROSE MEYERHOFF
Brussels, Belgium

Each time the S.S. searched the convent
grounds, the nuns would alert us and we children would leave our classrooms and start walking or running in the opposite direction. We had to
keep quiet and go fast, and we were very afraid.

*Rose Jacobowitz was only seven when the German army occupied Belgium in
1940. When the Germans took her mother away, a neighbor took her to a Catholic
convent, where she was given a false name and attended school until the war
ended. At age fifteen she came to the United States, alone, to live with an aunt and
uncle she'd never met.*

I knew the war had started because draft registration for the army was
in our school. My mother and I packed up and ran, to avoid the oncoming German armies. Jews, Catholics, hundred and hundreds of people
were walking away from Brussels, and we didn't stop until we got to
Paris. I don't know how many kilometers that is, but I know I complained a lot!

My parents were divorced, and my father, a cabinetmaker, was living
in Antwerp. I had a sister living with my aunt and uncle in Antwerp, and
they were supposed to meet us in Paris. Then we were going to get on a
boat and go to England. But we never made contact in Paris, and we
couldn't get to the North Sea because the borders were closed, so we
went back to Brussels. Later we found out my aunt and my sister were hit
by a bomb and killed. I don't know what happened to my father.

In September I came home one day from school, and a friend of my
mother's stopped me at the door and said, "The Germans were here,
took your mother away. Don't go upstairs to the apartment."

I trusted him because I had seen him many times at home, so I went with
him to the train station and we traveled to Louvain, where Benedictine
sisters were running an orphanage for Catholic children. There were
Jewish children already there when I arrived, and more kept coming.

We were all given a Christian name. Mine was Christiane DeGraef.
Every morning we would file into the chapel, looking all alike in our
black dresses, to go to Catholic mass before breakfast. At first the Jewish
children could sit in back and not participate, but later on the nuns got
nervous, and we were asked to kneel, and stand, and sit, and open the
prayer book, like the Catholic children.

The Catholic priest who ran our day camp was shot by a firing squad because he allowed Jews to attend, but those nuns decided to take in Jews anyway. Periodically, S.S. officers or Gestapo or German officials would come to the convent and say they had heard there were Jewish people hiding there, and they insisted on searching the convent grounds each time.

This was quite a large building, laid out in four squares with a courtyard in the middle, and about four stories high. Each time the Germans came, we would leave the classrooms immediately with one of the nuns. If they were coming up one staircase, we would be going down another. And if they would be going down, we would be going up. So we were always out of sight of them, and they would be satisfied, and leave.

They came probably six, seven times to search the convent grounds. It just sounds fantastic, I know, that a hundred kids could go up and down the stairs and not be discovered. But when I went back to visit in '74, there were a couple of nuns still there that had taken care of us, so then my husband believed it!

We knew when the liberation was coming because one teacher had an underground radio. She came every day with a map and little colored pins, so we could see the English and American armies advancing through France and Belgium. We laid the map on the floor and crouched behind her desk, hoping nobody would look in the windows and see what we were doing.

In the afternoon we would stand in the courtyard and count the Allied bombers, sometimes 200 at a time, flying over on their way to Germany. We started getting bombing in Louvain, and if the bombs came at night, we would run down to the basement and lie on the floor and try to sleep.

One night we looked out the window and saw white dots coming down from the sky, like snow. Pretty soon we could see these were parachutes coming down. We ran outside and there were jeeps and tanks and trucks filled with soldiers. We were hugging each other and screaming and jumping because we knew that now we didn't have to worry about getting killed, or caught, or sent away.

In January of '45 I left the convent because Jewish organizations were trying to find all the Jewish orphans. Nobody really knew what to do with us, though, because we were too young to be sent off into the world on our own. I was sent to a Jewish orphanage in Weisenbaek.

In the convent the older kids looked after me, but now I was taking care of the younger kids. In April of '47 HIAS located my mother's brother, who had come to New York in 1922. They told him there was this niece in Belgium, and he and his wife adopted me.

I stayed in that convent two and one-half years, and I still have a special feeling for Catholics, and nuns in particular. They were risking their lives for us.

I have a real hard time with Germans. I can't make friends with them. I can't watch Holocaust movies or read the books. I was going to interview people for this book, but I couldn't do it. I don't want to be reminded.

Where we live we are the only Jewish couple, and our kids were the only Jewish kids in the school. Maybe that's a reaction to the Holocaust, too, that we didn't go where all the Jews were.

VICTOR MINTZ
Warsaw, Poland

The brain is a computer. You start a new life
but you can never erase, never forget. You lost
dear ones, friends, you raise children with no
aunts and uncles, no cousins, no grandparents.
But life is life. It's going on.

Victor Mintz was descended from men who were both scholars and successful businessmen. He escaped the Nazis by fleeing to Russia, then Lithuania, then back to Russia, to Samarkand.

My father passed away when I was two years old, and I was raised by my grandfather from my mother's side, Moshe Sander Engelman. Engelman was one of the best-known Jewish families in Poland, scholars and rich, both together. About half of Poland's woods belonged to his father, so he was cutting and exporting lumber. He was a religious Jew, Orthodox.

When the 1914 war started my grandfather took us to the Ukraine, to Pruszkow, because his son-in-law was living there, and they were afraid in Warsaw because of the bombardments. Then in 1919 there came the Ukrainians with Petlura, the head of the Cossacks. On a Sabbath afternoon they killed 5,000 Jews in three hours, a pogrom. I saw them through the window, running with open swords, and after, they made a hospital in our house with over 100 injured people. I was ten years old.

In 1922 we came back to Warsaw and I graduated high school, and then business college in 1928. I was the main accountant in a bank.

In Warsaw was a Jewish *kehilla,* the community ruling itself, schools, welfare, taxes and tax collectors, like a Jewish government accepted by the Polish government. Jewish people could vote, like a regular election.

In Poland was also anti-Semitism. Some places they didn't let Jews in to live, and they used to stay by the Jewish stores and tell people not to buy. Sometimes you go into a park, young Poles would beat you up. University was a fight because they wanted Jewish students on the left side of the room and Poles on the right. I remember a big Jewish student demonstration, police in the middle, protecting us from one another.

The atmosphere was very harsh. In 1937 Jewish businessmen started to boycott German products. In 1938 the Germans threw out all the Jews who used to be Polish citizens, and a lot of those refugees came to Warsaw. You got Jewish writers, a lot of Talmudic schools, Hebrew schools, secular schools in Yiddish, Zionists, Socialists, Bundists—it was like a rainbow, everybody fighting something.

September 1, 1939, was the war. They called us Sunday morning to make trenches in the heart of the city. We came, and there were no shovels. Nobody knew what to do, so we came home. On Monday morning, September 4, my two cousins and I walked out of the city, going east.

On the highway airplanes were coming down very low, with machine guns shooting, and to the left and right of us, people died. We would run into the woods when we saw planes coming. Five, six days we were walking and running on the highway.

I went to Bialystok till the end of December, and then I smuggled the border to Lithuania because Lithuania was still a free country. When we smuggled the border, I was caught. This was Saturday morning, and it was still dark. The Lithuanian soldiers took me and the other two boys, to take us to the border to send us back to Russia. We saw a Jew going to synagogue, and I told him what is going on. The soldiers wanted money, so he told the soldiers to come to the synagogue, and they paid the soldiers there. In the middle of the night, they took our whole group by horse and buggy to Vilna.

I was in Vilna a few days. Then the Jewish community sent me to Telz. I got a job as accountant in a factory, got married.

1941, in June, started the Russian-German war, and we started to run again, going by foot. It was the same story on the highway, German planes coming down with machine guns shooting. Lithuanian partisans, anti-Semites, were killing Jews. We went in a freight train to Kovno, then to Riga. In the morning the Germans were already in Riga, but by a miracle, the train depot was on the Russian side.

There was no order, nothing. Nobody asked you who you are, what you are, where you're going. We went on the train to 200 miles before Moscow. The train stopped every fifteen or twenty minutes, and the people got off, because German planes were bombarding the train. But we came safely to a collective farm near Danilov.

I was there a couple of months working, and then I saw the front is coming nearer. Also it started to get cold, and my wife and I didn't have any warm clothing to wear, so I decided we will go south to Samarkand. We didn't have food to eat, we were sleeping on the streets, because a lot of refugees were there. Finally, I got a job. My daughter was born in Samarkand.

In May 1946 an agreement between the United States and Russia was that all Polish citizens have to be let out of Russia. We came to Lodz, everybody's gone. Warsaw, I didn't find Jews. The Holocaust I heard about, but now I see it! I'm looking for a relative, friends, I can't find anybody. I heard my sister and my brother-in-law, their little baby was killed, and they died on the highway on the way to the camps. My mother died. My grandmother, I don't know. By the gate at the cemetery was a little stone, and this was the grave of my grandfather. He had passed away a few months before the liquidation of the ghetto. Who put up the stone, I don't know.

Even most of the houses were gone, but my apartment was not destroyed. A man was living there, and I asked if I can see the rooms. "Yes," he said, and then he told me, "You've got a lot of books in the basement." But I was afraid to go down in the basement with that gentile because of the pogrom in Kielce, where Poles killed so many Jews after the war.

Our idea was to leave for Germany and from there to go to Palestine. But it was illegal to go, and I had a little daughter a year old, so I couldn't go illegally. My wife had in the United States two brothers and two sisters before the war, so in 1948 we came here.

In the war, the Americans, they had reconnaisance photographs, and they asked President Roosevelt to bombard the trains going to Auschwitz. He didn't do it. Now hundreds of thousands of refugees from Vietnam, from all over they let in, but the Jews they didn't let in.

In the churches they were always telling, through the centuries, that Jews are the God-killer, are poisoning their lives and their water and everything. But Jews were always studying, always the people of the Book. According to the Jewish religion, every life is sacred.

When I ran away from Poland in 1939, this was the day before Yom Kippur. A Polish farmer gave us soup to eat. This was the first time I was eating on Yom Kippur, and eating nonkosher food, but I was not eating in a couple of days. It's just the past few years I'm turning back to religion. You can't turn away from God.

I will tell you another story. I remember one time there was an Israeli saying Jews in Europe were going like sheep to the slaughter. But the Holocaust is like Babi Yar in 1941. Thousands and thousands of Jews were killed at Babi Yar, and nobody started a fight. But this had nothing to do with religion, with you're afraid. The killers had guns, machine guns, and an army. And you stood naked!

I don't believe in America we could have what happened in Germany. But you have surprises in history.

FAYE PORTER
Gorodok, Poland

We weren't organized, you know. That was the trouble.
No leaders, no place to go. The last minute, some
people fled, but everyone, if he fled, he fled by himself,
not knowing where you go, what you're going to do.

Faye Merrin Porter and her husband—their name was Puchtick, a name they changed when they came to America—fought with Ukrainian partisans against the Germans. Their son, Jack Nusen Porter, is the editor of Jewish Partisans: A Documentary of Jewish Resistance in the Soviet Union during World War II, *published in 1982.*

In 1939 the Polish army stopped to rest in our town, and the Russians sent out leaflets to surrender. They didn't give up, the Polacks, so the Russians sent twenty-five airplanes over Gorodok throwing firebombs. They destroyed the Polish army, but they destroyed all the houses, too. We went to stay in Mukacevo with the Ukrainians.

The Germans came in July 1941. They gathered men and said they're taking them to work. Then they prepared pits, graves, and killed them. They took Ukrainians to help them, and the Ukrainians told us.

My husband was a shoemaker and he worked for the Ukrainians free, so they drew up a petition that he can stay in Mukacevo. Then the Germans gathered us into a ghetto. In the ghetto was a miserable life. You cannot walk on the sidewalk, but my brother was walking on the sidewalk, so they took him in the police station, beat him up terrible. They tied my brother-in-law to a wagon and dragged him until he fell dead.

We wore a white *Mogen David* on our arm, then yellow patches in front and back, and patches, eight inches, on every Jew's house. The *shochet* wasn't allowed to make the meat kosher. We just had to leave it, eat bread, vegetables. All day we were doing nothing. We knew that something is hanging over our heads. My husband ran away and was with the Jewish partisans.

The last of 1942 the Nazis chased us out from the ghetto, and we knew that this is the last day of our life. They put us in the middle of the street, to be all together and counted. The children were so scared.

I said, "Let's burn the houses and run into the forest! When it's a fire, maybe they can't kill everybody." But nobody listened to me. My sister, she said, "No, I'm afraid to go." I saw a barn, so I ran in there.

Saturday morning they took everybody to the graves. All day Saturday, Nazis and police were coming in and out, in and out, but they didn't see me sitting there. My cousin was hiding too. Sunday, about three o'clock in the morning, it was quiet. I called to my cousin, and we crawled on our hands and knees into the forest.

This Polack took us in, and we stayed a couple of weeks in his woods. We used to go out at night and dig potatoes, and bake them outside. Then three boys found me and brought me to my husband.

A Ukrainian, a Communist in Kiev, had given him a rifle, 150 bullets, two grenades, and sent him back to organize the Jewish underground to fight the Nazis. When this group saw the grenades, the rifle, they kissed them. They made bombs and put them on tracks to destroy the trains, the Germans, and put in bombs to destroy the electricity stations, police stations, bridges.

The partisans went to the people and took clothes, food. I was the cook. In winter we were sewing white robes so they wouldn't be seen. Twice the Nazis came, but Ukrainians let us know, so we moved to a different place. There was an anti-Semite commander in the partisans, and his adjutant came secretly and told us we should keep our guard double and not sleep because he wants to destroy us. The partisans killed him, instead. We were together, Jewish and non-Jewish, in the partisans.

In spring 1944 the Russians let us know the war was ending. We cried and we kissed each other. I knew that all my family was destroyed, my parents, four sisters and four brothers, all their children. My parents had already sixteen grandchildren, and all were gone. We were alive, and we were free, and we didn't believe it.

We were living near Rovno, and my husband was working in an office where Ukrainians would bring in raw furs, and he gave them letters of exchange, or leather for boots. You could count maybe fifteen, twenty Jewish families in Rovno. The Russians were gathering all the orphan children to send away to Russia to schools, so every Jewish family took

Jewish orphans. We took a boy, fourteen, and a girl, ten, took them in like our own children, until the Brichah sent them to Palestine.

The Zionist organization was organizing people to go underground to Palestine. The Russians didn't like our talking about it, so we used to make parties, make-believe engagement parties, a wedding, to discuss how to go there.

Our son was born in 1944. Because we had a small baby, we couldn't go to Palestine, so young boys, Zionists, led us on foot through Poland, Czechoslovakia, to Austria, to a D.P. camp. A Jewish interpreter working with the Americans put my husband's name in the *Forward,* and his brother, who came in 1913, sent us right away papers to come to America.

LIBBY ROSENZWEIG
Breslau, Germany

After the war I went back to my home town.
Our Christian next-door neighbors had taken
our home, everything we had. They wouldn't
let me in even to take a look.

Libby Storozum was thirteen when war began. As a slave laborer in German factories, she says she did not know real hunger or mistreatment. But she still has nightmares about the horrors she witnessed.

My father came originally from Poland. He spoke German and Russian and Yiddish. He had a fruit store in Breslau, but when the Germans came to power he realized something is wrong, and he moved us to Modrzejow. He went back and forth to Breslau until 1935, when the Germans took the Jews' passports away. Then we had a stand, with live fish, in the market on Thursdays and Fridays.

The first we knew the Germans are coming was that this gorgeous synagogue across the river was on fire. When we saw the fire, we knew it wasn't war against Poland; it was war against the Jews.

We went to my father's family, five kilometers away. Then the S.S. troops with the black uniforms and red armbands were gathering all the Jews with beards. My father had a beautiful beard, and my sister went for a barber while I went to get bread. That was where my horror started because the streets were paved with bodies, with opened skulls and bellies.

I wore a white armband with a blue Star of David, and then I had the yellow Star of David front and back. We were enslaved. We had to dig ditches, clean the Germans' quarters, their villas. It was mentioned already about the ghetto, that they are moving the Jews closer together, so we had packed a suitcase and a knapsack.

They came early in the morning. I spoke German, so the caretaker took me to be the interpreter for our three buildings, even though I was only fifteen. I heard one S.S. say to the other, "If half the family is in work camp, the other half can go free." I didn't tell this to my parents, I just volunteered to work, and my parents were sent home. I didn't know that later they would do the same thing again, and then my parents would be gone.

They gathered 5,000 of us in a field, and I was one of sixty girls selected to go to a spinning factory in Arnau, Czechoslovakia. We went by regular passenger train. On the train I had my sixteenth birthday.

In the labor camp we were all thirteen to eighteen. We didn't have any freedom—it was barbed wire—but we were not treated badly. We had a German work commander, a woman, and a Jewish camp leader, and a German Jewish nurse. The flax came in big spools, and I had to bring it through water and gears onto little spools. We were making cloth for soldiers' uniforms.

We worked every day except Sunday, when we had to clean the factory. In the morning they gave us two sandwiches, one for breakfast and one for later on, for lunch or supper. A lot of things were made out of thickened blood and horsemeat, and being from a Hasidic home, I didn't eat them.

I was in labor camp for almost two years. The good Germans couldn't do anything openly to help because their lives were at stake, but in March '44 our director told us the small camps were being closed, so for us to stay alive he's going to transfer us to Bernsdorf, a paper-spinning factory.

Bernsdorf was run by S.S. We all got numbers, the yellow star with a number and a red triangle. That's all we were, numbers. We got half a loaf of bread for the whole week, and at night we got soup out of kohlrabi and potatoes.

The S.S. were brutal. If they caught somebody doing something they didn't like, they hurt us. If the American military succeeded, they hurt us. They brought girls from Auschwitz with the striped clothes, the shaved heads, skinny. The girls told us the horrors, that we can't expect any more. We lived in fear.

Spinning paper was horrible, and seeing the girls from Auschwitz, I didn't care any more. I let the machine go. They were threatening to send me to Auschwitz, to kill me. But then they put me in a sewing room. I wasn't really a seamstress and I didn't know how to do it right, but I had a beautiful voice and I was singing, and the girls used to give me half-done, so I would be able to make production and the S.S. wouldn't send me away.

I was lucky with food, too. I was assigned to a machine with the manager's wife, and she felt so sorry for me that in the morning she would put a sandwich with butter and things on top of the machine. I could understand Russian, and when we were liberated by the Russians I went to protect her. Just a plain "hello" to some Russian soldiers was invitation for rape, until the Russian Jewish officers put a stop to it. But in between, in a few hours, a lot of the girls were raped, heartbroken, crying.

Then a truck came from Waldenburg with men and women liberated a few days before us. I resembled my sister, and these people were recognizing me, so I knew my sister was alive in Waldenburg, but when she walked down the stairs, I didn't recognize her. My sister really went through the horrors of the Holocaust.

We went to Munich because we heard an uncle was alive there. It took days and days on trains, bribing guards with bottles of vodka, until we came to the American zone. There it was a different life, completely different. Freedom!

We stayed in a D.P. camp at Feldafing until March '46. I wanted to go to Palestine, but every time we started out, we were sent back. I never wanted to come to America because we thought everybody's rich here, and after a labor camp I didn't want to look up to anybody any more! Then I married, and he wanted to come to America so we came, and now I'm 100 percent American.

It really bothers me when people say the Jews went like sheep or didn't put up a resistance. There was no chance. Nobody knew that something like this could happen. In Poland, Jews were more afraid of the Polish people than the Germans!

On Channel 2 they had a film, "Breaking the Silence." They had children of survivors blaming their parents for "silencing" the Holocaust. My children, if they wanted to know about the Holocaust, they knew! They had to wake me up during the night, screaming, from a nightmare! The Holocaust should be shown. It should be taught. And it should never be forgotten, not just for the Jews but for mankind. We are all born with an Eichmann in us.

LUCY SMITH
Cracow, Poland

I am still in hiding, in a way. I could not go
forward, even professionally, like making exhi-
bitions of my painting. It took me a lot of time
to learn to be open, to talk.

*Lucy Kreisler was only six years old when the Germans occupied Cracow. Her
father, a chemist and paint manufacturer, fled to Lvov, and Lucy and her mother
went into hiding. When the war ended, she finally could go to school.*

My mother did not give me much Judaism. I did not know there were
Catholics and Jews or that I was Jewish. I knew there were holidays, and
my uncle took me to Temple a few times. I thought it was entertaining.

I was supposed to start school the year the Germans came. I went for
one month before I was told not to come any more. I also couldn't go to
public parks any more, but we went to the river and found places to play
in the street.

I did not have to wear a yellow star because I was under ten years old,
but gradually it became more and more clear to me that I was Jewish.
Some Poles occupied our apartment, and told my mother to get out. She
couldn't take any furniture or anything.

My mother came from a rather wealthy family. We went to Tarnow,
where my mother was born, and stayed a year in a little apartment. The
Germans were putting up posters, you have to come here, and here, at a
certain time. Her cousin said not to trust the Germans, and don't do what
they say, so she just didn't go. My mother had two uncles, almost her age,
and the Germans came, and both were shot in the street,

We were always hiding. A Ukrainian was assigned by the Germans to
administer this house that was ours in Tarnow. He was staying downstairs, and we were in the attic, and when the Germans were coming he
was saying no, no one was upstairs.

Then we were hiding in the ghetto. There was a cave for coal under
this house, and a man covered the door, put in bricks and left only a
small passage underneath. One could just crawl through on one's belly,
and then push a crate to cover this passage. There were maybe twenty of
us hiding there, sometimes for several days with just a little food.

The ghetto was not constant killing. At the beginning we played on the
balconies, and in the ruin of a synagogue next to our house. But the
Germans would come to the ghetto and take anyone in sight, especially

children and families with children, so there were less and less children. Finally, most of the children were gone.

My father got false documents, Catholic certificates of baptism, for us. My mother got in touch with a gang that specialized in getting people out of the ghetto for money. There was a house that one side was in the ghetto, and one side out of the ghetto, on the border. The house was being used for delousing people, and we went there pretending we wanted to get deloused. Then these people opened the door, and we just went across. The gang were waiting, and they took us to the train.

We went to Warsaw because nobody knew us there, so it was less likely that someone would recognize us with our false identity. There was a kind of apartment, and the woman who owned it was a part-time madame, but there was a bed for us. We were waiting for our belongings, and eventually some clothes came, and a very precious thing for my mother, the down comforter.

Mother had some jewelry, rings, which she sewed in her coat and was selling from time to time. She also had from my uncle's store combs and things for sale. But part of living in hiding was paying blackmail, and the gang was waiting to see how much they can still squeeze out of us, and after that they would denounce us.

We found another place and didn't tell this gang where we were going. We lived there almost a year with the wife of a prisoner of war, a Polish officer, and her two daughters. They didn't know we were Jewish, but they also kept a man they knew was Jewish, for the money. When the ghetto burned, one daughter said, "Let the Jews burn. Main Street used to be theirs!"

When the Russians and Germans started fighting in Warsaw, we walked, and walked, and walked, to Pruszkow, staying one night in a store where Polish women were so scared they were saying the "Hail Mary" absolutely the whole night. This was fall 1944.

My mother told a German officer we were Ukrainian and got permission that our group could go to Tarnow. It was absolutely quiet when we got to Tarnow because no one was there. We went to our basement cave, and after a while we heard sounds like soldiers. Someone went out to look, very quiet, and there were not German soldiers but Russians. We all rushed out, and that was the end of the hiding.

Now life started to be quite pleasant. Russians settled in this house where we were, and they shared food with us, and I could go to school.

When people were coming back after the war alive, everyone was surprised. My father didn't come back. When he came to Warsaw to bring those papers for us, one day there was sabotage on the train station by the resistance and the Germans took everyone close to the station, including my father. What really killed my father, though, was he sold one of his formulas to the Russians, a paint for trains, and this paint wasn't drying, so he was hiding from the Russians when they were taking people deep inside Russia. Those people survived, but my father did not.

In Tarnow, even after the war, they still had religion lessons in public school, Catholic. The principal of the school suggested that we don't say I'm Jewish, but a restaurant where we ate dinner was definitely a Jewish place, and a girl from school saw me going there. She put two and two together and made trouble for me after that.

Jewish people were leaving, some for Israel, but my mother was very ambiguous about it. She would say that we should leave, then she'd say she didn't want it. My mother's family had some houses in Tarnow, and she was selling them after the war. Also, we had relatives in the United States, and they were sending things for us to sell.

Initially I thought not much about being a survivor. I felt terribly alone, but I was taking things as they came. I went to France by myself and studied art. In 1959 I got married to an American, and in 1967 we came to the United States. When I came here, my mother followed me.

The Holocaust is being treated with soap opera sensationalism. When my son was in religious school, he was taught a lot of statistics and a lot of ghoulish stories, and it turned him completely off. Somehow these people become like historical objects, like mummies, and there's something emotional lost there. The film *Shoah* was good because even Germans come out as people.

I do not think Germans were particularly worse than other people. The United States sent those refugee boats back to Europe and interned the Japanese, so the potential is here. I also think that to be too obedient is not safe.

SABINA ZIMERING
Piotrkow, Poland

> A Holocaust starts or stops with every single human
> being. I was nineteen years old, and I said, "I don't want
> to let the Germans kill me. I don't want to die. Not now!"

*Sara Szwarc (Schwartz) was sixteen when war began. She and her sister, Helena,
survived because they looked and acted like Poles and because two of their Catholic
schoolmates became members of the Polish underground.*

I grew up in Piotrkow-Tryb, 100 miles southwest of Warsaw. In a
population of about 60,000 people, 12,000 were Jews, but we lived in a
Polish neighborhood. We celebrated all the Jewish holidays, but I grew
up with Polish friends, went to a Polish school. My Polish language was
accent-free, and I was very familiar with Polish customs and religion. My
Polish friends were saying, "Oh, you're such a fun kid! Why don't you
come with me to church and convert!' I told my mom, and she laughed.
But growing up this way gave me the confidence to pass as a Pole during
the war.

For weeks before war broke out, we had to practice covering the
windows in case of bombing attacks. September 1, 1939, a beautiful
Friday morning, I went with my mother to a farmer's market. We heard
the siren, but we all assumed it was another trial, preparation. A few
minutes after that, bombs were falling.

I was sixteen and remember thinking that our sleepy town will finally
have some excitement!

Our family tried to escape to the East. German planes were machine
gunning people on the ground, so we were hiding in the woods in
daytime and walked at night. In a whole week we put in only thirty miles,
so we went back home.

One month later, Piotrkow had the first Jewish ghetto in German-
occupied Poland. Our family of five was put in one room with another
family. You could hear the heavy boots of patrolling soldiers from blocks
away, always two and three together. Food was rationed and very scarce,
and people began dying of hunger and typhus.

The Germans turned over most of the job of running the ghetto to the
Jewish Council. The ghetto was beautifully run, food distributed, sick
people put in quarantine for typhus or sent to the hospital, but it was not
an easy job.

The Germans would say, "We need 20,000 *zlotys* in twenty-four hours.

If we don't get the money, 200 Jewish men will be shot or sent off." Once the Germans said, "All fur coats have to be delivered within forty-eight hours." Or they would say, "We need 500 strong men by tomorrow, 8 o'clock in the morning." Usually just part of the 500 came back, abused, beaten.

In spite of constant fear and hunger, we still lived like seventeen-year-olds. We had an eight o'clock curfew, but we would meet in the small backyard of our apartment building with other teen-agers, new boys from Lodz whose families were forced to leave their city. We had a group of maybe fifteen, twenty young people, a literary club. One of our leaders said, "Why don't we resist?" This was such a surprising thought, and we were just so shocked.

My Jewish high school was closed right away, as were Jewish grade schools. Jews were not allowed to congregate in groups of more than five or six, but education continued illegally. I was teaching children in their homes, and my friends and I continued our studies with Jewish professors.

My father was taken for work several times but returned. The adults were spending the evenings pondering the future, but whenever the discussion turned to approaching disaster—rumors about the liquidation of our ghetto—my grandfather vehemently protested, claiming that God would not allow this to happen.

I did not contradict my grandfather, but I did believe rumors that the Germans systematically were exterminating one ghetto after another and that our turn was coming soon.

I felt an inner revolt. My parents were saying, "What will happen to others will happen to us. Don't bother us." But I did continue to bother, and finally my mother had an idea. She contacted our Catholic childhood friends, two sisters whose mother was my grade school teacher, and asked if one of them could give me her passport. They said they will have to discuss it with their mother.

The punishment for Poles helping Jews was death. But a few days later our friends came and said, "Pick Polish sounding names. Get photographs. We will give you passports." I remember the expression on my parents' faces. A miracle!

October 20, 1942, shortly before midnight, the passports were put to use. Liquidation commandos surrounded the ghetto, and we could hear shots and screams. We took off our Star of David armbands and went into the scarey outside world.

At first our friends were hiding us in their attic. You couldn't move, you couldn't cough, because the father was against it. Then when he went to work, we could come down and eat and talk.

Out of 20,000 Jews in the ghetto, the Nazis keep 2,000 for work, our father and brother among them. Our mother was sent with the rest to Treblinka. Our father told us to go to the next town and sign up to work in Germany. There it would be easier for us to pass as Poles.

Now, for the first time in our lives, my sister and I had to rely only on ourselves. I was nineteen and she was seventeen. It seemed safer to pretend we were cousins, so I was Krystyna Slawinska and she was Helena Kowalska. We ended up in a road machinery factory in Neustadt-Orla, with hundreds of women from all over Europe. With each new transport, we could see girls that looked just like we were—not Polish, but Jewish.

Once in a while some German soldier seemed decent, not comfortable with what he was doing. Some of the German workers invited us to their homes, gave us clothes, food, shoes, things like that.

But there were remarks about our resemblance to each other, and we decided to run again. On a Friday evening we slipped out of camp and walked to town, where we were promptly arrested. Our camp director vouched for us, that we'd never done anything wrong before, but back at the camp one woman told us, "They suspect you are Jews. Don't stay." So we took off again, this time on a train heading south.

My plan was to cross into Switzerland, but our money ran out. We ended up in Regensburg, north of Munich. We found an employment office and applied for work, pretending we had been accidentally separated from our transport. We were told to go to the next building, where they might help us find our lost group.

The next building turned out to be Gestapo headquarters! We were subjected to a body search. They found a ration card for soap, with the name and address of our factory, but I quickly collected my wits, and said a Polish girl in Leipzig gave us this coupon. We were allowed to return to the employment office, where they were quite surprised to see us back.

We spent the remaining eighteen months in Regensburg, worried constantly about being recognized, working in the Maximilian Hotel, which served military dignitaries.

By April of 1945 our city was being shelled by heavy artillery. Retreating soldiers were sleeping in doorways, everywhere, some wounded. It was obvious the German army was collapsing. Concentration camp Jews were brought to clean up from the shelling, and every day when the prisoners were coming, I looked in hope that I would see my father there.

April 27 a very, very unusual quiet came over the city. People started to come out of basements where they were hiding, and then trucks full of American soldiers were driving through the city. They were whistling at us girls and shouting "Hitler *kaput!*" and throwing cigarettes and candy.

The Americans looked like kids. They had soft-soled shoes, and when they walked, you couldn't hear them. It was not like the Germans, with the boots and the stomping. The Americans walked like civilians!

Until 1950 I was in medical school in Munich. In psychiatry class a patient came out with an anti-Semitic tirade, and hundreds of German students were applauding, whistling, yelling approval.

What happened in Germany could happen here, if things get very, very bad and some demagogue gets hold of the nation. It's always easy to create hatred, to convince someone that it's somebody else's fault. Hate-filled people can impose their philosophy on a lot of people that are maybe slightly sympathetic or neutral, but they're afraid of speaking up.

To be a survivor, first of all was this very strong will to make it, not to give in. And some planning, and to be quick with an excuse. And just circumstances and luck. It's such a random thing. There's a whole family, and after it's over, some people you considered very valuable, very worthwhile, very deserving, are gone, and I am here.

Our Polish friends' mother was in a concentration camp, for smuggling information, smuggling weapons, between underground groups. The older sister was in jail, about to be executed, when the war ended. To show my appreciation for the risk they took for us, I sent packages and medicine and brought them over here in 1979 to visit. They were honored at our synagogue, and I also contacted Yad Vashem to issue a certificate of gratitude for them as Righteous Gentiles. That ceremony was at the Israeli consulate in New York.

Sabina Schwartz Zimering "passed" as a Catholic and worked as a maid at the Hotel Maximilian in Regensburg, Germany, from 1943 to 1945.

After the war in Europe ended May 8, 1945, Sabina Zimering helped teenage concentration camp survivors search for surviving family members.

MARIA SPIEWAK
and
DANUTA TRYBUS
Piotrkow, Poland

Translated from the Polish by Sabina Zimering

I, Maria, was fourteen, and Danuta was sixteen.
Our job was to smuggle documents, weapons,
secret newspapers. All of us in the underground were given cyanide we hid on ourselves.
If we were tortured and in danger of giving
away names of other members, we could take
our own life.

*Sabina Zimering and Helena Bigos owe their lives to the false identity papers they
got from their Catholic friends. Against their father's wishes, Danuta, Maria, and
their mother joined the anti-Nazi Polish underground.*

The original Nazi plan was to exterminate first the Jews, and next, the
Poles. From very early in the Nazi occupation the Polish nation became
mobilized in the underground movement, an army fighting the Nazis for
our country. At one point, in our small town, 90 percent of the people
belonged.

Our father did not participate. He was a professor of biology, a very
well-educated man, but he just didn't have the courage. Not everybody
can be a hero.

We helped our friends with papers and gave them a little cross to wear
on their necks to really look like Polish girls, and little Catholic prayer
books. We wanted to make sure they were complete Poles!

We also helped them by delivering letters to their father. If Sabina and
Helena had written letters to a Jew, they would have been finished, so
they wrote to us. The father would wait behind the barbed wire fence
where he was working, and we would give him the letter and quickly go
away.

We wrote to our friends news about the uprising in the Warsaw Jewish
ghetto because we were very happy about it and knew they would be, too.
We took a risk because it was very suspicious that one Polish girl, in
Poland, is writing to another Polish girl, in Germany, about a Jewish
uprising!

We were most of the time traveling on trains, delivering weapons or
documents. There was continuous terror of being caught. Some were

shot on the spot, some tortured mercilessly. Danuta was caught by the Gestapo and put in jail in Czestochowa just before liberation, but our mother was arrested in July 1944.

They tortured people with very hard beatings, rubber clubs with lead on the ends. They pulled out nails, put people under water until they were practically suffocating, burned them, hung them up so they couldn't touch the ground, continuously asking, "Tell the truth! Tell the truth!" Then our mother was in the concentration camp. She went through typhus, dysentery, got tuberculosis.

As the camps were liberated, the Swedish Red Cross was picking out really weak people and bringing them to their country for restoration. Our mother was in hospital in Malmo. They tried to bring her back to health, but she spent the rest of her life, eleven years, in bed.

When Sabina and Helena came back to Piotrkow from Germany in September of '45, we returned their very old, very beautiful, family Shabbat candleholders they left with us. Family pictures, clothes, we saved and gave back, too.

When we were honored at Adath Jeshurun synagogue, the rabbi said we were heroines. To us it was not a heroic doing. It was a normal thing to do for a friend in trouble.

We have an organization in Poland of all the people like us who were given medals and acknowledgment by Yad Vashem for helping Jews. It's called the Organization for the Righteous among Nations, and their names are shown in the Jewish Historical Institute in Warsaw. There are today 1,600 Poles that belong to that organization, and more than 6,000 Righteous Gentiles in Europe altogether.

PART 3

The Liberators

The term *liberator* is most often applied to the American soldiers who were the first to arrive at the barbed-wire enclosures surrounding Ohrdruf, Buchenwald, Dachau, Mauthausen, and other concentration camps.

It was springtime, April and May of 1945, and World War II was coming to an end. American soldiers had read about German atrocities in their newspaper, *Stars and Stripes*. But nothing they read had prepared them for the immense and intensely human dimension of what they found—the smells, the emaciated bodies stacked like firewood, and the survivors, many of whom looked like walking skeletons. One liberator said, "Only their eyes were human size."

To be a liberator, to see and talk to the victims, was an unforgettable experience, even for young soldiers who had spent many months in battle and had seen their close friends wounded or dying. Even today, more than forty years later, many of them begin to cry as they talk about the things they saw. They still stare silently, in disbelief, at photographs they took themselves. And many of them, like many survivors, do not want to be interviewed, because they find they still cannot talk about what they experienced in those few hours or days in 1945, when they discovered what so many Germans—people just like themselves—had done to other human beings.

Here are the stories of a doctor, a nurse, a surgical technician, a Special Services entertainer, a Nazi-hunting member of the Counter-Intelligence Corps, and nine American soldiers. They, too, are witnesses to the Holocaust.

RICHARD DARR
witness to Ohrdruf and Buchenwald

It was a total shock, to see people that had been
treated like this. I don't think there are any
words that can truly express the impression it
made on me. I—I can't. It's just impossible.

*Richard Darr was drafted in September 1942. As a squad leader in the 260th
Infantry Regiment, he saw active combat in Holland, Luxemburg, Germany,
and Austria. After the war he worked in Germany for the American occupation
forces.*

Our unit began in combat during the assault on Metz, and we continued east, engaging in spasmodic contact with the enemy. The war was
beginning to draw to an end, and German prisoners were coming in in
droves.

When we arrived at Ohrdruf labor camp, and then Buchenwald, the
guards had left. The prisoners there knew we were defeating the Germans, that we were coming, and they were hanging on the barbed wire
fences to greet us.

These camps were an unbelievable, shocking sight. The living looked
like cadavers, and in the open burial pit dead people were stacked,
literally stacked, like cordwood.

The buildings were one-story wooden structures, narrow but quite
long. Inside, bunks were five or maybe six high, no headroom, so people
in them couldn't sit up. The people crammed in there were too weak,
physically incapable of getting out, of standing up and greeting us. Some
could just hold out their hands.

We spent the night sleeping on the ground outside the barbed wire.
We were told not to mingle in the camp because of the danger of getting
typhus, but some of us went in. Some prisoners could speak fairly good
English, and I'd had two years of German in college.

We gave them everything we had, too much. We had K-rations in
boxes about the size of a Crackerjack box. Supper would be powdered
drink mix, a can of deviled ham, crackers, maybe a chocolate bar and five
cigarettes. Breakfast was canned eggs and powdered coffee, powdered
milk. But if one got chocolate bars from twenty troopers and had been
virtually starved for months—well, a person would have to reenter the
world of eating in a rather evolutionary way.

I returned to Germany in '48. I was on the three-man economic advi-
sory staff to General Clay, and then I was military governor in Baden-

Wurtemberg. We wore a sport coat or a business suit to the office. That was part of the de-Nazification program, wearing civilian clothes to re-educate the German populace to democracy.

There was a small Jewish D.P. camp in my area, and one day German policemen arrested a resident of the camp for selling black market meat. There was plenty of proof that Jews wouldn't have gotten a fair trial in a German court, so I asked the German policemen, "Do they raise cattle in the D.P. camp?" Obviously they didn't raise cattle. Then I told them, "Well, you will have to bring me the German farmer that sold the black market meat to the D.P. camp inmate." With that, the German police dropped the case!

DONALD DEAN
witness to Mauthausen

I still have some file sheets I took from the camp office. Typed lists, one line for each pris-oner. Nationality, last name, first name, date of birth, date of death, and the running total of how many people had died to that moment. The last number on the sheets was 21,388. And somebody was typing on those lists every day, keeping track.

Donald Dean graduated high school in 1929, the beginning of the depression. He enlisted in the army in 1942.

I was a warrant officer in ordnance. We repaired tanks that were shot up, other vehicles, field artillery, controlled all the repair parts—engines, axles, transmissions. We had forty trucks loaded with parts that moved into combat with the troops.

At Linz, Austria, word came that there was a concentration camp about fifteen miles south, so another fellow and I drove down there. As we got closer to Mauthausen there were inmates who had been liberated the day before. Most were so exhausted by the time they got across the road, they lay down to rest!

One little guy had gotten a machine gun, and he was having the biggest time. They'd find these S.S. troopers that worked in the camp, and they'd kill them right then and there. One fellow who had worked where they hung prisoners and shot 'em, he was lying there with a rake through his skull.

The commanding officer of the unit occupying the camp put out a proclamation, that civilians in the towns of Mauthausen and Diessen would dispose of the bodies. The Germans came in vests and fedora hats to help bury these people. There was a big ditch, a mass grave, and they'd pick the bodies up unceremoniously by the arms and legs, lay 'em on a wheelbarrow, push 'em over and lie 'em down in the graves. The stench was terrible.

We saw a big door that looked like a walk-in cooler. You opened that up and there was a room, I'd say twenty by twenty feet. In the ceiling were shower heads which actually were gas heads. The floor level was about three foot down below the level we were at, and this room was completely full of bodies, full three feet deep.

They'd kill them—the gas would put 'em away pretty fast, although some said the screaming and hollering was terrible—and then they'd put 'em into the ovens. The ovens were still warm, full of ashes.

Inside one building I saw the most gruesome thing. They'd taken bunk beds, three high, and pushed them all together so they actually were shelves. It was dark in there and it was wet, just dripping wet, and inside were people that had been so mistreated they were crawling around, just insane, and in such misery, like a bunch of animals.

This fellow who showed us around talked pretty good English, and he told us how they caught him eating a raw potato he'd stolen out of the kitchen. They stood him up on a footstool, put a rope through an eyebolt up in the ceiling. Then they tied his hands behind him, fastened the rope to his hands, and kicked the stool out from under him. So there he hung, in pain, until they finally cut him down.

The odor from the camp, it was in our hair, our clothes. We bathed and we bathed and we still had the odor. We finally burned our clothes! Somehow it was like the odor of a Turkish cigarette, and even today if I get a whiff of one of those things I think about that camp, the smell of things that were rotting.

I show my pictures to people, and they are amazed at how anybody could do such things. I have two boys, and they know about it, but my wife won't look at the pictures. She says they're too horrible. All you can do is hope it'll never happen again.

Survivors of Mauthausen, liberated in June 1945. *Photo by Donald Dean*

WAYNE D. HANSON
liberator of Dachau

> When I think of Dachau the thing that comes to
> my mind first of all is the trainload of bodies,
> fifty-two cars of human beings, all dead. You
> couldn't believe what we were seeing. And the
> smell is something you never forget.

Wayne Hanson enlisted in the army right after high school graduation and went overseas as staff sergeant in a machine gun platoon. In the Battle of the Bulge, 85 percent of the men in his platoon were wounded or killed.

Our division landed at Marseille December 9, 1944, and went up to the front on Christmas Eve. Early in the morning, when you couldn't see anything yet, you could hear the German patrols talking, looking for us, and the clinking chains on their half-tracks.

On the 29th of April, we entered Dachau, the first platoon to arrive. There were about ten guards still there. Some had put on prison garb to get away, but the prisoners were real happy to "accommodate" them. Some we captured, and they were real arrogant. It was like we were doing something wrong, interfering in this camp! It didn't appear to them like they had any kind of guilt.

This trainload of boxcars was sitting on the tracks going into Dachau. These were Jews, a Star of David on the boxcars. Some had been shot and were hanging out the openings, and the floor of each boxcar was covered with bodies piled on top of each other. The European boxcar is smaller than ours, so fifty people in there would be very crowded, just stuffed in. And on this entire train, this line of fifty-two boxcars, I saw one survivor.

We saw barracks like long warehouses. In one building, they laid them in rows waiting for the crematorium. We saw the ovens, which were warm yet.

There were some survivors in the compound, 250 or 300, nothing but skin and bones. Some of them could only crawl, and you wondered how a person like that could move, could make his body go.

We had one Polish fellow in our group who talked with some Poles in there, and he had a nervous breakdown afterwards.

The German people we had come in contact with were people exactly like us. But seeing Dachau, I lost a lot of trust in people. Those camp guards, I don't know how a man can become so calloused, have absolutely no compassion.

ARTHUR L. JOHNSON
witness to Buchenwald

Buchenwald was almost unspeakable. Seeing
those prisoners' faces—if there was any reason
for a "just" war, this was it!

*Arthur L. Johnson graduated college in June 1941, was drafted in October, and
landed in Normandy on D-Day plus 12. His company handled 200,000 tons of
ammunition in some of the heaviest fighting of the European war.*

Our company was backing up the First Army during the Battle of the
Bulge. We got shot up and our ammunition dump got blown up and we
had casualties, but we came out relatively lucky.

Buchenwald was a shocker. Here were the Germans, civilized people,
and the reports in *Stars and Stripes* were almost unspeakable. People
dying like flies and piled like cordwood because the Germans ran out of
fuel to run the furnace to incinerate the bodies.

General Eisenhower wanted the world to see this, so reporters and
civilians came from Washington and other places, and it was open for us
to see, too.

Many prisoners were still there. They were too weak to go, and there
was no place to go before the war finished. There were gaunt faces and
sunken eye sockets, people who were emaciated, but there was a smile on
their faces. Now they had hope.

Many were still wearing their striped prison uniforms, others had
picked up parts of American uniforms. Some who spoke English told me
about the filth and stench, and one little spigot for a water fountain for a
thousand men. One bathroom, dysentery rampant, no food. Many
crawled under dead bodies to keep warm, six or eight of them in one
little cubicle. Sitting and talking to them, we felt almost numb.

Then we saw the crematorium. Maybe 150 feet square, a wall around it
five or six feet high, brick. When I got there the bodies were gone, but
the stench of dead human flesh was still permeating the area.

A guy took us through and described what they did. They took the
dead bodies and the people who were dying or too weak to work, and
dumped them all down a hole. People down in the hole would put them
up on hooks in the wall, just like sides of beef, hang the bodies up on
these hooks until they were ready to burn them. I still remember going
through that L-shaped building with the hooks on the wall like meat
hooks. They had room for maybe forty or fifty bodies in this area, nice

and efficient. They had whitewashed the walls after liberation, but you could still see on the walls the human bloodstains from the shoulder blades, buttocks, and heels, from people's bodies dripping blood!

Then they showed us the elevators that would take them efficiently from the basement area up to the incinerator level. And then they'd take the ashes out of the ovens and maybe send a letter to the family that so-and-so had died, and for a small fee we'll ship them in this urn to you. The urns were still there, where they put the ashes and sold them to the families. It was a modest money-maker! The image of those furnaces, that building, still haunts me.

I remember touring the commandant's house, where his wife, the "bitch of Buchenwald," Ilse Koch, got some strange, morbid satisfaction making lamp shades out of human skin because they had interesting tattoos on them. I saw it with my own eyes! And at the same time there were records in the room—Beethoven, Brahms, Wagner.

It still puzzles me that here was Buchenwald, just ten or fifteen miles from Weimar, and all these people in Weimar just didn't know anything about what was going on. The paradox of Germany, with its cultural achievements, its Nobel prize winners, playing Beethoven or Mozart while this kind of barbarity was going on. I've pondered on it many times since, how people could have compartmentalized their lives, how thin that veneer of civilization is, how quickly even we could slip into that type of horror!

Some people are saying the Holocaust is a hoax, invented by Jews. But the prisoners at Buchenwald were not all Jews. There were political prisoners, Polish Catholics, prisoners of war. And I was there. I saw Buchenwald with my own eyes.

WILLIAM KAMMAN
witness to Dachau

Germany was in a depression, and people had
their own problems, and chose to ignore what
was happening. I have a very difficult time with
Germans even now, but the scarey thing is that
people are pretty much the same wherever you go.

*Drafted in 1943, at age nineteen, Bill Kamman went into Germany as a recon-
naissance man with the 101st Airborne. He stood outside the fence at Dachau but
could not make himself go inside.*

In December 1944 we landed at LeHavre and joined the 101st Airborne
just as they were breaking out of the Bulge. Across the Rhine and into
Germany, most of the time we were on scouting missions ahead of everybody else, riding in jeeps and armored cars.

The war was starting to wind down and there was a lot of confusion,
people wandering the countryside, German soldiers, civilians, a lot of
people coming out of the camps.

We were also hunting for S.S. men, supervisors, the upper echelon.
We knew they had escaped into the forest. We had captured lots of
weapons, pistols and small arms, and I remember giving them to prisoners and saying, "Here, you go find them." They would go into the forest
and pretty soon we'd hear shots.

I chose not to go into Dachau, but these people in their blue and
white striped clothes were Jews, so I stood outside and watched. The
most amazing thing to me was that some of those people were still able
to walk because they looked like they were dead. They were the thin-
nest, most emaciated people I've ever seen. But still they were walking,
and they were surviving, and they were looking for food, in garbage
cans, everywhere.

There were units coming in behind us to take care of resettlement and
everything, so we left the area. The war ended, and in December of 1945
I was discharged.

We just wanted to be home, get on with our lives. We very seldom
talked about what went on in the war. I never talked about Dachau, but
for a lot of years I had bad dreams, nightmares. It's amazing how it still
pops back in your head every once in a while.

I've always felt very Jewish. Not observant, but I grew up in a Jewish
neighborhood, and the high school I went to, half the kids were Jewish. I

played all the sports, and we ran into quite a bit of anti-Jewish feeling at other schools, and you defended yourself. We were tough kids.

I've always felt that Jews are very unique people, not good or bad, but they survived. And if something happens to someone that's Jewish, you react. That doesn't mean we love each other or sometimes even like each other, but we know what's happened to the Jews historically, the Holocaust.

There's plenty of anti-Semitism out there now, only more subtle. Hopefully the world is more civilized, but I don't really think it is. There are too many areas of the world where life is cheap, where they kill people like crazy.

WILLIAM LANDGREN
witness to Dachau

I'm used to seeing dead soldiers from battle, but
you see a little girl's head sticking out, with the rest of
the bodies around it, and then it hits you, how they
must have suffered, how ugly it was to just starve to death.

Drafted at age twenty-five, Bill Landgren went overseas in 1943. He was assigned to the 45th Division just before the amphibious landing at Anzio. The 45th was in combat for 511 days in Italy, France, and Germany.

I graduated in agronomy at Iowa State and took ROTC for two years, field artillery. When I was drafted I thought, "It's a cinch I'll get into field artillery." Then the sergeant says, "You're in the infantry now, brother." I was a "ninety-day wonder"—graduated Officers' Candidate School as a second lieutenant in ninety days. I was commander of a machine gun platoon.

Going into Munich, I followed the train track into Dachau, behind our riflemen. I'd picked up an old camera and fifteen or twenty rolls of film, so I got a lot of pictures. There they are, a cluster of German guards and their dogs, dead, and more than forty coal cars and enclosed boxcars, full of dead. Outside the crematorium was a huge pile of bodies, twice the size of my living room, and you can see how thin they were, just skeletons, and they'd started to deteriorate.

The town of Dachau was about two or three miles away, and of course those people claimed they didn't know what was going on. So the Americans brought them out, made them bring their wagons and their horses. They made them parade through town with the bodies, and then bury them in a mass grave outside of town. There's a picture of the guy using ice tongs to pick up those bodies because they were so badly decomposed.

I sent the film to my mother and father. They didn't know what was on them, and they took them down to the photographer and told him to develop them. When the photographer saw what they were, he made a display in his window. My mother wouldn't even look at them.

I knew the photo album was up in the attic, and then I got to thinking about it, and then seven or eight years ago I got it down. I'd show it to people, our friends around here, but I never showed the pictures to my kids.

My wife and I took a trip to Germany, and we had a German woman taking us on a tour of Munich. I said, "I'd like to go to Dachau, where the concentration camp was. I was there during the war." "Nothing's there," she says, "you're wasting your time. It's all gone." Back home, my son's wife's sister says, "What do you mean there's nothing there? They've got the barracks, there's a museum, here are the pictures."

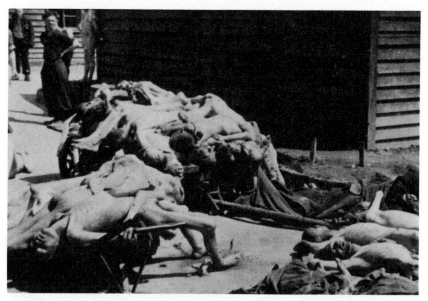

American soldiers who liberated Mauthausen found bodies piled high. The Germans had not had time to burn them, or to bury them in mass graves. *Photo by Donald Dean*

American soldiers ordered German civilians to load starved, skeletal bodies of Dachau victims onto wagons and drive them through nearby towns, May 1945. *Photo by William Landgren*

Former prisoners and camp guards continued to take bodies to the crematorium after Dachau was liberated by the American army in 1945. *Photo by William Landgren*

ROBERT ELIOT MATTESON
witness to Mauthausen

I'll never forget going to Germany in 1937 and
seeing how the trains were running on time, and
all that. It impressed me, that Hitler was really
putting the country back on its feet. Then a Czech
fellow told me about the Nazis and the "real Germany."

*Robert Matteson taught political science at Carleton College before enlisting in the
army in 1943. He was awarded the Silver Star for capturing Germany's number
2 Nazi, Ernst Kaltenbrunner.*

The war was on, but I was deferred because I had a wife and child, so I
found a job in the State Department. I spent about seven months sitting
behind a desk, then asked my draft board to induct me.

I went to England as a private in the 80th Infantry division. After
Normandy we started racing across France and then went toward Austria. By this time I had a battlefield commission and was in charge of the
319th regiment counterintelligence corps.

About the end of April 1945 we started to clean up the Nazis that were
left behind. We had a list of people you could contact when you got to a
village or city. In Bad Ischl our local man had information that General
Ernst Kaltenbrunner was in Strobl, about fourteen kilometers west.

Like Hitler, Kaltenbrunner was born in Austria, and in 1930 he became a member of the Nazi party. He impressed the Nazis by the ruth-
lessness with which he carried out the security service function, so after
the assassination of Reinhard Heydrich in 1942, Kaltenbrunner became
head of the Gestapo—secret police, criminal police, and intelligence, all
combined in one. His signature had to appear on all orders that con-
signed people to concentration camps, and he did his job with great
thoroughness.

In Strobl the Nazi *burgomeister* was so frightened, he was trembling! I
asked him where Kaltenbrunner was, and he said, "He's in a villa outside
of town." Then I found out that Kaltenbrunner had gone up in the
mountains, to a cabin on top. Hitler wanted to come there, and they were
going to have a Wagnerian last stand, with rockets shooting down and
the whole place going up in flames.

The local leader of the resistance got four Austrians from the village who knew the mountains and knew everybody. An American
officer, who'd been sent to take charge of stolen art treasures the

Nazis had hidden nearby, decided to send a squad of soldiers with me, to provide fire support in case we needed it. The plan was for me to act like a passer-by. The four Austrians, with their rifles with telescopic sights, would form a ring about 250 yards down the slope, behind some large rocks. The American soldiers would stay 300 or 400 yards behind.

We met at midnight. About six in the morning we got to where we could see the hut. There was no smoke coming out of the chimney, and all the shutters were shut, so it looked like it might be a dead lead. As I walked toward the cabin, I could hear a whistle. I thought it was a signal, but it was just a bird. I felt about as lonely as the bird did! I knocked on the door, and there wasn't any response, but I could hear heavy breathing coming through the shutters to the left of the door, so I knocked on the shutters, and somebody opened them.

I knew Kaltenbrunner was six feet three, weighed 220 pounds, was forty-three years old, and had dueling scars on both sides of his face. This guy didn't fit that description.

I said to him in very American-sounding German, could I come in, the transportation had been knocked out. He looked over my shoulder, and I looked around, and these four Austrians with rifles had come out from behind the rocks! He turned and walked across the room and took a revolver from some trousers hanging beside the bed. I got off the porch, and he slammed the shutters shut.

The Austrians gave a signal to the American squad, and they came up and joined in a semicircle around the cabin. There was a rock in back, so there wasn't any way out of the rear. We waited ten minutes, and then we went up on the porch and started knocking down the door.

Four men came out with hands over their heads. One was dressed in a doctor's uniform, but he had the dueling scars, and he was six feet three, and there was no mistaking who he was. In the stove I found Gestapo badge number 2 and Kripo badge number 2. I also found the last message Kaltenbrunner had radioed back to Hitler, saying he was ordering Stuka dive bombers to wipe the concentration camps off the face of the earth, so the Allies would find no evidence of what we all knew they'd done.

We interrogated Kaltenbrunner, and then he was sent to London, where he continued to say his main area of responsibility was intelligence, not the concentration camps and the exterminations. In September 1945 he was taken to Nuremberg for the major Nazi war crimes trial. He was convicted and hanged at Nuremberg, October 15, 1946.

I stayed in this little town in the Alps another month and arrested 150 people, an amazing collection of puppet governors and Nazis from eastern Europe, Germany, and Austria. It was like fishing a well-stocked trout farm!

Toward the end, going from Gemunden to Bad Ischl, we found out from the resistance that there was a camp, Ebensee, that was part of the Mauthausen system. It was surrounded by barbed wire and guard towers, but the guards had all left, so we broke the lock and went in.

The inmates took me first to the hospital. There were huddled bodies lying there on shelves with just rags over them, people crawling with lice. They put out their hands for food, but we didn't have any.

Then they took me to the crematorium and a room piled high with bodies, stacked in there because they couldn't burn them fast enough. And out behind the crematorium was a chemical ditch in which they'd throw bodies to decompose.

I came out and reported it, and they sent military government people with supplies for them.

The more I learned, the more abhorrent it became. Then in 1956 I went back to Austria and I had tea with Prince Hohenlohe, one of the people I'd arrested. He'd hidden Eichmann, and he was knowledgeable about art treasures the Nazis had stolen. Then I was on Austrian television with a Nazi intelligence agent I'd arrested, Dr. Wilhelm Hottl.

The war was fast action, but it's like a slow movie when you relive it.

DR. WILLIAM McCONAHEY
medical officer at Flossenburg

> I don't think I can understand what it was like
> to be there without having really been there.
> The hopelessness of it. No way out. Only torture,
> only misery, only starvation, and finally death.

As a surgeon with the 337th Infantry, Dr. William McConahey was in charge of a front-line first aid station.

We were on the "first team," which meant we went in at Utah Beach on D-Day plus 2. I marched my men inland to rendezvous with paratroopers who had jumped ahead of us, and we dug foxholes for our first night on shore. The next day we got our jeeps in, with our medical equipment.

I was as far forward as medical officers got, about a mile behind the front lines, or less. We had the Red Cross front, back, on our helmets, both arms, and on our jeeps. The German army respected the red crosses—usually.

I had about fifteen surgical and medical technicians and a couple of jeep drivers. Our job was to get the wounded out of the front lines, splint bones, stop bleeding, dress wounds, stop shock, stop pain, and get them back where they could get surgery, suturing, more care. I'd have to use lights at night, so I'd set up in a house or barn or in an orchard. We would be in a position maybe two or three days, maybe two or three hours. We could close up and hop in a jeep and be gone in ten minutes!

As we moved into Germany we started hearing about the concentration camps at army briefings. April 23 our division liberated Flossenburg, and I went in there next day.

Flossenburg held 15,000 prisoners but there were only about 1,500 left. The German guards had marched out about 13,000 toward Dachau, to get away from our advancing army. It was a very poignant, sad-looking road because they were marched out carrying blankets or maybe a jacket, but they were too weak to carry things, and they'd dropped them along the way.

A few very emaciated prisoners were wandering around in blue and white striped prison garb. My jeep driver spoke German, so he had conversations with many of the prisoners. They were from all over Europe—Poles, Russians, Czechs, French, Belgian, Spanish. They had a lot of Jewish people there, of course, but many were political prisoners, from the underground, or just people picked up by the Gestapo because they thought they were anti-Hitler. They all bore the scars of beatings and being knocked around.

The camp was laid out in very neat barracks style, with two big barbed wire fences around it. Running through it was a little railroad with a little pushcart like you see in coal mines, pushed by hand, to haul bodies to the crematory.

Three inmates, pretty much zombies, were still burning bodies in the crematory because prisoners were still dying left and right, and for sanitation you had to do something! About sixteen corpses were lined up to be burned. They were just skin and bone, each one weighing about forty pounds, I'd guess, because you could pick them up with one hand. One fellow opened the furnace door, and there were a couple of bodies in there, sizzling away.

We saw the beautiful houses where the S.S. guards lived with their women. Then I walked into the barracks, very drab and cold, with three tiers of bunks on each side. It was nothing but boards—no mattresses, no straw, nothing. Each bunk was big enough for one, but they said three slept there every night.

I visited the "hospital" where they brought prisoners to die. They'd put them on the bare wooden floor with straw on it, and they'd lie there in their own excrement and vomitus, until they died.

Some prisoners, their spirits were broken, they were just shells and they'd lost the will to live. Some were so close to death you couldn't feed them because they hadn't eaten for so long their stomachs were atrophied, and if they got food in, they vomited and bloated and obstructed. We tried to get them back on small feedings very slowly, over a period of weeks, but we couldn't save them. We felt terrible. They were dying under our eyes, and there was nothing we could do.

After the war ended, we drove to Dachau one day. Dachau was much bigger than Flossenburg. Again, we toured the barracks and saw the crematories, six big ovens. Outside were thousands of jars stacked up, the charred bones and ashes of people who had been burned there. I was told they used these for fertilizing the gardens, and that sometimes they would send a political prisoner's family a box of bones, anybody's bones. We saw the whipping posts, the torture chambers. It was obviously degradation and terror and horror and suffering, just like Flossenburg, only on a bigger scale.

It was those concentration camps that made us realize what we were fighting for. We really felt this was a holy crusade to wipe out this diabolical regime. We have sadistic bums and misfits and psychopaths in this country who could do what the S.S. did in Germany, but Hitler gave them a rank, a uniform, a purpose and a mission, and encouraged them.

The infantry medical corps was not like "M.A.S.H." or the movies. Unless you're there, unless you're in combat, and fight the battle, and crawl on your belly under machine gun bullets, and dig a foxhole in the rain, and get shelled, you can't understand what it's like. We were with the infantry, having the same life as they were having, and the same death they were having, too.

The war marked me for life. I realized that making a lot of money or being a big shot, that wasn't as important as doing something worthwhile. To really be a person was what counted.

EDMUND MOTZKO
witness to Gardelegen

I saw this pile of bodies, still smoldering. And
sitting there on a cement ledge, charred black, a
father and son. They knew they were going to
die, so they just put their arms around each
other and that's the way they died. The son
must have been sixteen, maybe eighteen.

*Ed Motzko lives in Sauk Centre, Minnesota—"Main Street, U.S.A." He couldn't
find a good job after high school, so he joined the National Guard in June 1940.
He fought with the 102nd Division in Holland, Belgium, and Germany.*

We landed on Omaha Beach in September 1944. After the Battle of the
Bulge, they transferred us into this outfit of zootsuiters from Detroit. We
weren't too anxious about going into combat with them, but overnight
they turned from boys into a first-class fighting unit.

If you were captured, the officers told us, torture was one of the big
items, but you only give your name, rank, and serial number. We also
saw how the Germans killed our men. We found one of their "souvenirs"
alongside the road, where they took this American soldier and put this
German Luger in his mouth, killed him, and left the Luger sticking in his
mouth. They ambushed four of our trucks, and took the American
soldiers in these vehicles and shot 'em in the back.

We opened up this slave labor camp, and they just stood there and
looked at us, couldn't believe they were free. Later I was downtown, and
a lady come running across the street to me, a German, and says in
perfect English, "You can't let those people out of there, they'll kill us!" I
says, "That's tough. These people have suffered, and whatever they
need, you have to give it to them. It's their turn now."

After this we're moving up to Gardelegen in April of 1945, and it was
the D Battery of the 548th that run into this atrocity, on Friday the 13th.
Our commanding officer told us, "There's probably some of you people
that can't look at it. You have to see it to believe it, and then after you see
it, you still won't believe it!"

It was something I'll never forget, piles of bodies still smoldering and
you can imagine the stench. I was selected to guard the eight or ten
survivors because we figured the Nazis would try to get somebody in to
kill these witnesses.

One survivor was a Hungarian Jew who spoke English. He said him
and another fellow got away from the building before the fire. An S.S.

trooper's dog sniffed them out and the S.S. shot the other fellow, but this Hungarian laid there pretending to be dead, and then he hid until the Americans arrived.

He told me this group of 2,000 men had marched 600 miles in about twenty days, with meager food and water rations. Hanover was supposed to be their destination, but the city was taken by the Ninth Army, so the Germans marched the men into this building about twenty-five by forty feet, a big brick barn with a tile roof. It had a dirt floor with about a foot-and-a-half of straw on it. They saturated the straw with gasoline and closed the big doors.

The first attempt at setting it on fire, the prisoners squelched the fire with their human bodies by laying on it. Then the S.S. blew a hole in one end of the building with an anti-tank weapon and threw in phosphorus grenades, and with that the fire took off.

Some of the prisoners had tried so hard to dig under the dirt, they wore down flesh and bone up to the second joints of their fingers. Some were blown to pieces by the grenades. Phosphorus burns added to the horribleness. Wherever phosphorus got on human skin, it just turned green, and continued to burn into the skin until it ran out of oxygen, so there were some pretty horrible burns.

I saw those people charred black from that smoke and fire, and I can recall it as vividly now as then. Some were war prisoners, one American soldier and some Russians, but most had the Star of David on their clothes, their identification. Some seemed to be very young, fourteen and sixteen years old.

They'd buried 500 of these people before I got there, in a bulldozed ditch right back of the barn. They'd put in one tier, cover 'em with dirt, and then start another tier. The ditch was better than half full already.

To see what they can do to people in other countries is just unbelievable. The Nazis need no sympathy whatsoever. When it comes to Memorial Day, I think how fortunate I am, to be home when all the fellas that were killed in the war aren't here, so every Memorial Day I march in the parade. People don't appreciate it, this freedom we have here.

KAY BONNER NEE
witness to Buchenwald

I would rather not talk about Buchenwald, but
our children must know that this was real, it
happened. If they don't know, how can they be
instruments of peace? How can they help us to
see that it never happens again?

*In 1943 Kay Bonner went to England as an entertainer attached to Special
Services, assigned to the Fifth Corps of the First Army. Kay and her partner were
the first women to land in Normandy after D-Day.*

If you had the ability to sing, dance, do funny sayings, and play a
musical instrument, and could learn to drive a two-ton truck, you could
work with Special Services. Our assignment was to entertain where the
big stars couldn't go. They needed stages and equipment; we needed
nothing but our truck. It had a piano, a microphone, and a side that let
down to make a stage.

We performed while soldiers watched from their foxholes, and V-1
rockets buzzed overhead. When the buzzing stopped, it meant the rocket
was going to land, and you'd better head for cover—fast! At Eupen,
German parachutists were landing and we were being strafed, and finally we left in the dark, with tracer bullets the only light we had to see
by. Katie Cullen, the girl with me, was killed.

When we came to Buchenwald, most of the Germans had fled. Their
goal had been to eliminate all their prisoners and burn their remains, so
that when the Americans arrived there would be an empty camp. But
there was not enough time.

As I entered the camp, I was overcome with the horrible stench of still-
burning flesh and hair, decaying bodies, and unsanitary conditions. I
remember thinking they can take photographs, they can write about
Buchenwald, but it will be impossible to describe the terrible odor.

The greatest number of prisoners were Jews, but the camp also contained political prisoners of many nationalities. There was a Belgian
general whose friends brought his old uniform and put it on him. The
uniform just hung, because there was nothing left of him but skin and
bones, and he was not going to survive. But his friends were marching
him along, holding him up, and tears of happiness were streaming down
his face.

Inside the camp office the furnishings were lavish. It was here that the wife of the commander, known as the "bitch of Buchenwald," displayed her lamp shades made from the tattooed skin of prisoners.

Outside the office were contraptions on which they hung prisoners by first tying their hands behind their backs, and then attaching rope to the hands and pulling them backwards and upwards, to hang from the posts. A prisoner did not have to hang very long before the arms were detached from their sockets.

At the right as you entered the camp were the crematoriums. The ovens were still smoking, with half-burned bodies inside. Beside the ovens were the emaciated bodies of prisoners they had not had time to burn, naked men and women together, stacked as you would stack your fireplace wood.

I remember thinking, "No one will believe this, I must take pictures." But my hands, my whole body, were shaking so, that I jammed the shutter and dropped the camera.

These emaciated, skeletal figures were real people, human beings. They had all lived and breathed and talked and loved, as is the right of every human. To end in the ovens, stacked like cordwood on the ground or piled in a cart, seemed the most inhuman of ends to a human life.

Not far from the ovens was a cement torture chamber. The walls were three feet thick to muffle the screams. There was a drain in the cement floor so they could hose away the blood. On the walls were great meat hooks where they hung prisoners like chunks of beef until they died. The prisoner who was pointing out these instruments of torture told me that his wife and two sons had died on the hooks.

Further down from the torture chamber, to the left as you faced it, were the barracks. Wooden beds with no mattresses reached to the ceiling. And the last barracks contained people so ill, so emaciated, that they were more dead than alive. It was impossible even to tell whether these people were old or young. They were the living dead, so starved and mistreated they couldn't even remember where they came from.

Some were still conscious enough to know that liberation had come. And then this good American, out of ignorance, did the worst thing she could have. I gave them all the food I had, chocolate bars and cheese and K-rations, concentrated food, richer by far than regular food. When the medics came, they fed them a gruel made of dried potatoes and watered powdered milk, but I had no experience, no training in medicine, and it did not occur to me that the rich food would be impossible to digest for people who had been starved for so long.

Many of these living dead did die, and I have always feared that I contributed to their death by my foolish action. The medics tried to comfort me, but it still haunts me.

The next day we brought the townspeople out to Buchenwald, and showed them through the camp. "You did this," we told them. And the people answered, "No, not us, it was Hitler." "You allowed it to happen," we said, "you are responsible." They said, "No, no. We didn't even know the camp was here."

The prisoners said they had been taken into town to fix roads and repair buildings. They said villagers had taunted them and thrown stones. How could they not know the camp was there? I wondered that they could not at least smell it!

I looked into the eyes of death in these prisoners, and I wondered what their lives had been like before Buchenwald. I hugged and kissed them, and cried with them, and murmured to them in a language most did not understand. And I watched them die. One person's hand turned stiff as I held it.

I was in Buchenwald for about a week and a half, and then the army was moving on and I had to go with them. Later I used to see people from the camps, carrying little bags over their shoulders or pushing a two-wheeler cart they had found. And the thing you almost could not stand was, they don't know they're going back to a country that has been blown away, to homes that no longer exist, to family who have disappeared.

When you're growing up, your ambitions are to have a reasonable amount of money and a lot of fun. But this unbelievable experience changed my values, my attitude, my whole life. I had not been politically active or even aware before the war, but I became so afterwards. And whenever I feel that one person cannot do much, or that what I'm doing is not important or not having any effect, I remember the Germans saying, "No, we are not responsible," and our answer, "Yes, you are. You allowed it to happen."

Buchenwald was liberated in 1945. Survivors of the death camps and people like me were asked to be silent. "It is all past," people told us, "we want to forget all that." Then in 1982 I was asked to speak at a Holocaust memorial program, and it was all there. I could see the camp, smell it, go step by step through the whole thing. Buchenwald survivors in the audience came to me afterwards and said, "You told it just like it was."

DONALD NOST
liberator of Hemer, a prisoner-of-war camp

> That fat German burgher was furious. "The
> prisoner swine are eating my rabbits!" he
> said, and sure enough, those poor, starving
> skeletons from the camp were slaughtering
> those rabbits, and eating that raw rabbit meat.

*When the Japanese attacked Pearl Harbor, Don Nost enlisted. Until he went
overseas, he taught U.S. soldiers about chemical warfare, demonstrating the use of
toxic gases, smoke, and explosives.*

In January of '45 I was in the 23rd Armored Infantry battalion, racing
at breakneck speed into Germany, and about April 10 we came to this
town called Hemer. It was a meat-packing town, and the people looked
it!

The prison camp was in an open area near Hemer, big, gaunt, dark
buildings surrounded by layers of barbed wire, with steel posts set in
concrete. I remember looking down one perimeter and it just went on
and on, it seemed like blocks.

I was up there in front when our tanks smashed the gate and let out
the skeletons that could still walk. The guards, of course, had fled as
soon as they heard Allied troops were near, and we found their uniforms
all over because they tried to melt into the civilian population. We freed
23,000 Allied soldiers there—Russians, French, British, Poles, and a
dozen or so American air crews that had been shot down.

They were wearing drab, grey, raggedy clothes that just hung on
them. They didn't have any undershirts or anything, and it was cold in
Germany that April. This was a quiet extermination camp, without any
crematoriums, without any smokestacks, without any gas chambers.
They weren't going to waste knives or ropes or bullets. They had a
simple plan—just nice, quiet starvation.

Some of those people were so starved one of them broke into the first
aid knapsack and ate DDT. The poor guy, he thought it was a little can of
white flour, and he's dipping this into his mouth, and the first aid man is
shaking his head to signal no, and the man was probably thinking,
"Here's another cruel soldier."

When it began to get dark, little spots of fire sprang up all over the
hillside, where freed prisoners were taking little cans they'd find, soup
cans, and they'd put water in, and grass, and make grass soup.

We gave the prisoners everything we could. Then medics arrived and the quartermasters had come up with food they could use, not rabbits and DDT and grass soup, but something that was good for their poor bodies—milk and soft cereal.

My sister married a German in Chicago, who was a member of the Brown Shirts. The guys had a Nazi flag, and one night in '37 they were singing the "*Horst Wessel*" Nazi song. Dorothy got up and started to sing "Rule, Brittania" and they threw her out bodily, into the street. But all the time I was in Germany, I only met three Nazis. All the others would look you straight in the face and tell you they were not Nazis!

LEONARD PARKER
liberator of Dachau

Many times when I was lying in a foxhole, or
sweating out an artillery barrage, or lying in the
rain pinned down by enemy fire, I asked myself, "Why am I here?" After what I saw at Dachau, I had the answer.

Leonard Parker enlisted in the army at age nineteen. He and his squad were scouting ahead of their unit when they came to a small town named Dachau. Parker knew Yiddish, so he could talk with Dachau prisoners about their experiences.

I enlisted in the army for no good reason, except I thought it would be an adventure. I was fourteen months in combat, ending up a tech sergeant in charge of a platoon. My platoon was out in front when we came upon this little town not far from Munich. The sign said "Dachau."

As we were approaching the town, there was a terrible odor. German civilians were looting the stores, and no one seemed to be paying attention that we were coming through. There was no evidence of German soldiers or anything.

What the odor was, was a railroad siding where there were flat cars just loaded with bodies. There were young children and women and men, machine-gunned to death by the S.S. because they couldn't be taken along by the retreating Nazis. Those bodies had been laying out there in the sun for three days, and the stink was terrific.

When we got to the far side of town we saw stone walls, with piers and barbed wire and metal fencing. You could see buildings through the wire. We stopped because we didn't know what to expect, and the commanding officer sent me, with one squad of my people, to see what was going on.

As we approached the camp, out of the gate came three prisoners dressed in blue and white striped prisoner clothes with prisoner caps, so thin they looked like sticks, very timidly coming toward us. Then the first one yelled at me in English, "Boy, are we glad to see you!" He was a U.S. Army captain, who had parachuted into France on a secret mission and been captured!

Then a flood of human skeletons came out of the gates. The seven of us were just surrounded by these prisoners, with their terrible odors, and they grabbed our hands and kissed them, many of them crying in Yiddish, "Thank God you've come to set us free!" These were women, children, and men, too, crying with joy, half mad with happiness. Many of us had eyes overflowing with tears, too.

When I started answering them in Yiddish, they just went crazy, and then I start to sing for them, "My Yiddische Mama," and they're all crying, and I'm crying. They couldn't believe there were Jewish soldiers in the American army, and when I told them I was an *unter-offizier* one asked if I would write my Jewish name for him on a piece of paper. Soon I was scribbling it for them all, on dirty scraps of paper that appeared in their hands like magic, as a souvenir from the American Jewish soldier.

We spent about an hour talking to them, listening to countless stories about the cruelty of the Nazis. I reported what was going on to our battalion commander, and we guarded the camp for three hours, until the American military government moved in to take over.

Dachau was a permanent installation like one of our military camps here. The buildings were solidly built, brick and stone, with guard houses all around, a mess hall, paved streets. Evidently they got overcrowded because they built like a billet, before the main camp, surrounded by two layers of fence and barbed wire, and as they had to expand more and more, it began to look more and more temporary.

We went through where they gassed people, and we saw and smelled the furnace room, giant ovens with pieces of bones and ash still in them. We went through barracks full of people who were too sick and too weak to get up. They were just lying there dying, in incredible filth.

We took no German prisoners that day. All that we captured, maybe 50 S.S., we killed.

I had my squad in a house in the city of Dachau, and the lady who owned the house, we asked, "Didn't you know this was going on?" "Oh, no." Of course, we didn't know whether they approved, or whether they felt helpless to do something about it or didn't want to do anything about it. But the insistence that they didn't know what was going on, that was a lie. I still cannot understand how the German people persuaded themselves that what they were doing was somehow right or useful, or how they could do something like that, and still live with themselves.

GLENN STRANBERG
medical corpsman at Dachau

Wherever there's war, there's hell. Dachau is
hard to believe, but it still bothers me that I
came home, and I was trying to talk to people
about it, and they didn't believe it.

Glenn Stranberg lives on the farm where he was born. He spent three years as an army medic during World War II, including an entire month at Dachau, where he cared for survivors after the camp was liberated.

I was drafted July of 1942. Being a farm boy and a hunter and a trapper, I figured I'd be an infantryman, but the army put me in the medics. I trained as a surgical technician so I could work in the operating room as a scrub nurse or a surgical technician. We had a team, a doctor, a nurse, and a technician, together twelve hours a day, seven days a week.

We were an evacuation hospital, what's now called a "M.A.S.H." unit, the first unit that took care of patients as they came off the line. We had seven operating tables, but sometimes you'd go to work and twelve hours later you'd come out and some of the people lying in the hall still hadn't gotten in, and sometimes their arms or legs would be too far gone when they came in because they'd waited too long. We were pretty callous by the time we got to Dachau.

We were just one day behind the troops. We walked in along the railroad track and saw the boxcars with the bodies in, and people laying dead along the track. Some were still alive, but they were unable to move any more. You'd just see them twitch, that was all.

We came through the gate, and there was that sign, "Work will make you free." Our military made people from the city of Dachau bring out wagons, load up bodies in the camp, and haul them out to a mass grave. Our job was to get the hospital unit set up right away. We tore the insides out of the S.S. barracks and set up in there. We were a 450-bed hospital unit, but in Dachau we had 1,500 patients.

Some of the prisoners started heading toward home with prison uniforms on—dirty, but so glad to go, they didn't care if they had anything on! Others were too weak. You could see their bones, the ribs sticking through. Some were teenagers, but if they'd been there any length of time they looked old.

First we gave the prisoners a bath and issued clothing, and blankets for the ones in the hospital. Then we fed them regular rations, potatoes and meat and vegetables, but their bodies couldn't tolerate real food. They got diarrhea, all 1,500 of them! After that we fed them cereals, dried foods. In the morning we'd take out the ones who'd died in the night, maybe ten or more at first, out of about sixty in each ward.

You tried to communicate by sign language that you were trying to help them because a lot of them, their minds were deranged from what they'd been through, and they still had the idea they were going to be killed. One young fellow, we got him all cleaned up, new pajamas on, got him into bed, and he jumped up and jumped out the window. Just like that, zip and out he went, killed himself.

Most were wearing the yellow star, but many were non-Jewish—Polish people, German people, even captured American soldiers.

I was at Dachau about a month. I visited the crematory ovens when they reenacted it for magazine photographers, showed how it was done. They handled the bodies with ice tongs. One would take hold by the head and one by the feet, put them onto the slab and slide them into the oven.

When you first came home, it has hard for people to believe. My brother-in-law, whose dad came from Germany, of course they didn't believe this. But I'd bring the pictures out, that's why they're worn, and I didn't give up. Ten years ago our son Kevin went to Poland and he rode in a bus where the driver spoke some English. Kevin told him about me, and he told Kevin he'd been in Dachau, and said, "Thank your dad, and the American people."

DOROTHY WAHLSTROM
nurse at Dachau

I spoke with a Holocaust survivor in 1985,
about the pain and anguish we shared. It was the
first time I could talk about things that had been
graven on my mind for more than forty years.

*Dorothy Wahlstrom was a nurse, a captain with the 127th Evacuation Hospital,
when her unit entered Dachau on May 3, 1945.*

The dead and dying were all around us. Piles of naked dead were
stacked beside the crematorium and inside. Dachau was certainly a calcu-
lated attempt by the Nazis to desecrate not only the body, but also the
mind and spirit.

We set up ward units in the S.S. barracks. Dead dogs lay in the kennels
nearby, killed by our military after survivors told us they were used to
tear away parts of prisoners' bodies on command. Survivors told us
infants were torn limb from limb as their mothers watched. They told us
that prisoners who could no longer work were used as live targets for
machine gun practice. They mentioned other unspeakable atrocities—
medical experiments, torture chambers—horrors too terrible to think up
without having experienced them.

Each of the two hospital units at Dachau, the 127th and the 116th, was
equipped to care for 450 patients at one time, but each unit cared for
1,500 or more at peak times.

We felt we were dancing with death. We couldn't get away from it, and
wondered if it would ever stop. We couldn't care for everyone, and often
we could not admit a patient until another one died or was discharged
from the hospital. It was truly heartbreaking for our medical officers to
have to choose the people they thought might live and leave the sickest
ones to die. Of those we thought would live, seven or eight stretchers
were lined up in front of each ward in the morning—people who had
died during the night.

The severely malnourished did not tolerate increased rations too well,
and dysentery was out of control. We had double bunk beds for our
patients, and the diarrhea was so severe it leaked from bed to bed. Many
were so emaciated that even with the care we gave them, it was too late.

The diseases were those that go with filth and lack of sanitation. One
and one-half tons of DDT powder were used in dusting the camp to get

control of the infected lice that spread typhus. Perhaps 20 percent of the camp population had active tuberculosis.

I wish I could describe the smells and the silence of death. Even now, certain sights and sound can remind me of that pain, that suffering, that sorrow and loss and anguish and degradation.

I find comfort in the sacred Scriptures that record that the Lord will vindicate His Israel, and that there will always be a House of David. I am truly grateful to the Lord for having allowed me to serve His people.

AFTERWORD

The Power of the Witness

DEBORAH E. LIPSTADT

The past two decades have seen a proliferation of historical investigations, books, movies, and documentary studies of what has become known as the Holocaust. Few if any areas of this terrible tragedy have not been probed by historians, philosophers, theologians, and social scientists. Without doubt there are still grave lacunae in this body of research, but in a relatively short period of time a significant amount of material has been amassed. These works examine many different aspects of the Nazi destruction of the Jews including the complex role of the perpetrators, the experience of the victims, and the response of the Allies, the neutral nations, and agencies and religious bodies, notably the Vatican. The research draws on vast documentary archives, diaries, journals, newspapers, photographs, and even newsreels.

The most important and powerful historical source, yet one that is the most transitory, is that of the direct witness—the participants. Historians have long recognized the critical importance of the victims' personal accounts. Although documents and correspondence provide us with crucial information, the witnesses—and in this case, specifically the victims—speak with a particular moral force. They can speak in the first person: "This happened to *me.*"

At the same time that we acknowledge the importance of their testimony we also recognize that their accounts are not foolproof. They may be limited by the vagaries of memory as well as by the fact that each victim "only" witnessed a small portion of this vast enterprise we call the Holocaust. Some lived in countries where Nazi rule was in place for an extended period of time prior to the beginning of the war, such as Germany, Austria, and portions of Czechoslovakia. Others were taken by surprise, as was the case in France, Poland, and the Soviet Union. Some individuals lived in ghettoes, while others were taken directly to camps. The situation in certain ghettoes differed radically from that in others. Life, and ultimately the way in which life was taken, differed from camp

to camp. In certain instances survivors can only estimate dates, the dura-
tion of events, or the precise number of victims involved. Sometimes
their memoirs may be influenced by ex post facto accounts of others.
The ensuing years and the painful memories of their experiences have
further made the act of remembering a difficult one.

For these reasons historians do not build the historical record solely on
the recollections of the survivor. But despite these shortcomings of oral
history, the memories recounted in this volume and the hundreds of
other interviews now being collected worldwide together constitute the
"still, small" but most powerful voice that cries out in bitter testimony.
These survivors felt the consequences of a world that went mad. They
were there.

The voice of the witness has come to be important for yet another
reason. Although denial seems impossible to imagine, some individuals
attempt to deny that the Holocaust occurred. One is tempted to dismiss
them as the historical equivalent of the "flat earth" theorists, but their
claims have made some inroads. Certain anti-Semitic groups have enthu-
siastically embraced them. Others have used these claims for political
and racial purposes. This small but industrious lot ignores the incredible
number of facts that refute their "theory," including that the perpetrators did not deny their role. Echoing traditional anti-Semitic charges,
they argue that the Holocaust is a great hoax perpetrated by the Jews on
the entire world.

If only extreme anti-Semites accepted such ludicrous notions, there
would be little room for concern. But some people—particularly those
born after the Holocaust—seem willing to accept the validity of such
arguments. Students and young people in this country, many of whom
have a most hazy—at best—sense of history, are especially susceptible.
The psychiatrist Walter Reich has observed that many young people
seem willing to listen to these claims on the grounds that everything
should be open to debate and that they can accept nothing as true if they
do not personally see or experience it.

There are a variety of ways of responding to these specious claims,
which deny the mountains of recorded fact. One tempting strategy is
simply to ignore them. It is neither wise nor productive to enter into a
debate with these so-called revisionists. To do so would grant them the
validity they crave. Anyone subscribing to such outrageously false ideas
is not likely to be bound by truth, so there is little to be gained by trying
to engage him or her in normal intellectual interchanges. Moreover, for
those who would try to deny the existence of the Holocaust, publicity is a
lifeline. Without it they cannot make their voices heard, and their claims
may well die a quick and merciful death.

There are, however, better ways of responding to these malicious charges. One is to educate potential listeners, to make it clear that the evidence of the Holocaust is so overwhelming that those who attempt to deny its existence are not really interested in pursuing truth but have other goals in mind. Facts may not deter the deniers, but they will demonstrate to others—particularly those born after the Holocaust—that these are not disinterested individuals engaged in a benign historical quest.

The other means of responding is to give the witnesses voice. Let those who were not there hear from those who were, who saw their families perish, who watched the trains bring thousands of unsuspecting individuals into the camps, who watched their parents and children be assigned by a Mengele or others like him to the wrong line, never to emerge from the buildings where they were sent to supposedly shower. No one individual can tell the whole story, but together the voices of those who survived have an unparalleled impact.

These witnesses' voices will be available to us for only a few more decades. The youngest possible survivor of a concentration camp is now in his or her late forties. Survivors of the death camps are even older. Soon there will be no one who will be able to say "I was there. This is what was done to me." That is the importance of this collection of voices. They are not ponderous. They are profound in their simplicity. They only seek to tell their individual stories and to convey their recollections of what happened to them and to their families. Many refrains repeat themselves, but one is most chilling. Over and over again survivors say, "I am the only one of my family who survived, all my relatives—parents, siblings, spouses, children, aunts, uncles, and cousins—were consumed by the fires of the Holocaust."

Another refrain is heard among the victims' voices: "I kept quiet for many years, but soon I will be gone and now I must tell my children." It has taken the survivors a very long time to be able to tell their stories. Many were convinced that the world was not interested, that once again, as had been the case while the Holocaust was in the making, their agony would be met with disbelief. While their speaking is of great historical importance for generations to come, it is also an act that can provide some healing for them personally.

There is another set of voices in this collection: that of the liberators. Although the American army did not liberate the death camps in Poland, they witnessed the terrible brutality of camps such as Buchenwald, Bergen-Belsen, and Dachau. The recollections of those who came upon these places before they had been sanitized and the survivors removed are critical because they were witness to the atrocities of the Third Reich. But they have value for yet another reason. They indicate how little those outside the whirlwind understood or were able to imagine what it was like. One reporter who accompanied the American troops to the concentration camps wrote on the first night after he entered Buchen-wald: "I had heard stories such as these but I always attributed them to foreigners with some ax to grind." Others admitted that they had as-sumed the reports of atrocities were propaganda to arouse hostility to-ward the enemy. Only when they came face to face with the reality of the camps did they realize that these were not exaggerations, that this truth could never be exaggerated.

Why had the world resisted this truth? The Holocaust unfolded slowly. Had the German people or the rest of the world wished to stop it in its early stages, they might well have succeeded. It is clear that the Nazis had tested the world to see how far they could go without encoun-tering its wrath. In most instances the political and moral bodies of the world stood silently by. An important lesson is to be learned in the universal acquiescence to both the initial persecution and the ultimate horror. The one who stands silently by becomes a party to the crime. Standing mute in the face of evil is to cast one's vote on the side of the evil doer.

There is, however, an even more chilling lesson to be learned. The Germans did not conduct special tests in order to choose the most brutal and diabolical among them to participate in the annihilation of millions. The people who guarded the camps, ran the trains, delivered the sup-plies, gathered the Jews from their homes, and in a myriad of different ways made the Holocaust a reality were people who previously had led normal lives. An evil system and a diabolical leadership were able to elicit uncivilized behavior from a civilized people. The Holocaust was not committed by a cadre of sadistic beasts. Before the war—and in many cases after it—these people were doctors, lawyers, architects, teachers, clerks, farmers, and students. No apparent historical, social, cultural, or biological difference existed between these people and the rest of the world that would make such behavior predictable. This does not mean we are all capable of such atrocities. It does mean that it takes relatively little to turn "normal" humans into creatures capable of the most sadistic acts. This observation is not meant to suggest that it was simply the system that was at fault and the participants were guiltless. But until they crossed the dividing line between good and evil, they were relatively average, nondescript people.

Not all the perpetrators were beasts, not all the victims were heroes. Many victims felt simply lucky to have survived, but in order to have survived they needed a unique strength and fortitude. Nor were all the liberators heroes. Some were simply soldiers whose paths led them to witness one of the great horrors of our times. Here too their voices teach us how the mundane can be transformed into the unfathomable, the everyday into the unimaginable.

Ultimately, the fundamental lesson of this collection is that if we let history and memory fade we risk letting such events happen again. The recollections collected here help form our defense against the repetition of history. The Hasidic teacher, the Ba'al Shem Tov, taught long ago that "in remembrance is the secret of redemption." The victims are not alone in their need of redemption. A world that allowed such crimes to happen and that continues to tolerate incredible evil in its midst is in continuous need of redemption. If we pay careful attention to these voices, they may lead one step closer in that direction.

Deborah E. Lipstadt, Ph.D., is a fellow at the International Center for the Study of Antisemitism, Hebrew University, Jerusalem.

GLOSSARY

achsherah "Training farms" in Europe and the United States during 1930s for young city dwellers who planned to emigrate to Palestine.

affidavit Permit papers refugees needed to emigrate to the United States; had to be signed by a U.S. citizen who guaranteed that the refugee would not need public assistance.

aliyah To emigrate to Palestine or Israel; literally, "going up."

aliyah bet Hebrew name for illegal immigration of Jews to Palestine during the Hitler era.

armband Jews under Nazi rule were often required to wear a yellow or white armband with a six-pointed Star of David.

Aryan, Aryanized Linguistic term that symbolized the myth of German superiority; a Caucasian gentile, especially one of Nordic stock; non-Jewish, having no Jewish ancestors.

brichah Underground route of escape to Palestine after the war; British Mandate policy continued to deny permission to most would-be emigrants.

Bund, Bundists Yiddish-speaking Socialist group.

children's transport Evacuation of Jewish children during the 1930s, mostly from Germany, to England, the United States, Argentina, Brazil, and other countries; organized by HIAS and JDC.

concentration camp Organized in early 1930s for "preventive detention" of political opponents of Nazi regime. Later used for Jews, gypsies, prisoners of war, members of the resistance, and as source for forced labor and raw material for medical experiments by S.S. doctors.

Cossacks Peasant soldiers in Ukraine and other parts of Russian Empire, part of Czar's military forces; associated with attacks on Jews known as "pogroms."

D.P. (displaced persons) When World War II ended, there were an estimated thirty million displaced persons in Europe, only 3 percent of them Jews. D.P.s included slave laborers, political and other prisoners, and people who had been forcibly removed from their homes, who had fled, or whose homes or cities had been destroyed. The Allies set up D.P. camps in former military camps, apartment complexes, hotels, and so forth, to provide temporary housing, food, and other support services.

Eichmann, Adolph   Head of the Jewish Office of the Gestapo; planned and organized destruction of Europe's Jews.

einsatzkommandos   Special military units recruited by Hitler and Himmler to exterminate the Russian Jewish population and Communist leaders; killed an estimated two million Jews, usually forcing them to dig their own mass graves and then mowing them down with machine gun fire.

the Forward (*Jewish Daily Forward*)   American Yiddish-language newspaper with nationwide circulation, estabished in New York City in 1897; became a contact point for survivors and relatives after World War II.

German Socialists   Political organization that became the basis for the Nazi party.

Gestapo   Secret police organized by the Nazis.

ghetto   A compulsory place of residence for Jews, in a prescribed area of a city.

GPU   Russian secret police, organized after 1917 Revolution; in 1934 its functions were transferred to the NKVD, which is also responsible for forced labor camps.

gymnasium   European equivalent of American high school.

Haganah   Underground Jewish defense organization in Palestine, established to protect Jewish life and property against attack by Arabs; literally, "defense."

Hashomer Hatzair   Jewish Socialist organization for young people, similar to Boy Scouts or Girl Scouts.

hasidim, hasidic (also chasidim, chasidic)   A hasid is a member of a particularly pious community of Orthodox Jews; hasidic is the adjective, hasidim the plural.

HIAS   Hebrew Sheltering and Immigrant Aid Society, international organization established in the United States in 1884.

high holidays   Jewish New Year; includes Rosh Hashonah and Yom Kippur (Day of Atonement), a fast day.

Hilfsverein (Hilfsverein der deutschen Juden)   German Jewish Relief Association; German government-sponsored agency that helped Jews emigrate from Germany; disbanded in 1939.

Hitler Youth   Militaristic youth organization emphasizing hiking, camping, and sports, but also precision marching, war games, political indoctrination, discipline, ritual, and symbolism.

Iron Cross   German military decoration; many German Jews won the Iron Cross in battle during World War I.

Iron Guard   Romanian political party that attacked Jews.

JDC   See Joint Distribution Committee.

Jewish Agency   Established 1929 by the World Zionist Organization to represent the Jewish people in negotiations under terms of the British Mandate for

Palestine; coordinating agency for transportation and resettlement of Jews in Palestine.

Jewish Family and Children's Service (also JFCS, JFS)   Local community organizations in the United States that helped arriving refugees find housing, training, jobs, English lessons, and so on.

Jewish National Fund   International organization for buying land and planting trees in Israel; founded by Theodor Herzl about 1900.

"the Joint"   See Joint Distribution Committee.

Joint Distribution Committee   Founded 1914 to provide emergency aid for war victims in Europe.

Judenfrei   Without any Jews (German).

Judenrat   Jewish Council; originally elected by taxpaying members of a Jewish community, empowered by the government to make laws and administer affairs of the Jewish community. Under the Nazis, the *Judenrat* was forced to manage the ghetto.

kapo   Concentration camp inmate chosen to supervise other inmates; some kapos were Jews.

kehilla   Jewish community council; a governing body.

kibbutz   A cooperative colony in Israel where all members share the work and share equally in profits; originally farming communities.

kosher   Food prepared according to Jewish dietary laws. Animals and poultry are inspected to make sure they're healthy, then killed quickly and humanely. Pork and shellfish are forbidden. Meat and milk products cannot be served at the same meal.

Kripo   Shortened name for Nazi criminal police, merged with S.S. in 1938; German abbreviation for *Kriminalpolizei*.

Kristallnacht   November 9, 1938, "night of the broken glass." Anti-Jewish riots instigated by the Nazis in Germany and Austria; in one night, 20,000 Jews were arrested and sent to concentration camps, hundreds were killed, 101 synagogues were burned, and 7,500 Jewish-owned businesses were looted and destroyed.

labor camp   Prison camps where Jews, Poles, and other prisoners were forced to do factory work, road construction, and so forth.

liquidation   Systematic mass killing of all or most of the residents, or a selected group (such as all children under age ten or all people without jobs) in a city, town, or ghetto.

matzo   Unleavened, crackerlike bread eaten during the eight days of Passover.

Mein Kampf   Book written by Adolf Hitler, proclaiming his beliefs, which became the Nazi credo.

melamed   Hebrew word for teacher.

Mengele, Dr. Josef   S.S. captain at Auschwitz who used living Jews in sadistic medical experiments.

mezuzah   A tubular case of wood, glass, or metal three or four inches long, containing a Hebrew prayer; the mezuzah is nailed in a slanting position on the upper part of the right doorpost.

mussulmen   Persons who have lost the look of a human being; human skeletons whose minds are no longer functioning.

Mogen David   Six-pointed Star of David, symbol of the Jewish faith.

Nazi   Abbreviation for the German National Socialist Workers' Party.

NKVD   Soviet secret police. Also supervised forced labor camps in Soviet Union.

Orthodox   Observing all the ancient rules of Jewish ritual and religion.

Palestine   Historic region on the eastern shore of the Mediterranean, comprising parts of modern Israel, Jordan, and Egypt; also known as the Holy Land. During World War I the British gained control of Palestine and continued to govern it until 1948, under a mandate from the League of Nations.

Partisans   Underground resistance groups in southern and eastern Europe, mainly operating in forests of the Ukraine, Poland, and Lithuania, who fought the Nazis by sabotage and other methods.

Passover   Eight-day spring festival of freedom, celebrating the biblical exodus of the Jews from slavery in Egypt.

People of the Book   Jews are sometimes referred to in this way because the Jewish religion is based on the first five books of the Bible ("the book").

pogroms   Systematic massacres and murderous attacks on Jews; some of the worst took place in Russia in the nineteenth and early twentieth centuries, some in Polish cities after World War II.

quota   Restrictions enacted by the United States in 1921 and 1924 (the Johnson Act) limiting immigration, especially from Eastern Europe, to small percentages of those nationalities already resident in the United States. U.S. State department and consular officials used quotas and bureaucratic red tape to prevent Jews from immigrating to the United States during the 1930s; despite the flood of applicants, many quotas went unfilled.

Red Cross "brief"   During World War II the International Red Cross tried to transmit messages between people in Germany and Austria and their relatives who had escaped. Messages were limited, sometimes to only twenty-four words. *Brief* is German for "letter."

Resistance   Organized underground and guerilla opposition to the German occupiers.

Righteous Gentiles   Non-Jews who risked their lives to save Jews during the Nazi era despite potential penalty of death, often for the entire family.

Rosh Hashonah   Jewish New Year, in September or early October; literally "the beginning of the year."

S.A.   German organization begun secretly, to supplement the small regular army Germany was allowed under the Treaty of Versailles; abbreviation of *Sturm Abteilung,* or Storm Troopers.

Schindler, Oskar   Wealthy German industrialist who risked his life during the

Hitler era to save Jews who worked for him in his factory at Cracow-Plaschau and later in Germany.

selection   Process in which newly arrived groups of prisoners at labor or concentration camps were separated into two groups; strong, youthful people were saved for work or medical experiments, but most children, old people, pregnant women, and people who appeared sick, crippled, or weak were "selected" to be killed immediately.

shabbos   Yiddish name for Sabbath, the day of rest, from sundown Friday to sundown Saturday.

shochet   Man trained and authorized by the Jewish community to slaughter poultry and animals in accordance with dietary laws.

shofar   Ram's horn blown like a trumpet at religious services on Rosh Hashonah and Yom Kippur; in biblical times, a signal.

shtetl   Small town or village in Eastern Europe.

sidecurls   Earlocks, untrimmed sideburns, worn in ancient times and still worn by some Orthodox Jews.

S.S.   Black-shirted troops organized as Hitler's personal bodyguard, later assigned to organize and staff the concentration camps; literally *Schutz Staffeln*.

Star of David   Six-pointed star, also known as the Mogen David, symbol of King David (Old Testament); adopted by Zionists as the Jewish national symbol.

swastika   Ancient symbol used as a religious emblem to ward off evil spirits; Hitler employed it to denote Aryan racial superiority.

Third Reich   The First Reich was the Holy Roman Empire; the Second Reich included the German Empire (1871–1919) and the post–World War I Weimar Republic (1919–33); the Third Reich was the Nazi state under Adolf Hitler, 1933–45.

Torah   First five books of the Bible (Five Books of Moses, in the Old Testament), handwritten in Hebrew on a parchment scroll.

UNRRA   United Nations Relief and Rehabilitation Administration, organized November 1943 by forty-three nations to provide food, clothing, medical supplies, and other assistance to refugees and people awaiting repatriation.

V-E day   Victory in Europe day, May 8, 1945. Germany surrenders.

Volksdeutsch   People of German descent.

Wallenberg, Raoul (Ralph)   Swedish diplomat who saved many Hungarian Jews by arranging false passports and establishing "safe houses" in Budapest.

Wehrmacht   German army.

Weimar Republic   German democratic government, 1919–33.

Yad Vashem   Holocaust Memorial Museum in Jerusalem.

yellow star   Jews in Nazi-occupied countries were forced to wear an identifying armband with the six-pointed Star of David on it or to sew a yellow fabric star on their clothing; in some countries, the stars were blue on white.

Yiddish   Polyglot dialect spoken by Eastern European Jews, composed largely of German but including vocabulary from other countries Jews had lived in.

Yom Kippur Day of Atonement, a fast day. The most solemn holiday of the year.

Youth Aliyah Organization that brought children from Europe to Palestine and cared for them.

Zionism, Zionist Movement to make Palestine the Jewish homeland, dating in its modern political form from the First Zionist International Congress, convened by Theodor Herzl on August 28, 1897, in Basel, Switzerland.

zloty Polish monetary unit.

APPENDIX

A Guide for Teachers and Discussion Leaders

CAROL WIRTSCHAFTER

The survivors' and liberators' reminiscences in this book are rich in the personal details that humanize history. To assist teachers, question sets were developed to bring out the unique aspects of each story and to identify the commonalities in the Holocaust experience. In this way the patterns of planned extermination and the strategies for survival become clear to the reader.

The question sets include generic and specific questions that address three issues: 1) recall of events described in the stories (i.e., "What examples of resistance to the Nazis does Sam Ackos give?"), 2) interest in persons and events beyond the text (i.e., "Who was the Raoul Wallenberg that Robert Fisch mentions?"), and 3) opportunities to make personal value judgments (i.e., "If you were a grandparent, would you do what Sam Bankhalter's mother did?").

The question sets are also designed for a simulation of a Holocaust survivors interview. Students can be divided into groups of six to ten, with each given a different survivor or liberator story and a tag with that person's name on it. Each student is instructed to read the story in the first person.

One member of each group takes the part of the oral historian, who uses the set of eighteen questions as a script and initiates a discussion with the group after the stories have been read. Students answer in the first person, building identification with the survivor or liberator in the story. In this way students can learn about the Holocaust experiences of others in the book without necessarily reading each one.

Many different groupings are possible for the simulation of a Holocaust survivors interview. One that has been found effective arranges the group so that there will be a diversity of national backgrounds, Holocaust experience, and gender. The following groupings are suggested with eighteen participants. Educators and conference planners are encouraged to arrange additional groupings.

I	II	III
Charlotte Hirsch	Hinda Kibort	Seva Scheer
Sam Ackos	Henry Abramowicz	Sam Bankhalter
Reidar Dittmann	David Eiger	Robert Fisch
Peter Gersh	Edward Grosmann	Henry Oertelt
Dorothy Wahlstrom	Edmund Motzko	Glenn Stranberg

Needed for the simulation are 1) as many copies of the interviewer's questions as there are groupings, 2) one copy of each of the survivor and liberator stories being represented, 3) as many copies of the generic questions as there are participants, 4) as many copies of examples of specific questions as there are survivor and liberator stories, and 5) name tags for all participants.

The simulation can be staged at any point in a World War II or Holocaust curriculum, or it can stand alone as an exercise in the study of ethical and moral decision-making or the uses of oral history. In an ongoing classroom setting, the stories should be assigned in advance of the simulation, and answers to the generic and specific questions should be written out so that a student will be better prepared to respond as a survivor or liberator. The role of the interviewer can be expanded to include a summary report of the simulated "group interview." This summary can be the basis for an additional discussion, and copies given to all participants to bring closure to the experience.

The simulation makes use of oral history to overcome the numbing effect of the phrase "six million victims" by creating personal identification with single survivors or liberators. It transforms the reader into a witness.

INTERVIEWER QUESTIONS

These questions are to be asked by the person designated as the oral historian conducting interviews at a reunion of Holocaust survivors and liberators living in his or her area. After each student has read his or her story, the interviewer asks each these eighteen questions, as well as any other questions that arise as a result of the group interview. The interviewer should encourage students to ask each other questions.

1. What is your name?
2. Where were you born?
3. What can you tell me about your family?
4. How old were you when the Nazis came to power?

5. What were your first experiences with the Nazi occupation?
6. Did you have non-Jewish friends before the war?
7. To whom did you or your family turn for help?
8. Which family members were the first to be separated?
9. What happened to them?
10. What were the hardships of the ghetto?
11. Which labor camps or concentration camps were you taken to?
12. Can you describe the deportation experience?
13. Were you in a death camp?
14. What do you think made it possible for you to survive?
15. What do you remember about your liberation? Is there a liberator in the group?
16. What was your military occupation specialty? What was your impression of the camps?
17. What happened to you immediately after the war?
18. What do you tell your children or grandchildren about the Holocaust?

GENERIC QUESTIONS

These are questions students should answer as each of the survivors' stories is read.

1. Where was this person born?
2. What languages did this person speak?
3. How old was he/she when the Nazis came to power?
4. What experiences with anti-Semitism had this person had before the Nazi regime?
5. What was the education/occupation background of this person?
6. What actions did this person attempt to maintain his or her freedom after the Nazis came to power?
7. To whom did this person turn for help in avoiding imprisonment?
8. To whom would your family turn if your lives were in danger?
9. What do you think made it possible for this person to survive the Nazi terror?
10. What were this person's experiences in the months immediately following the end of the war?
11. What further questions would you like to ask this person?

12. What do you think they tell their children/grandchildren and friends about the Holocaust years?

SPECIFIC QUESTIONS (EXAMPLES)

Henry Abramowicz

1. What example does he give of the Jews as second-class citizens in Poland?
2. What does he remember about the German occupation of Lodz?
3. How was the Abramowicz family able to escape the Nazis?
4. Why didn't the family return to Lodz after the war?
5. How did the war affect his professional life?

Sam Ackos

1. What anti-Semitic experiences did he have before the Nazi occupation?
2. How did the Greek people manage to get news from the Allies after the Nazi occupation?
3. What examples of resistance to the Nazis does he give?
4. How was he able to survive the war?
5. In what ways are his sisters' experiences different from his?

Sam Bankhalter

1. Why did his mother carry her grandchild during the Auschwitz selection process? If you were a grandparent would you do what his mother did? Why?
2. What does he think the legacy of the Holocaust is to his own children?
3. Why does he say, "As a Jew, I don't think you can feel as good anywhere as you can feel in Israel"?
4. What dangers does he see in America today?

Reidar Dittmann

1. What was his response to the German occupation of Norway?
2. What does he mean by saying he was like an S.S. recruitment poster?
3. What do the young people look like in the U.S. armed forces recruitment commercials today? In what significant ways do they differ from Nazi recruitment posters?

4. What differences in treatment of prisoners did he observe at Buchenwald?

5. Compare his liberation from Buchenwald to that of Sam Bankhalter.

David Eiger

1. What were his experiences with anti-Semitism before the German occupation of Poland? How do they compare with the experiences of other Polish Jews?

2. What immediate restrictions did the Nazis place on the Jews in Radom? What was the purpose of confiscating radios? What would an occupying power need to do to achieve the same results in the United States today?

3. Why did the Nazis choose to kill all the doctors and lawyers in Radom?

4. Humor is one way people have of dealing with tragedy. What example does he give of this kind of humor?

5. Why did he and his father decide not to go back to Radom after the war?

Robert Fisch

1. He mentions several non-Jews who helped Jews. Describe two of these incidents.

2. Who was Raoul Wallenberg? How was he able to save fifty thousand Jews? How many people would have needed to act as Wallenberg did to save six million?

3. What does he mean by saying, "History, unfortunately, never avoided Hungary"? How does his own experience reflect that statement?

4. What were the personal cruelties he suffered? Did he have cruel thoughts toward others? What did he do after the liberation when he saw Germans who were hungry? How do his life choices show a high regard for human life?

5. What does he mean by "Roosevelt knew exactly what was happening, so why were the trains not bombed to stop the concentration camp activities?"

Peter Gersh

1. Compare his description of the fall of Poland to that of Sam Bankhalter.

2. Find examples in his account of Polish people who helped Jews and Polish people who harmed the Jews.
3. Why does he remember the camp commander at the Plaschau labor camp?
4. Was he out of danger once he was liberated? Describe the dangers he encountered immediately after the war.
5. Why does he say, "When I heard that the Russians occupied Poland, I thought, God should see to it that they're there for a thousand years"?

Edward Grosmann

1. He refers to the Spanish Inquisition. What was the Spanish Inquisition? What choices did the Jews who were victims of the Spanish Inquisition have that were not allowed the victims of the Nazi Holocaust?
2. How was his experience from 1941 to 1944 different from the previous survivors' experiences?
3. Why did the Nazis tattoo numbers on the Jewish prisoners?
4. How was he able to survive the winter of 1944?
5. What anti-Semitism did he encounter in the United States?
6. Why did he leave the synagogue? Why did he return?

Charlotte Hirsch

1. How did her mother respond to the news of what was happening to Polish Jews? Why do you think she responded this way?
2. In what way does she say the Nazi occupation was particularly threatening to Jewish girls?
3. Why do you think her father decided not to attempt an escape to Romania?
4. How did she try to save her mother?
5. What methods of killing people did the Nazis use in the camps in addition to the gas chambers?

Hinda Kibort

1. What does she mean by "We did not have time like the German Jews did, from '33 until the war broke out in '39"?
2. What was the attitude of the non-Jewish Lithuanians to the Jewish Lithuanians once the Germans occupied their country? Give examples from Kibort's experiences.

3. What initiatives was she able to take against the Nazis? What skills did she have that might have enabled her to do these things?

4. Why did the Nazis make the Jews build the gallows for the baker? Why did they make it a public hanging?

5. What survival skills did she learn from Frau Schmidt?

6. Do you agree with her about the role of the bystander? What could the bystanders in her town have done to resist the Nazis?

Edmund Motzko

1. What was his opinion of the military outfit from Detroit?

2. What were the American soldiers told about how the Germans treated American soldiers? What proof did he have of the German army's treatment of American soldiers?

3. What preparation did the commanding officer give his men for seeing the victims at Gardelegen?

4. What atrocity does he describe?

Henry Oertelt

1. How did Hitler's rise to power first affect Oertelt's life?

2. What example does he give of the indoctrination of German youth that occurred during the Nazi period?

3. Why do you think the S.S. men came for him at two in the morning?

4. Why does he call the prison guards' brutality "a game"?

5. What acts of kindness from Germans does he recall from his experiences?

Seva Scheer

1. What does she mean by "Whatever bad happened, the Jew always was the scapegoat"?

2. Why was it important to have a job in the ghetto?

3. What did she do in order to buy bread in the ghetto?

4. What is her definition of a survivor? What does it mean?

5. What accidental harm did the American soldiers do when liberating the prisoners at Bergen-Belsen?

Glenn Stranberg

1. What was his civilian occupation? What was his military occupation?

2. How old was he when he was sent to Europe?
3. What did his unit do when it arrived in Dachau?
4. What atrocities does he describe?
5. What was the response of his relatives when he returned and told them about Dachau?

Dorothy Wahlstrom

1. Compare her description of Dachau with that of William Landgren and Wayne Hanson.
2. What were some of the atrocities that were described to her by survivors?
3. Why did she feel that the medical unit was "dancing with death"?
4. What does she mean by the "dehumanization of the dead"?
5. What conditions in the camps led to the diseases that she witnessed?

OPTIONAL ACTIVITIES

Write a fictional story based on this person's experiences from the point of view of a friend, neighbor, or schoolmate who acts in some way to rescue the survivor or members of his/her family.

Dramatize several of the key individuals in a particular story.

Illustrate the story.

Carol Wirtschafter is a human relations curriculum consultant and Holocaust educator. She has her Ph.D. in educational psychology and is assistant director of the Jewish Community Relations Council/Anti-Defamation League of Minnesota and the Dakotas.

ABOUT THE EDITOR

Rhoda G. Lewin earned her B.A. and M.A. in journalism and mass communication and a Ph.D. in American studies at the University of Minnesota. She is an independent scholar, an oral historian, and a columnist for *American Jewish World*. She writes and lectures frequently on the Holocaust, the American Jewish immigrant experience, and Jewish history. She currently resides in Minneapolis, Minnesota.